DESTINATION GULAG

*The tragedy and triumph of deportations
and exiles to Siberia*

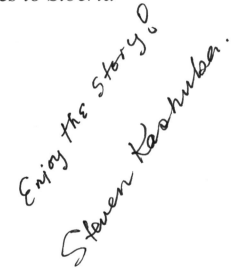

Enjoy the story!

Steven Kashuba.

STEVEN KASHUBA

Order this book online at www.trafford.com
or email orders@trafford.com

Most Trafford titles are also available at major online book retailers.

Artwork associated with images used in the story: Mariana Medvid-Yurkiv
Destination Gulag is available directly from the author at kashtwo@telus.net

Printed in the United States of America.

ISBN: 978-1-4669-8312-0 (sc)
ISBN: 978-1-4669-8311-3 (hc)
ISBN: 978-1-4669-8310-6 (e)

Library of Congress Control Number: 2013905245

Trafford rev. 09/11/2013

 www.trafford.com

North America & international
toll-free: 1 888 232 4444 (USA & Canada)
fax: 812 355 4082

CONTENTS

DEDICATION

To the memory of Andrij Kashuba

*D*estination Gulag* is dedicated to the memory of my father who lived long enough to witness the lessons that he and my mother instilled in each of their children. The road my father walked was often a difficult one, from his service in the Austrian Army to his immigration to Canada. It has been said that the ultimate measure of a man is not where he stands in moments of comfort and convenience but where he stands at times of challenge. My father met many challenges. Yet, he was one of the lucky ones. He could have been born into a kulak family in Soviet Ukraine and deported to Siberia as was his cousin Alexei Kozlov.

Andrij Kashuba, 1900-1976.
Passport photo taken in 1928.

ACKNOWLEDGEMENTS

Writing a story that has to do with the complex and sometimes dark history of the Soviet Union, a closed society for so many years, is not without difficulty. Even today, at a time of openness triggered by Gorbachev's *perestroika* and *glasnost,* there are those in Russia who do not take too kindly to foreigners undertaking research into the history of the Gulag. To them, this is tantamount to digging up old bones better left undisturbed. To do otherwise could well be hurtful to the image Russians have of themselves.

This story would not be possible without first traveling to Russia. We interviewed countless citizens, university students, and veterans of the Great Patriotic War. Each had a story to tell. In fact, it was difficult to find a Russian who did not have an ancestor who spent some time in the Gulag, not so much of their own volition but rather as a result of Stalin's scheme to populate the most desolate regions of Siberia with political dissidents. In the end, Stalin killed most of them.

In particular, I want to thank the Gulag History Museum guides in Moscow and Perm for making the horrors of political repression come to life. Thank you, Mariana Medvid-Yurkiv of Lviv, Ukraine, for improving the quality of images used in the story. My special thanks to my daughter, Nicole, for accompanying us on our journey to Siberia and assisting with the interviews. Most important, I want to express my deepest gratitude to my wife, Sharon, for assisting with the research, interviews, and editing each draft of this story.

PROLOGUE

When I wrote *Once Lived a Village,* a story about my trip to the Soviet Union in search of my ancestral village, I did not suspect for a moment that circumstances would soon propel me to a write another book. However, unlike the first book where it was relatively easy to retrace the steps that my parents took to come to Canada in search of democratic freedoms and my time in the Soviet Union in 1967, this story was much more difficult to research and write. More difficult because it is a story about one branch of my extended family that was banished to Siberia and seemingly vanished in its vastness. And, trying to get at the facts surrounding their deportation to a closed society which to this day continues, in many respects, to be a police state, was virtually impossible.

As a result of some preliminary genealogical research, I speculated that there might well be a surviving descendant of my father's cousin, Aleksandr (Alexei) Kozlov. However, while it is one thing to make an assumption about a surviving descendant of one's family, it is quite another to undertake research to confirm such a hypothesis. In order to prove (or disprove) this assumption, I knew that I would have to undertake a trip to Siberia. After all, a simple research of information contained in Russian archival records, be they NKVD or KGB, would, in all likelihood, prove fruitless.

Going back in history to a time following World War I, the Kozlov family, much like my parents, lived near the Polish-Russian border. However, unlike my parents who resided in Poland, the Kozlov family resided in Soviet Ukraine. There was one other unfortunate aspect surrounding the Kozlov family. Although in distance they were separated from my parents' families by only a few kilometers, the Kozlovs were independent landowners and considered by the Bolsheviks to belong to the middle class. That, as it turned out, was most unfortunate.

Josef Stalin (General Secretary of the Communist Party from 1922 until his death in 1953 and the Premier of the Soviet Union from 1941-1953) launched his first Five-Year Plan in 1928. It was his belief that Russia was *fifty years behind the advanced countries* and, therefore, *must make good this distance in ten years.* According to him, it was, *we either do that or they will crush us.* With this objective in mind, Stalin created a system of collective farms, called kolkhozes, which stretched over thousands of acres of land and had thousands of peasants working on them. The creation of kolkhozes destroyed the kulaks as a class. While the plan encouraged industrialization, it actually damaged Soviet agriculture to such an extent that it did not recover until after World War II. In fact, many believe that Russia and Ukraine to this day have not fully recovered from Stalin's policies.

In 1930, the Kozlov family, branded as kulaks, was among the first victims of Stalin's wayward policies. They were promptly shipped off to Siberia. Against their will, they became prisoners within the Gulag system.

As can be expected, this is not entirely a first-person story. Much of the information contained in this book comes from relatives of prisoners who survived the Gulag, as well as from the Gulag archives in Moscow and Perm-36, located near the city of Perm. Archival information was often quite ordinary: the day-to-day activity of the Gulag administration; inspectors' reports, financial accounts, and letters from the camp directors to their supervisors in Moscow. Yet, when reading these documents, the full extent of the Gulag system and its importance to the Soviet economy does come into focus. Many of the details contained in this story were made available to me by a surviving descendant of the Kozlov family. To my surprise, he continues to feel that he is vulnerable and subject to arrest. As a consequence, his name and whereabouts in Russia are not being disclosed. Perhaps one day this will change. I truly hope so.

From the archives, we now know that there were at least 476 camp systems, each one made up of hundreds, even thousands, of individual camps or *lagpunkts,* sometimes spread out over thousands of square miles of otherwise empty tundra. The vast majority of prisoners in them were peasants and workers and, with a few exceptions, the camps were not constructed for the purpose of killing people. Stalin preferred to use firing squads to conduct mass executions.

Nevertheless the camps were, at times, very lethal. Nearly one-quarter of the Gulag's prisoners died during the war years (1939-1945), while others escaped, completed their sentences, or were released into the Red Army. There were also frequent amnesties for the old, the ill, pregnant women, and anyone else no longer useful to the forced labour system. Unfortunately, these releases were invariably followed by new waves of arrests.

We now better understand the chronology of the camps. We have long known that Vladimir Lenin (Communist revolutionary who served as Premier of the Soviet Union, 1922-1924) built the first ones in 1918 (at the time of the Bolshevik revolution), as an ad hoc, emergency measure to contain *enemies of the people,* prevent *counter-revolution,* and *re-educate* the bourgeoisie. Archives have also helped explain why Stalin chose to expand the camps in 1929. The plan led to millions of arrests. Kulaks were forced off their land and imprisoned. It also led to an enormous labour shortage.

It was during an earlier assignment in Ukraine that my interest in the deportation of the Kozlov family was tweaked when I met a veteran of the former Soviet Union Air Force. He told me that while on a highly sensitive assignment during the Cuban Missile Crisis he worked with a person by the name of Dutkewycz, a non-commissioned officer holding the military rank of a *Mladshiy Serzhant* (Junior Sergeant). *Could it be,* I asked myself, *that the Dukewycz family is related to the Kozlov family? Is it possible that this Air Force veteran holds the key to tracing any descendant of the Kozlov family?*

In retrospect, without the chance meeting of Commander Korab and the discovery of three important letters, the presentation of this shocking story would not be possible.

Welcome aboard. I hope you enjoy the journey as much as I did.

INTRODUCTION

The origin of the Soviet Union lies in the First World War of 1914-1918. This war demonstrated that millions of men would, without question, obey orders to fight and die for causes abstract and distant. New states were created from virtually nothing and large groups of civilians in the Soviet Union were moved or eliminated. The most important political vision was that of a communist utopia, *Workers of the World Unite!* With a summons to political and moral transformation, Marxism inspired generations of revolutionaries to work for an end to capitalism and replace it with socialism. It was their belief that through this political process the working masses would be liberated. When the Russian Empire (the House of Romanov was a dynasty that reigned Russia from 1613-1917) crumbled in 1917, Vladimir Lenin, with his vision of communism, made his move.

By the end of World War I, Central European nations were tired of war and conflict. In the Treaty of Versailles enacted in 1919, the territories inhabited by Belarusians and Ukrainians were divided between Bolshevik Russia and Poland. With the ultimate defeat of Germany, a vacuum was created and the Russian Red Army marched on Poland in 1920, only to be pushed back by Marshal Pilsudski's troops in Warsaw. In Poland, two-thirds of the population of 27 million was of Polish heritage, with about 5 million Ukrainians, 3 million Jews, and one million Belarusians. Although the Treaty between Poland and Bolshevik Russia, signed in Riga, Latvia, in 1921, established Poland's eastern border, the accord ensured that Ukrainian and Belarusian lands would continue to be a bone of contention for years to come.

By merging the Russian Soviet Socialist Republic, the Transcaucasian Soviet Socialist Republic, the Ukrainian Soviet Socialist Republic, and the Byelorussian Socialist Soviet Republic, the Soviet Union was established in 1922. The Soviet Union immediately centralized its power, banned all other political parties, and terrorized political rivals. Cheka, the Bolsheviks' secret police responsible for security, killed thousands of people in the attempt to consolidate a new soviet state.

With the death of Vladimir Lenin in 1924, Josef Stalin consolidated his power and searched for ways to finance the communist march to state control of production and distribution. In 1928, by the terms of his first Five-Year Plan, Stalin proposed to seize farmland through a policy of collectivization, force the peasants to work in shifts under state control, and treat the crops as state property. As Stalin made his case for modernization, he was also staking his claim to power. He looked upon Ukraine as a source of food and, consequently, the means through which Russia could be rescued from poverty and isolation.

During this process, however, Stalin discovered that not everyone looked upon communism with favour. As a result of this opposition, he searched for ways to enforce his vision to make everybody equal. All classes would be eliminated and all men made brothers.

Stalin's solution was to create a repressive system by interrogating, arresting, and deporting dissenters to concentration and labour camps in Siberia. It would be here that the deportees, branded as enemies of the people, would be rehabilitated into the image of a good soviet. This plan soon had unintended consequences leading to the destruction of families and unnecessary deaths. Beginning in 1929, the establishment of thousands of camps which formed a part of the Gulag, took on a new significance. Stalin decided to use forced labour both to speed up the Soviet Union's industrialization and to excavate the natural resources in the Soviet Union's far north.

The prisoners worked in almost every industry, including logging, mining, construction, factory work, farming, and manufacturing. They lived in isolation, a country within a country, almost a separate civilization. Over time they developed their own literature and their own heroes and villains in camps surrounded by barbed wire and in isolated camps from which escape was impossible. Some former prisoners went so far as to say, years after being released from the Gulag, that they were able to recognize fellow deportees by the vacant look in their eyes. These camps operated long after Stalin's death in 1953, and were not dismantled until Mikhail Gorbachev began to dissolve the Soviet Union's political camps altogether in 1987.

Yet, until recently those living in Western nations knew very little about the history of deportations and exiles to Siberia. I first became aware of the pervasiveness of forced labour camps in Siberia when I spent a summer in the Soviet Union in 1967. I also discovered that much of the Soviet Union's military might during World War II did not necessarily come from mainland European Russia but rather from Siberian Russia. Suddenly, the importance of Siberia within the Soviet Union took on a new meaning.

But, that was only the start of my education. Days later, in a small village near the Ukrainian city of Lviv, I was arrested by the KGB on two counts: first, for straying into an area which was out of bounds to tourists; and second, for allegedly being involved in the black market. After exhaustive interrogation and with visions of Siberia ever on my mind, the KGB released me from house arrest with, "*It would be a great expense to the Soviet Government to pursue the matter further. You are banished from the Soviet Union for 25 years.*"

What is curious about Josef Stalin and the Gulag, which took millions of lives, is the indifference or outright boredom evident in the West towards this phenomenon in contrast to our condemnation of Adolf Hitler, World War II, and the Holocaust, which also took millions of lives. This analogy can be extended to Stalin's collectivization program in Ukraine which led directly to the Holodomor and the loss of over 7 million lives in 1932-1933. To many people, the crimes of Stalin do not inspire the same reaction as do the crimes of Hitler. The absence of hard information backed up by archival research made it difficult, if not impossible, to unlock the horrors of the Gulag. Archives were closed and access to camp sites was forbidden. Unlike Auschwitz, which came under the scrutiny of the West, no television or cameras ever filmed the Soviet camps or their victims.

Although I was aware that I could return to Russia and any former Soviet Bloc country as early as 1992, I did not return to Ukraine until 1997, six years after the breakup of the Soviet Union. It was at a border crossing into Ukraine that I discovered that the KGB continued to maintain information in their computer database about my 1967 trip to the Soviet Union. From this, I could only deduce one thing: the scepter of the former Soviet Union continued to rear its ugly head even in the independent state of Ukraine. As a result of this particular border incident, I was most reluctant to consider a trip to Russia or Siberia. It was only after a chance meeting of two individuals in Lviv that I felt duty-bound to set out in search of members of my extended family deported to Siberia so many years ago.

While on assignment in Lviv, Ukraine, in 2004, a veteran of Soviet Union Air Force informed me that the first Soviet labour camps were set up in Siberia after the Bolshevik Revolution in 1917. Unfortunately, these labour camps soon became the destination for thousands of Ukrainian farmers who had accumulated considerable wealth. Their agricultural expertise became a liability. Robbery of kulaks was glamorized and murder became an accepted part of the struggle for the dictatorship of the proletariat.

Looking back, it was not only my interest in the Gulag that caused me to pause and write this story, but also my interest in genealogy. I wanted to pursue the history of my family, to record and preserve the past for future generations, and to garner a sense of self-satisfaction in accurate storytelling. While undertaking research for the book, I discovered that Stalin's political policies spelled disaster, not only for millions of those living in Soviet Bloc countries, but especially for my father's cousin, Alexei Kozlov and his family.

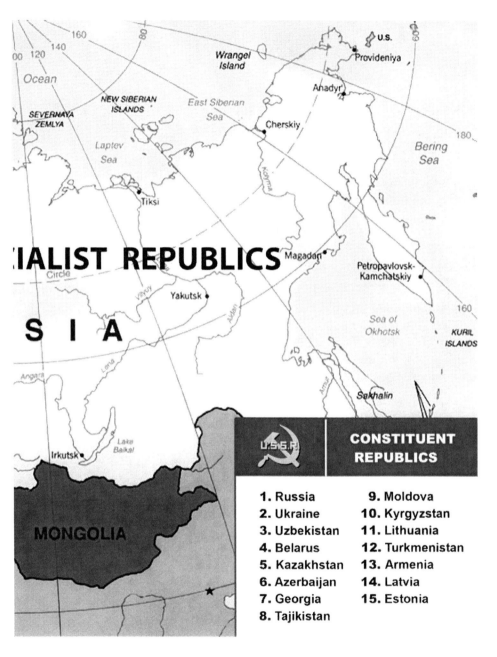

Map of The SOVIET UNION, 1945-1991.

PART 1

THE SEARCH

Chapter 1

STALIN—THE FOCUS OF CONCENTRATED EVIL

For many in Eastern Europe, the allure of communism lives on

As the jet plane taxied down the runway of Edmonton's International Airport in preparation for our flight to Ukraine, I had a lot on my mind. This was confirmed when a security agent rushed up to me saying, *"Sir, your passport. You forgot your passport!"*

Sponsored by the Government of Canada, I was on an international assignment to provide consulting services to a small family-search firm in Lviv, Ukraine. Knowing that the flight time to Europe would be long, I had plenty of time to think about genealogy and the meaning of family. But, my thoughts were not about family alone; they were also about Poland. After all, May 1, 2004 was quickly approaching and that would be the day upon which Poland, a former Eastern Bloc Country, would join the European Union.

Like thousands of others, my father left Poland in 1928 for a faraway land called Canada, a land that he knew very little about. My mother followed in 1931. But, they were among the lucky ones. They came to this great land on their own volition and not as a result of family conflict or repressive government policies. Extenuating circumstances existed for their decision—poverty and lack of employment opportunities among them.

Knowing that my upcoming assignment in Ukraine would focus on family searches and genealogy, my thoughts were not so much about the dispersion of members of my family within Europe or Western democracies, but rather with those who were taken against their will to what one survivor characterized as *'the end of the earth.'* To this survivor and to millions of others, this place, which evokes visions of depravity and terror, is Siberia. It is here that a vast network of labour camps was set up across the length and breadth of the Soviet Union by Josef Stalin. I could feel the hair on the back of my neck stand on end as I thought about the *Gulag* and the belief expressed by my father that the Kozlov family was swallowed by its vastness. *Why?* That question was uppermost in my mind.

Flying over the northern reaches of Canada on the first leg of my journey, I thought about all of those individuals and families I had interviewed, several of whom tearfully told me of the impact of punitive government policies upon their families. Many were forcibly moved from a village in which they had lived for generations to a new location without even having time to say goodbye to their family or their friends. Just a few days earlier it was a long-time resident of Edmonton who said to me, *"Imagine the stress and horror of suddenly being removed from your home in the middle of the night to a place called Siberia, never to be heard from again."*

Another interviewee, upon reflecting about the Gulag, had this to say, *"Deportations were not only to the Gulag. My family was forcibly moved from one location in Poland to another just because they were ethnic Ukrainians!"* Carried out under the code name *Operation Vistula,* this particular program came on the heels of Soviet-enforced population exchanges between Poland and Soviet Ukraine at the end of World War II. My Aunt Anna, whose family had been touched by this punitive government policy, characterized the program as a form of ethnic cleansing. However, this, in her view, paled in comparison to the pain felt by those individuals and families who were suddenly deported to Siberia.

As the plane descended in preparation for a landing in Lviv, Ukraine, I once again recalled the words of my father who, so many years ago remarked, *"I wonder what happened to my cousin Alexei Kozlov and his family? Did any member of that family survive their banishment to Siberia?"*

This question had been on my mind the previous night when the stars, moon, and even the planets all seemed visible to the naked eye. The natural light sources in the night sky seemed to light up the whole sky. I thought about how the farmers of Ukraine would use the state of the night sky as a calendar to determine when to plant crops. *What a pity,* I thought, *that so much of this magic was taken away from Ukrainian farmers in the 1930s by Stalin.*

For good reason, I wanted those shining stars to commemorate the deportation of Ukrainians and Poles to Siberia. I wanted those celestial stars to shine brightly all night to honour those soldiers, intellectuals, educators, doctors, professionals, members of the clergy, and ordinary citizens—men, women, and children—who vanished into the far reaches of Siberia. Most became victims of collective executions, deaths in concentration camps, and starvation. And, what were their crimes? Their only crime was that they were members of an identifiable group that Josef Stalin wanted to eliminate in the name of communism.

Awaiting our turn to get clearance at the airport in Lviv, I was suddenly brought out of my daydream when I heard someone say, *"Pan Kashuba? Are you Steven Kashuba?"*

"Yes, yes. I am Steven Kashuba. Are you Anatoly Kamenchuk?"

"Welcome to Ukraine, Pan Kashuba. Welcome to Lviv. I am the President of Living Family Searches. I look forward to being your host for the next couple of weeks."

After the introductions and some small talk, I was suddenly struck with the thought that my diminutive and bespectacled host was no ordinary scholar but rather a nationalistic Ukrainian. Yet, as we talked and got to know each other better, I was left with the impression that he could not or would not dispossess himself completely of his earlier Soviet influence. Maybe he even longed, in some small way, for the halcyon days of the Soviet Empire. *Is it possible,* I thought, *in this day and age of enlightenment for anyone who understands Russian history to harbour any feelings of warmth towards the Soviet Union's dark and bloodied past and its leader Josef Stalin?*

In the coming days, as I reflected upon those first moments of our meeting, I was convinced that deep within the soul of my host lived two distinct individuals—one who reflected the hopes and aspirations of a new nation while the other clung to the ashes of a vanquished empire, the Soviet Union. *This,* I concluded, *must also reflect a dilemma currently faced by many citizens of Ukraine even though they voted to confirm the nation's independence on August 31, 1991.* In the end, perhaps it would be this one person, more than anyone else, who would lay down the cornerstone for my desire to delve into the past.

Anatoly Kamenchuk's comments took me back to 1967 when I spent a couple of weeks in Moscow. I recalled my brief visit to the University of Moscow, following which I had motored past the imposing-looking KGB headquarters. At that time, my thoughts were of the tight surveillance and control the KGB had over all tourists to Russia. In contrast, my thoughts on this day turned to the NKVD and the Gulag. *What dark secrets does that KGB building harbour about Stalin's victims who perished in Siberia? Could the KGB archives provide some evidence of what happened to the Kozlov family?*

If nothing else, I wanted to do something in memory of my dad.

With the Soviet Union and the Gulag on my mind, I recalled reading about an observation that Sir Winston Churchill made in October of 1939, just after the outbreak of World War II, when he said, "*I cannot forecast to you the action of Russia. It is a riddle, wrapped in a mystery, inside an enigma; but perhaps there is a key. That key is Russian national interest.*"

From personal experience, I could understand Winston Churchill's assessment that it would be difficult to predict what actions Russia might take in a particular political situation. What really resonated with me were the words, '*That key is Russian national interest.*' Having the fondest regard for the wisdom of Churchill, I had an uneasy feeling that my search for any surviving members of the Kozlov family deposed to the Gulag might not be possible. After all, it is common knowledge that political decisions and actions within Russia have been a state secret for a long time. Many have tried, but without success, to unlock those secrets. As I set out in search of the truth, I would soon learn that what happened during Josef Stalin's Reign of Terror was more bizarre than anything that I could have imagined.

By 2004, I had already made several trips to Ukraine and Poland in search of my ancestral village and any surviving members of my family who might still be living in these two countries. I say surviving members because over the past century, wars, famines, deportations, exiles, and instances of ethnic cleansing have taken their toll. During those trips I met, for the very first time, first cousins who managed to survive these tragic events. Each had a story to tell. In many cases the story was told in hushed whispers, somehow as though the mass murderer, Josef Stalin, were still listening.

Vladimir Ilyich Lenin, 1870-1924. "The goal of socialism is communism."

Josef Stalin (born Iosif Vissarionovich Stalin), 1879-1953. "A single death is a tragedy, a million deaths is a statistic."

Winston Churchill, 1874-1965. "Socialism is a philosophy of failure, the creed of ignorance, and the gospel of envy, its inherent virtue is the equal sharing of misery."

Young Bolshevik Revolutionaries in Saint Petersburg, 1917.

Even though Stalin was long gone, the shadows of the past seemed to cast a spell over many members of my family as though another calamity were about to unfold. Still, the year did mark a significant change in the purpose of my trips to Eastern Europe. Unlike previous trips which involved a search for members of my own family, I was now on a business consulting assignment. The timing of these assignments could not have been better. They would provide me with additional opportunities to delve into the complex political histories of Ukraine, Poland, and Russia—the three countries which have had the greatest impact upon my family.

I knew a lot about the history of my family as told to me by those who were still living. In contrast, I was about to learn something about those of my relatives who left no footprints. No footprints because of the misguided political decisions of tyrannical despots who shredded the very fabric of my family. What puzzled me most was that the political decisions of one particular tyrant not only destroyed families, but also the hopes and aspirations of nations themselves.

While standing under the shadow of the Adam Mickiewicz monument on Svobody Prospect near Hotel George in downtown Lviv, I could not get out of my mind how a number of those dastardly deeds perpetrated by Stalin had befallen so many families. Perhaps it was this monument dedicated to the memory of a Polish-Lithuanian romantic poet who, after his 5-year exile to Russia in 1824, best expressed his feelings of love and longing for his beloved homeland in a poem entitled *The Pilgrim* in which he asks,

Why does my heart forever still bewail,
Far-distant lands, more distant days of old?

Monument to Adam Mickiewicz, 1796-1855, Lviv, Ukraine. Revered Polish poet whose efforts stimulated a movement to shake off the Russian conqueror.

The Poles hold Mickiewicz in high esteem and like to claim the poet as their own. Ukrainians also like to claim Mickiewicz as their own. Ukrainians find solace in Mickiewicz's words when they recall the devastation of the deportation of kulaks to Siberia in 1930-1931. After his deportation to Siberia, Mickiewicz never returned to his homeland. He died of cholera in Constantinople (Turkey came into existence in 1923 at which time the name of Constantinople was changed to Istanbul) and his body was transferred to Krakow's Wawel Castle, the resting place of Poland's greatest men.

Living Family Searches was a firm specializing in family searches, genealogy, travel, and accommodation. Anatoly Kamenchuk, its CEO, held degrees in languages, tourism hospitality, and history—well suited to the objectives of the firm. Born in Kulbyshev (now Samara), Russia, which is situated on the confluence of the Volga and Samara Rivers, a city where much of the Soviet armament during World War II was manufactured, Kamenchuk had an uncanny grasp of Soviet history. His work in family searches and knowledge of Russian history would soon have considerable impact upon my future plans.

As I listened to Kamenchuk, I could not help but remark, *"Your English is impeccable. Your command of the English language surprises me. How is that?"*

"I majored in history and English as a second language in university. Later, I immersed myself in a study of tourism and hospitality."

Not only was Kamenchuk proficient in English, a skill necessary to his work with those who came from the United States, Canada, and Europe to seek his assistance in their search for family, but he also had an extensive knowledge of the history of the Soviet Union. If nothing else, Kamenchuk's birthplace and background helped me realize that Lviv continued to have a strong Polish and Russian presence and influence.

As my assignment was coming to a close, I decided to take a weekend trip to the city of Ternopil, home to several members of my extended family. Our chauffeur for the trip was Anatoly Kamenchuk's associate, Ostap Korab. Korab and Kamenchuk had been friends for a very long time and worked as an effective team in furthering the mandate of *Living Family Searches*. Korab, unlike Kamenchuk, spoke only a few words of English. As a result, all of our conversations and interviews were conducted in Ukrainian. Korab drove a classic old Volga, which he characterized as the Cadillac of the Ladas. In response to a question, he said that the car was, *"A gift to me for my work."* I assumed that it was for his work while serving in the Soviet Union Air Force.

I recall how Korab would accelerate his Volga to a high rate of speed going uphill on the highway bound for Ternopil and then kill the motor to allow the car to coast downhill. Out of curiosity, I asked Korab, *"Why do you go through all of those dangerous manoeuvres?"*

"That, Comrade, is a habit of mine. I get paid only so much for this trip by Kamenchuk. If I can save a few hryvnias on gas, I make extra money. Razumiyish (Understand)?"

When we arrived back at Lviv late that evening, the major street taking us back to our apartment hotel was absolutely backed up with traffic. Making any kind of progress was nearly impossible. *"What's going on in Lviv, Ostap?"*

"This is Friday night. It is football night in our city."

The next thing I knew, Korab drove his car onto the sidewalk and proceeded to get around the traffic jam, through the adjoining city blocks, and finally back onto the major thoroughfare. Throughout this dubious detour we passed several uniformed police; however, not one jumped out to stop Korab. I marveled at all of this and concluded that he must possess some special privileges. *Was it the car or the driver?*

When we met the next day, Korab told me more about himself. Throughout, I was struck with the manner in which he presented himself—his posture ramrod straight and head, with copious amounts of salt and pepper grey hair held high, reflected the true image of a military officer. *"You know, Steven,"* he stated matter-of-factly at one point, *"I am a decorated military veteran with a rank of Commander. I served with distinction in the Soviet Air Force during the 1960s. If you knew what I went through in the Soviet Air Force, you would have to concede that driving a Volga up and down those hills is child's play."* As if to prove his point, Korab reached into his satchel and pulled out several black and white photographs saying, *"Look at these pictures!"*

"You say that this is a picture of you? The guy standing next to you looks familiar. Who is he?"

'*That is the General Secretary of the Soviet Union, Nikita Khrushchev.*"

"*Nikita Khrushchev? Have you been drinking too much? Are you kidding me? And, the military aircraft behind you? What is all that about?*"

"*That, Comrade, is a Russian military transport plane camouflaged in brown so that it would not be identified as a military plane on a secret mission. We wanted to make it look like a passenger aircraft.*"

"*You were on a special mission?*"

"*Tak, tak. It was a special mission, a military crew flight to Cuba. On that plane we had a nuclear warhead. We were about to teach President John Kennedy a lesson or two. In what way? I cannot tell you. That is a state secret.*"

Born near Buczacz, Ukraine, with a degree in economics and trained as an airplane pilot assigned to special operations, Korab reminded me of the Canadian Air Force officers I got to know while on assignment with the Department of National Defense in Germany in the 1960s. Although a chain smoker, he looked healthy enough to wrestle to the ground any grizzly bear in Alberta. With that faraway nostalgic look in his eyes, he spoke with great pride about the glory that was once the Soviet Union. There was something very special about the pride he took in recalling old memories about his home town which was a part of Poland during the inter-war years and within the borders of Soviet Ukraine after World War II. "*You know,*" he explained, "*Buczacz has been witness to ethnic cleansing, population exchanges, and Operation Vistula. It was also a staging ground for many atrocities committed during and after World War II.*"

During the next few days I had further opportunities to discuss with Korab his role in the military during and after the Cuban Missile Crisis of 1962. The way he described it, it was a confrontation between the United States, the Soviet Union, and Cuba. At the time, Fidel Castro did not want missiles in Cuba, while Khrushchev did some arm-twisting to get his way. It would not be until much later that Soviet officials would admit that during the 1962 Cuban missile crisis, Soviet nuclear warheads had been deployed to Cuba and could have been launched at American cities within a few hours.

"In my view," said Korab in hushed tones, *"the October showdown in 1962 between President Kennedy and Chairman Khrushchev over the Soviet attempt to install a nuclear missile force in Cuba is the closest the world has come to a nuclear disaster. I was there. I should know."*

According to Korab, it was in July of 1962, that he first discovered that something very secretive was happening under the code name of *ANADYR* (Anadyr is the name of a river flowing into the Bering Sea which separates Alaska from Northeastern Siberia). It was in this desolate region that the Soviet bomber base was located. The special operation called for an expedition to Cuba under the cover of flying to a very cold region. In reality, the crew would be flying intercontinental ballistic missiles (ICBMs) to a site on Novaya Zemlya, a large island in the Arctic where nuclear weapons had long been tested. To strengthen the concealment, many units were outfitted with skis, felt boots, fleece-lined parkas, and other winter equipment. *"The deception under the direction of a magician by the name of Dutkewycz,"* boasted Korab, *"was so thorough that it fooled even senior Soviet officers sent to Cuba."*

"Good Lord," I interjected, *"are you telling me that the person who was responsible for camouflaging your military aircraft was a Dutkewycz? Are you serious?"*

"Of course, his name was Pyotr Dutkewycz. Why do you ask?"

"Strange, very strange. I ask this only because my father had family by that name. They lived in the village of Lisovody."

According to Korab, the Soviet transport plane deployed to Cuba included agricultural experts, several missile construction specialists, and other military experts whose job it was to determine whether the missiles could be deployed in secrecy. Korab recalled how the Soviet Ambassador to Cuba took the Cuban Defense Minister Raul Castro aside to explain that Engineer Petrov in the group was actually Marshal Biryuzov. Soon, Raul Castro escorted the group to meet Fidel Castro.

As I reflected upon my conversations with Korab, it was not so much that he was involved in some form of international intrigue, nor was it about the pride with which he spoke of his role in the Soviet military. What really got my attention was that he served in the Soviet Air Force with a person by the name of Dutkewycz.

Since the Cuban Nuclear Crisis occurred during Khrushchev's watch, I wanted to learn a bit more about Korab's assessment of Khrushchev. His answer to my question seemingly came without much deliberation, *"Khrushchev opened the doors and windows of a petrified structure. He let in fresh air and fresh ideas. He produced changes which time already has shown to be irreversible and fundamental."*

Obviously, Korab continued to be drawn to those days of the Soviet Empire and the Cold War between the Soviet Union and the United States. Perhaps it is not so much that Korab served with distinction in the Soviet Air Force as it was with his reflection on the development of comradeship amongst the members of the Soviet Air Force during the height of the Cuban Crisis.

What is it that has drawn this individual to bury the misdeeds of tyrants such as Stalin and Khrushchev in favour of a few positive memories? What is it that makes so many Soviet-era veterans and present-day pensioners who survived the purges of a tyrant and the horrors of World War II to be drawn as if by a magnet to the memory of those Communist despots and their impulsive and unpredictable policies? How is it possible that Khrushchev's evolving national policies following the death of Stalin in 1953 had such a lasting impact upon so many?

Even in today's Ukraine, when the horrors of communism are known to just about everyone, many social democrats continue to denounce and undermine private property rights and seek to replace them with some form of collectivized property. Since the late 19th century, many Ukrainian intellectuals have been hostile to private property rights and have advocated, if not outright communism, at least some third way closer to it than to a regime of full-fledged private property.

Perhaps it is a case where communist states, from 1922-1991, adopted planned economies. Many of those who grew up under the communist regime believe that the Communist Party is a vanguard of the proletariat and represents the long-term interests of the people. Maybe it is the memory of state-sponsored organizations integrated into the political system that draws its adherents. Representation in these organizations was guaranteed. The social organizations were expedited to promote social unity and cohesion, to serve as a link between the government and society, and to provide a forum for the recruitment of new communist party members.

When my assignment with *Living Family Searches* was completed, I registered in Hotel George, located in downtown Lviv. The next day, May 9, was the traditional day set aside by the former Soviet Bloc Countries to honour their war veterans and to celebrate their victory over the Nazis in World War II, the Great Patriotic War. It was a rather quiet morning when I was suddenly awakened by the loud sounds of drums and military bands. As I looked out our window, I was startled to see hundreds of war veterans and citizens, many wearing their old military uniforms and medals, marching in a procession to the sound of military music. I decided to go out on the boulevard to see what all of the clatter was about. One of the marchers, noticing my curiosity, broke rank, asking me, *"Why don't you join the march, Comrade?"*

Looking at what appeared to be a decorated war hero, I said to myself, *"Why not? Sure, I'll join you!"*

Marching along with that raggedy-looking group of veterans, I felt completely out of place. Without fully realizing it, I was suddenly a participant in the Victory Day parade in commemoration of the Great Patriotic War in a city of permanent denial of everything Soviet, especially communism. Later, I was to learn that I had marched with members of the Communist Party brought from Moscow to Lviv specifically for the Victory Day Celebrations. During the march, hundreds of war veterans and citizens gathered near the Lychakivska Cemetery where Soviet soldiers had been laid to rest. Having paid their respects, the marchers wended their way along Lychakivska Street to The Hill of Glory, the site of hundreds of graves of war heroes. They then held a rally at the Eternal Fire.

As I listened to some words of patriotism and the meaning of Victory, I was surprised to note that several speakers praised Stalin and drew parallels between Nazi insurgency and today's, " . . . *quiet occupation of Ukraine,"* while others talked about the consequence of " . . . *the struggle of the mighty capital for the occupation of our country."*

Looking directly at me, a war veteran who had a lot on his mind remarked, *"My generation has seen a lot and it is not falling for the enemy's treachery. I do not believe in dollars. It's all about propaganda and American occupation. Communists are the only ones doing something in this country, but they have no shortage of obstacles put up before them."*

15

"Obstacles and problems? Do you see problems with democracy?" I asked the veteran.

"Tak, I do. All Lviv is going to do now is serve as an industrial and military garbage disposal for the West. The status of our military in the eyes of citizens has already deteriorated. Nowadays, no one respects the soldier. The army does not have the respect it once had."

As I made my way back to Hotel George, I could not get out of my mind what I had witnessed. Clearly, there were two visions of the Soviet Union in Ukraine. I wondered why so many still embraced the ideals of communism when it was clear that so many millions had lost their lives, willingly or unwillingly, in support of the communist dream.

As I called for a taxi to take us to the Lviv Airport for our flight back to Edmonton, I could not help but characterize Stalin as being the *focus of concentrated evil.* However, to my surprise it was not a taxi that showed up, but rather Ostap Korab.

"Pan Kashuba," declared Korab, *"I am here to drive you and your wife to the airport.'*

"Are you kidding me? You want to drive us to the airport?"

"Tak, I do. And, the ride is free. It is on me. I remembered something about 1962 and I want to share it with you."

Korab knew how to keep me in suspense. En route to the airport there was not one word about what he was about to tell me. With our luggage on the conveyor belt and with the last farewells, Korab called me aside and sprung the shock of my life upon me, *"Steven, when I served in the Soviet Air Force, I did meet a Pyotr Dutkewycz, but what I forgot to tell you was that we had a pact. I wrote a letter to Pyotr's brother in Tyumen. It's a long time ago, but I do recall that his brother's name was Konstantin Kozlov. But, with all the KGB security, I do not think that Kozlov ever got my letter."*

"You wrote a letter to Kozlov and you were concerned about KGB security?"

"Tak. During the days of the Cold War, domestic mail may not have been of importance. However, mail destined for other countries was frequently opened by the KGB. Since I never got a response from Kozlov, I am convinced that the letter was never delivered."

"Can you tell me what was in the letter?"

"Nyet, I cannot. The message would be of no use to you. However, if you ever find Kozlov and he is a relative of yours, ask him about the letter. Tell me about Kozlov's answer."

Back in Edmonton, with the words of Anatoly Kamenchuk and Ostap Korab still ringing in my ears, it seemed as though some irresistible force had taken possession of me. I suddenly felt compelled to set out in search of the truth: when and why was the Kozlov family deported to Siberia? By whom? Did any members of that family survive? Was there any truth to the story as told to me by Commander Korab? If so, was there any connection between Dutkewycz and Kozlov?

My interest in the Kozlov family was further heightened when I met Dr. Vasily Morozov, a Russian medical doctor from Tyumen attending a conference in Alberta. I was thankful that his command of the English language was sufficiently good to respond to a question. *"Dr. Morozov,"* I asked, *"I met a Soviet pilot in Lviv. He told me that he once wrote a letter to a person living in Tyumen by the name of Kozlov. I know that Tyumen is a large and modern city. However, I do want to ask you a question. Have you ever heard of a family by that name?"*

"Da, Kozlov is a very common name in Russia. I think that there are several families by that name in Tyumen. Why don't you plan a trip to Tyumen and look for this person yourself?"

As I considered the words of Kamenchuk, Korab, and now Morozov, I asked myself, *is it possible that there is a Kozlov living in Tyumen with ancestral roots in Ukraine? Could it be that this Kozlov is a descendant of Alexei Kozlov?*

Like it or not, the time had come to set out in search of some answers.

However, I had a strange feeling that the Russian authorities might treat my application for a travel visa to Russia in the category of persona non grata.

Chapter 2

THE SEARCH BEGINS

Saint Petersburg, the cradle of communism

M y decision to travel to Siberia came six years after my 2004 assignment in Lviv, Ukraine. During those intervening years the words of my father—*I wonder what became of the Kozlov family when they were deported to Siberia*—kept popping into my head. Making the decision to travel to Siberia was the easy part, putting the plan into place was quite another. There would be no shortage of obstacles.

In retrospect, it might have been easier to get a tourist visa, board a plane, and fly directly into the heart of Siberia. But, I wanted to travel a route similar to that taken by the kulaks from Ukraine. However, unlike the kulaks and political prisoners who were transported in cattle cars under heavy guard, I wanted to make the trip from Moscow east in the comfort of the world-famous Trans-Siberian Railway. This, I thought, would give me time to reflect upon the hardships experienced by the deportees during the earliest days of the Soviet State when people were sentenced not for what they had done, but for who they were. It was my goal to set out in search of a descendant, any descendant, of the Kozlov family.

Yet, right from the very start, obstacles to my plan began to materialize. To my surprise, my initial visa application to the Russian Consulate in Toronto was rejected, without explanation. In fact, the Consulate didn't even have the courtesy to inform me of the rejection. I only learned of the rejection after repeated calls to the Russian Consulate. The explanation from a Consulate official was short and to the point, *"Yes, your application was rejected. First, if you are to visit family in Siberia, the Consulate wants to know the name and residence of the relative, and second, the Consulate requires a letter of invitation from that family member."*

"That," I pointed out to the official, *"may be difficult to accomplish. Difficult because I don't even know for certain that I have a relative living in Russia."*

"Why then," asked the official *"did you, in your application for a visa, list the purpose of your trip to be family research?"*

In the process of explaining to the official why I listed family research as the purpose of my trip, I was interrupted with, *"That is the problem with your application. Doing family research in Russia requires special permission from a Russian Embassy or Consulate. You should have applied for a business visa."*

"A business visa? What if I did not want to undertake any research, but rather seek a visa to simply visit Russia, to travel to Siberia as a tourist?"

"You would need a tourist visa, that is all."

As our brief conversation was coming to a close, I sprung another question, *"Has my trip to the Soviet Union in 1967 anything to do with this refusal? Is that the problem?"*

A direct answer, if I had expected one, never did come from the official. At least I had the name of an official in the Russian Consulate to whom I could direct my inquiries. As a result, every phone call that I made in the coming days was routed directly to an official by the name of Igor. However, during this process Igor's surname was never given to me. This begs the question, was his name really Igor? After several calls and without an explanation, Igor surprised me with, *"Your file, Gospodin Kashuba, is being reviewed by officials in Moscow."*

By this time, I wondered if I had done irreparable damage to my application. However, it mattered little now. Even if I did apply to travel to Russia as a tourist, the officials would still have my initial application on file in which I had stated that the purpose of my trip was to undertake family research. And, to Russian authorities, family research would only have one outcome, an outcome in their eyes that would not be complimentary to Russian history.

Somehow, I now had to undo the damage I had done. First of all, I would have to retract the statement that I had made earlier about family research in Siberia. After all, the very purpose of my trip to Siberia was to prove the hypothesis that I did have family living in Siberia. To do otherwise would bring to my doorstep a considerable amount of suspicion from Russian authorities as to the very purpose of my trip.

There was one other concern. During those years when I set out in search of family in Ukraine and Poland, it was not unusual for a person within a particular community to come forward with the claim that they were related to me in some way. Of course, the purpose of such a subterfuge was invariably a financial one. In their eyes anyone coming to the *Old Country* in search of family was rich, very rich. Why not tap into this largess? This realization made me very wary of establishing any relationship without first confirming it to be true. In reality, this meant that genealogical research that was tied in any way to the sad history of Stalin's deportations to Siberia was a *nyet, nyet.*

With these obstacles before me, I made another application to travel to Russia. Only this time I applied for a tourist visa through a recognized Russian travel agency. Even as I took this step, I realized that in place of the state-operated Intourist Agency that coordinated my travel to the Soviet Union in 1967, it was now an authorized Russian travel agent that would coordinate all of my travel to and within Russia. Things may have changed politically in Russia; however, it seemed as though the procedures for travel remained as though frozen in time.

From all of this, I could only assume that the presence of the KGB would not have diminished over time and would be similar to what was in place in 1967. To sort out all of this documentation, accommodation, travel itinerary, train tickets, and places that I intended to visit took a considerable amount of time. Finally, my pleas to Igor seemed to be paying off. At least I thought they were.

Here it was April 23 and our plane was scheduled to leave Edmonton on Monday, April 26. However, the Russian Consulate was still in possession of my passport as well as those of my wife and my daughter who would be traveling with me. Without passports and visas, our planned trip to Russia would come to a sudden halt. I made a number of calls to Igor's office inquiring about our visas and passports. Finally, on April 24 Igor said to me, with a chuckle, *"Gospodin Kashuba, you are very persistent. I do have some good news for you. I had to plead with my Director to allow you and your family to travel to Russia. Finally, and reluctantly, my Director agreed to grant you and your family the necessary visas."*

"Igor, you say that your office approved our application? Has the Consulate changed any part of our itinerary?"

"Nyet. None of your plans have been changed. The authorities now know where you will be staying and how you will be traveling while in Russia."

"There are no restrictions?" was my question.

"Da, to yest pravda (that is true), there are restrictions. Stick to your plan and do not take photographs of sensitive industrial or military sights. Do not discuss or undertake research about Russia's history or other sensitive matters. If you discover that you have family in Russia, you must report the name of the family member to the authorities as well as the relationship of that person to your family."

"When I am in the towns or cities noted in my travel plans, am I free to travel to the countryside, to talk to the local people?"

"Da, you can travel to places off the major tourist routes. It is our understanding that such side-trips will be undertaken with a qualified Russian driver."

On the Friday before our scheduled Monday flight to Frankfurt via Air Canada, we still had not received our visas and passports. At that point I contacted our Russian travel agent and asked whether they were ready to refund all of our money in the event that our trip was canceled.

"Da, of course, your money will be refunded, all but an administrative fee."

By this time, most everyone at Edmonton's Purolator office was fully aware of our dilemma and continued to monitor any new developments. Finally, on the Sunday evening before our planned departure just hours away on Monday, Purolator indicated that our documents from the Russian Consulate were about to leave Toronto. However, the question remained—would these documents get to Edmonton in time for our 2 P.M. departure? To our relief, I picked up the package from the Purolator office at 11:30 A.M. on Monday, April 26.

On the way to the Airport, I remained convinced that the Russian Consulate deliberately delayed sending us those travel visas. Maybe they wanted to play a little bit of Russian roulette with us. First of all, Igor had not convinced me that the matter of my expulsion from the Soviet Union in 1967 was *not* a problem. Second, Russian authorities were obviously discouraging any research into the history of deportations to Siberia, and third, one still had to pay in advance for all accommodation and travel while in Russia. Yes, the official Intourist Travel Bureau may have been dead for some time, but the procedures put into place so many years before the disintegration of the Soviet Union in 1991 were very much alive on this day.

With a stop-over in Frankfurt, Germany, we had plenty of time to review our itinerary and to reflect upon the history of Russia. The Lufthansa flight from Frankfurt to Saint Petersburg reminded me of my journey by motorcar from Warsaw, Poland, to Moscow, Russia, taken so many years ago. I tried to visualize the changes that might have taken place over the years, especially since the break-up of the Soviet Union in 1991. The more I reflected on the manner in which the Russian Consulate handled our request for travel visas, the more convinced was I that change in Russia's attitude to tourists was slow in coming. Driving from the Pulkova International Airport to our hotel in Saint Petersburg also confirmed that improvements in Russia's infrastructure left a lot to be desired.

There is little doubt that the historic city of Saint Petersburg, Russia, the seat of government to the Tsars, was the most logical place to begin a search for answers to the question of exiles and deportations of millions of citizens to Siberia and Far East Russia. I suspected that an examination of this important question, a question that Soviet and Russian leaders had for so many years tried to bury, might also lead to some answers as to how and why the Kozlovs were deported to Siberia in 1930.

Although it is true that the Trans-Siberian Railway officially starts in Moscow, for me the real starting point for the most famous and fascinating railway system is Saint Petersburg. As a result, I wanted to start our journey to Siberia on a railway system that played a pivotal role in the development of Siberia.

Finally, the time had come to retrace the steps that took the Kozlov family from Soviet Ukraine to a labour camp in Siberia. Yet, the seriousness of my trip to Siberia was in sharp contrast to the beauty of Saint Petersburg, a stately, complex, and imperious city with a hedonistic and creative temperament which continues to place a high priority on pleasure and happiness.

Built by Peter the Great (Pyotr Alexeyevich Romanov, 1672-1725) on an uninhabited swamp starting in 1703, today the city has matured into the ultimate Russian diva. Even though it is constantly in need of repair, *Piter*, as it is affectionately known by local residents, retains the power to seduce all who gaze upon her grand palaces, glittering spires, and gilded domes. Saint Petersburg, Europe's fourth largest city and a UNESCO world heritage site, sits astride the Neva River surrounded by man-made canals which embrace unbroken facades of 18th and 19th century palaces, mansions, and golden-domed churches along with a spellbinding collection of cultural storehouses.

At the top of the list of interesting places to visit was the incomparable Hermitage Museum that is set in the Winter Palace, dressed up in stunning green, white, and gold columns, windows and recesses with its roof topped by rows of classical statues. The first phase of the Winter Palace was constructed in 1711 for Peter the Great as Domik Petra. It subsequently housed Russian monarchs until the Bolshevik Revolution of 1917. Housed inside 1,057 rooms with 117 staircases is a collection of over 3 million items depicting the history of Russia and Western Europe.

Nicole and Steven Kashuba in front of the Hermitage Museum, Saint Petersburg, Russia, 2010. Founded by Catherine the Great in 1764, the museum has a collection of nearly three million items.

While absorbing the beauty of the city, I had to remind myself that the main purpose of being in Saint Petersburg was not as a tourist, but rather as a researcher. Still, I wanted to visit the Palace Square *(Dvortsovaya Ploshchad)*, one of the most impressive and historic spaces in the city, the Church of the Resurrection modeled after St. Basil's in Moscow, the Russian Museum, and especially Kazan Cathedral that is influenced by St. Peter's in Rome. It would be in this awe-inspiring place of worship that I would spend a few precious moments in remembrance and prayer for all those who gave up their lives in building Saint Petersburg.

Industrialization brought a flood of poor workers and the associated urban squalor to Saint Petersburg. Revolution against the monarchy of Tsar Nicholas I was first attempted in the short-lived coup of December 14, 1825. The next revolution against Tsar Nicholas II was in 1905 when more than a hundred people were killed and hundreds more were injured after troops fired on a crowd which was petitioning the Tsar outside the Winter Palace. The Tsar's government limped on until Vladimir Lenin and his Bolshevik followers took advantage of Russia's disastrous involvement in World War I to instigate the third successful revolution in 1917. Again, Saint Petersburg was at the forefront of the action.

After a couple days of sightseeing, I turned all of my energies to the matter of exiles and deportations. Through interviews of university students visiting the Hermitage, it did not take long to find a couple of students whose great-grandfathers were exiled to the Chita region of Siberia. *The chickens,* as they say, *were coming home to roost.* However, to my surprise, the students were not overjoyed at talking about exiles and deportations to Siberia. Perhaps their attitude exemplified the attitude of the government of the day—*it is best to let sleeping dogs lie.* If nothing else, all were proudly Russian, glad to be away from Siberia and in the home of the city in which their ancestors grew up. Still, I was surprised to hear them talk about the Gulag with a great deal of respect and awe. However, their portrayal of barbed wire and watchtowers lent real meaning to the horrors of the Gulag.

"What about the school curriculum," I asked one of the university students whose command of English was surprisingly good, *"did you learn of the horrors of the Soviet-forced labour camps?"*

"The school curriculum? Da, of course, there was a lot of Soviet history being taught. But, in terms of forced labour? I think not. Even today, it would be unlikely to see in the curriculum anything about forced labour."

"Where, then, did you learn about the Gulag?"

"I learned from my grandfather about the enormous size of the Gulag system. He spoke of the vast network of camps across the country, about the colossal construction projects driven by prison labour."

"Were members of your family involved in any of these major projects," I asked the student.

"Da, of course. My great uncle was involved in the Volga Canal project that cost hundreds of thousands of lives. I also heard about a camp on Vrangel Island, one of the most remote and inhospitable places in the country. Other members of my family ended up in that God forsaken place."

What impressed me most about the student was the matter-of-fact manner in which he discussed, even with pride, his hometown in Siberia. He seemed not willing to attach any blame to the despots of the day, even though the Gulag, in actual fact, touched every second family in Russia. To him, much of this was common knowledge, but to me quite a revelation.

"You must understand," were his final comments, *"I am aware that forced-labour camps were created in 1919, shortly after the Bolsheviks seized power. I also know that after a series of organizational changes in the 1920s, the system was consolidated as the Gulag in 1930. My grandfather told me that by 1936 the Gulag held some 5 million prisoners."*

"What," I asked the student, *"are your personal thoughts about the Gulag?"*

"My personal thoughts? I try not to think about it. I accept what Russian leaders say about the Gulag. It was necessary to develop the country."

"Russian leaders? Who are these Russian leaders that say these things?"

After a long silence, *"I am sure that you know who the leaders are. Most members of my immediate family are happy with Russian leadership. Every country has had its share of problems. Just like Russia."*

If I thought that I would be the benefactor of some special or unique insight into the operation of labour camps in the Gulag, I would have been greatly disappointed. Like several other students that I interviewed in Saint Petersburg, their thoughts were much more about the future than with the past. After all, the Gulag did not affect them directly. I concluded that the Russian people are somewhat content or at least accepting of the horrors associated with the Gulag. It seemed to me as though most Russians harboured far too much apathy towards a system that murdered millions of people. If they had any interest in the tragedy of the Gulag, they certainly kept quiet about it.

Having completed my research in Saint Petersburg, it was time to board a Trans-Siberian train bound for Moscow. Even this part of the journey made me feel uneasy. After all, it was just a few months earlier on November 28, 2009, that the Nevsky train bound for Saint Petersburg from Moscow was bombed by what is believed to be Chechen rebels. As a result of the bombing and the subsequent derailment, 25 passengers lost their lives and over 100 were seriously injured.

Worse yet, the subway train that would take us from the railway station in Moscow to our hotel had been blown up by rebels just two months earlier. Once again, Russian President Dmitry Medvedev blamed rebels from the Republics of Ingushetia, Chechnya, and Dagestan as being responsible for the bombings. Others believed that the two female suicide bombers blew themselves up as retribution for the loss of their husbands at the hands of Russian police. Little wonder that I broke out in a cold sweat just thinking about our planned visit to Red Square and the Gulag Museum in Moscow.

Upon leaving Saint Petersburg, I soon discovered that not all trains that plied their trade under the banner of Trans-Siberian Railway were the same. I say this because the train that took us on the first leg of our journey to Siberia was not an express train. Not more than two hours into the eight-hour trip, our train pulled over onto a railway siding to allow an express train, also bound for Moscow, to pass us. When my wife Sharon asked why we took the slow train, I quickly told her, *"Well, the survival rate on a slow train is much higher than on a fast train."*

"How is that?"

"If we are bombed by Chechen rebels, a slow train will come to a complete and final stop much quicker than a fast train. Fewer people would be injured."

If nothing else, we learned a lot about our accommodations in a sleeper car made for four people. And, as luck would have it, a fourth passenger never did materialize, leaving the sleeper compartment to Sharon, Nicole, and me. Over a leisurely lunch, we read and discussed Russian history. The topography of the region, inundated with muskegs, swamps, and sloughs brought home to me the reason why Hitler's attack on Saint Petersburg (named Leningrad during this period in history) was doomed to failure from the very start.

From the very beginning, travel by train in Russia gave us an opportunity to reflect upon the history of a countryside that still bears memories of the feudal system. The dark-grey wooden houses in the small villages, each with a small garden, reflected the continuing life-style of Russians. Much like other regions of Europe, serfs who occupied a plot of land were required to work for the Lord of the Manor who owned that land. In return, the serfs were entitled to protection, justice, and the right to exploit certain fields within the manor to maintain their own existence. Serfs were often required to work on the lord's fields as well as his forests and roads.

Ivan the Great (1440-1505), the Grand Duke of all Russias, consolidated many surrounding areas under Moscow's control. His grandson, Ivan the Terrible, was the first officially crowned Tsar of Russia in 1547. The 16th and 17th centuries brought established settlements to Siberia, the discovery of the strait between American and Asia, and the birth of an expanding Russian Empire. The Romanov Dynasty gained control of the nation in 1613. Peter the Great, a Romanov, who ruled from 1689 to 1725, was responsible for bringing economic ideas and culture from Western Europe and implementing them into Russian society. Catherine the Great (1729-1796), the wife of Peter III (who was assassinated in 1762), continued this effort and helped establish Russia as a leading international power.

In 1812, Napoleon Bonaparte invaded Russia. After several grueling battles and some successes, Napoleon was forced to retreat with only 10 percent of the initial invading forces surviving the Russian army and the frigid winter cold.

Peasant unrest and suppression along with a growing liberal political movement under the rule of Tsar Nicholas II (1868-1918), made the Romanov dynasty unstable. With the onset of World War I, rioting broke out in major Russian Empire cities leading to the Russian Revolution and the overthrow of the Romanovs in 1917. At the close of this revolt, the Bolsheviks, under Vladimir Lenin, a Marxist politician, claimed power in the capital city of Saint Petersburg and in Moscow. The Bolsheviks established themselves as the Communist Party, created the Red Army, and triumphed over the anti-socialist monarchists in a civil war. From this victory, the Soviet Union was formed in 1922, and once again established Moscow as the capital of Russia.

During World War II, Adolf Hitler (1889-1945) discovered that history can repeat itself. Between the years of 1941 to 1943, the Fuhrer met a fate similar to that of Napoleon when his army attacked Russia in 1812. In what was perhaps his single biggest decision of World War II, Hitler passed up a chance to attack Moscow during the summer of 1941. Instead, he clung to his original plan to take Leningrad. Hitler ordered his troops to *flatten the city*. Unfortunately, the fall rains and mud turned to snow and frigid temperatures in November. The once mighty German military machine ground to a halt in Russia. The illusion of invincibility that had caused the world to shudder, much as was the case with Napoleon, had vanished forever.

As we traversed the region between Saint Petersburg and Moscow, the image that the culture of Russia is of a blended variety was reinforced. Obviously, the very soul of Russia was influenced by the multiple nationalities that played a role in the region's past. Historically, the culture has been dominated by the Russian nationality, language, and the Russian Orthodox religion, thereby creating a politically motivated desire to create a soviet culture. At the same time there have been

31

spontaneous periods of campaigning to preserve such other cultures as Tatar, Ukrainian, Chechen, and Armenian.

With the dissolution of the Soviet Union in 1991, the country had begun to experience a reviving interest in heritage and an attempt to return the character of ancient cities to the Great Russian writers and artists who helped establish them. In stark contrast to the attitudes which I observed during my 1967 visit to Russia, the university students and citizens we met in Saint Petersburg reflected a curiosity about Russia's great history and legendary rulers of the past. Interestingly, students did not shy away from expressing a personal opinion, even though this view may have been at odds with the opinion of Russia's current political leaders.

With so much Russian history dancing about in my head, I was looking forward to spending a couple of days of relaxation in Moscow. Saint Petersburg may have been responsible for bringing many ideas from Western Europe to its doorstep; however, today it is Moscow that is the major political, economic, cultural, scientific, religious, financial, educational, and transportation center of Russia. In fact, Moscow was recently listed as having more billionaires than does New York City.

Yet, these impressions, statistics, and facts had little meaning for me. My interest was focused upon one issue and one issue only—deportations and exiles to Siberia. I felt optimistic that I might be able to uncover a few secrets about the shocking history of what is generally known as the Gulag. Even more important, I wanted to learn more about how and why Siberia swallowed a branch of my family.

Chapter 3

MOSCOW AND THE KREMLIN

Life within the Kremlin was shrouded in impenetrable secrecy

We arrived in Moscow late in the evening without incident, took a taxi rather than the underground to our hotel, and settled in for the night with visions of the Kremlin dancing in our heads. The next morning when we boarded the metro which would take us to Red Square, we noted that the banners and preparations for a celebration were not so much about May 1, the traditional International Workers' Day, but rather about the upcoming Victory Day Celebration to be held on May 9.

Before the break-up of the Soviet Union in 1991, May 1 of each year was an important day for the celebration of workers. It continues to be an important day for a small number of communist nations in the world. However, Red Square was being prepared for Russia's Victory Day celebrations to commemorate the day in 1945 when Nazi Germany surrendered to the Soviet Union and to the Allies. Although we would not be in Moscow for the Victory Day celebrations, we were looking forward to attending similar national celebrations in Tyumen, Siberia.

Research into the history of the Gulag must of necessity start in Moscow's Red Square. For many Russians, this is the very center of the universe and, as if to punctuate this impression, all major streets in Moscow spread from here. The Kremlin and Red Square (Krasnaya Ploshchad) were together recognized as a UNESCO World Heritage Site in 1990. Both are inextricably linked to Russian history since the 13th century.

While absorbing the beauty of Moscow's Red Square, we visited the nearby Gulag Memorial, which is located on Lubyanka Square near the KGB headquarters. Founded in 1992, shortly after the breakup of the Soviet Union, the Gulag Memorial helps to promote the revelation of the truth about the historical past and to perpetuate the memory of the victims of political repression exercised by totalitarian regimes. Russia has set aside October 30 of each year as the day of remembrance for the victims of political repression.

Sharon and Steven Kashuba at the entrance to the Gulag History Museum, Moscow, 2010.

Entrance to the Gulag History Museum, Moscow. Source: Gulag History Museum, Moscow.

Memorial to the Victims of the Gulag. Source: Gulag History Museum, Moscow.

Memorial to the Victims of the Gulag. Source: Gulag History Museum, Moscow.

In the midst of all of those swanky shops on Moscow's Petrovska Street, an archway leads to a courtyard that is strung with barbed wire and hung with the portraits of political prisoners. This is the entrance to a unique museum dedicated to the Chief Administration of Corrective

Labour Camps and Corrections, better known as the Gulag. Guides describe the vast network of labour camps that once existed in the former Soviet Union and recount the horrors of camp life.

Millions of prisoners spent years in these labour camps made famous by Alexander Solzhenitsyn's book, *The Gulag Archipelago.* According to historians, during its peak years from 1929-1953 more than 18 million people passed through the Gulag system. The Gulag became a chilling symbol of political repression, as many of the prisoners were serving time for antisocial or counter-revolutionary behaviour. This museum serves as a history lesson about the system as well as a memorial to its victims.

The bilingual guide told us that, *"The Soviet labour camps left precious few landmarks and any remaining ruins are scarce."* According to her, aside from the memorial and museum in Moscow, only *Perm-36* proved to have a full-scale Gulag museum in the barracks of an actual camp which local historians rebuilt, establishing a camp that was reminiscent of Gulag logging operations. *"At the present time,"* the guide informed us, *"Russia does not have a national museum."* When I asked her why this was the case, she either ignored me or pretended that she had not heard the question.

Today, access to some of the secrets held by the Gulag is unlocked through research at the KGB archives in Moscow. Until recently, the entire terrain of Stalin's *special settlements* had remained a state secret throughout the Soviet era. Even the use of the term *special settlements* was forbidden. From the beginning in 1930, the state decreed that the image of special settlements would be a forbidden topic, appearing neither in the press nor in published records. All documentation on the special settlers was subject to the highest order of archival classification and remained top secret until the early 1990s. Soon after the inglorious demise of the Soviet Union in 1991, the new government of the Russian Federation under Boris Yeltsin took the first step toward reforming what had been the Soviet archival system. In 1992-1993, a series of new laws eased researchers' access to the archives and initiated a partial process of declassification.

"These and other files," according to our guide, *"contain an endless variety of previously classified materials, including unpublished legislation, policy commission papers, official protocols, numerous genres of reports, statistical materials, and communications from all branches of party and government."* Overseen by the Health, Labour, and Welfare Ministry, the archival documents are contained in the form of cards with about a dozen categories including the name, date of birth, and travel records of prisoners. However, two important archives remain virtually inaccessible to the public—the archives of the Federal Security Bureau, which stores the greater part of the Secret Police Records, and the Kremlin archives.

Although there may exist an apathy on the part of the ordinary Russian to all things Gulag, the very essence of the Gulag is still everywhere. Some prisoners' camps were incorporated into newer and still functioning industrial-production prisons, especially in Western Siberia. Other former labour camps continue to function as state farms. Oddly, many Russians continue to minimize or rationalize the horrific crimes committed by Stalin. For the millions banished to the Gulag, countless prisoners might have embraced this labour camp proverb: *He who has not been there will get his turn and he who has been there will never forget.*

Most of our time in Moscow was spent in and around Red Square, a fortified stronghold just outside the Kremlin's north wall. Built in the 1150s, it became the headquarters of the Russian Orthodox Church in 1350, and expanded with new walls and towers at the end of the 15th century. It was Stalin who in 1935 had the imperial double-headed eagles removed from the wall's five tallest towers and replaced them with the distinctive red stars which continue to grace the walls to this day. And, of course, a visit to Red Square would not be complete without visiting the resting place of the founder of communism, Vladimir Ilyich Lenin.

Vladimir Lenin died in 1924; however, his mausoleum (tomb) would not be constructed by slave labour in Moscow's Red Square until 1930.

Moscow's original Kremlin wall was constructed between 1485-1495. Today, the stately Kremlin Towers and Red Square project a sense of Russian history.

It seemed to matter little about all of those interesting historical places one might visit. My thoughts seemed always to be of Josef Stalin and his grandiose plans for Siberia. Despite the countless changes in the appearance of Moscow itself, the presence of police (many with their guard-dogs), plain-clothes agents, and security cameras had not diminished. This included the process used to check us into the hotel where we had to relinquish our passports, to the tight security when boarding an underground train. The same care was taken by officials at the Yaroslavsky Vokzal, the train station that would launch our journey to Siberia. Here, officials carefully checked our passports and train tickets before granting us the boarding passes even though they had been prepaid. Obviously, the security for railway passengers was all as thorough as was the security for passengers boarding any international flight.

Wanting to make sure that nothing went wrong, we were at the train station well in advance of our departure time. It did not seem to matter that we were dressed in a manner so as not to draw attention to ourselves. Our first serious encounter occurred in an upscale coffee shop when out of the blue a stranger purchased three huge chocolate desserts for us. He did not speak English and his motive was not known to us. Shortly, however, he was joined by two other men before beginning to follow us everywhere that we went in the huge train station. At one point he managed to step between me and our daughter Nicole. I do not know whether it was his intent to separate us from our luggage, to rob us, or to seek some funds. However, I was not about to risk our safety. Pointing to the great beyond, I loudly ordered him, *"Beat it, get lost."*

We then made a bee-line directly to our train and took a position as near as we could to security officials while awaiting clearance to board. When I told a police officer of the dessert incident, in the best Russian I could muster, his response surprised me when he said, *"Gospodin, train stations are rarely safe, especially for foreign tourists. Stay together and be careful."*

"What about away from the station; away from Moscow? Is it safe?"

His response of, *"Perhaps, perhaps,"* seemed so typically Russian-non-committal.

"What about the trains? Are they safe?"

"We try to make them safe. But, we are not always successful."

The comments of the official seemed to fly in the face of much of the information we found in travel brochures and on web sites. Still, I was thankful for his words of caution. Finally, we were cleared for boarding our carriage that would take us from Moscow to the city of Perm, beyond the Ural Mountains, and into Siberia. When we first entered our sleeping compartment (*spalny*), constructed to accommodate four passengers with two upper and two lower sleeping bunks, we hoped that we would be the only passengers in the sleeper. But, this was not to be. Just before the train left the station, a fourth passenger entered our sleeper compartment, introduced himself as Vlad, and made himself at home. Noting that he had a very good command of the English language, I wondered if his appearance was an indication of the long reach of the KGB.

"Vlad, eh," was my way of opening the conversation. *"Is this a business trip for you?"*

"I live in Nizhny Novgorod which is a city of over one million people. We will be going through Nizhny in about one day's time."

"Do you work in Nizhny Novgorod?"

"Da, sort of. I am an electrical engineer representing a large electrical company."

Right from the moment that he thrust his bear-like hand to greet me, to an explanation about who he was and his occupation, he struck me as though he was no shrinking violet. Even as I introduced Sharon and Nicole to him, I had this uneasy feeling that he already knew who we were, our destination, and the purpose of our trip.

"Canadians, are you not?"

"Yes, we are from Canada. What about you, Vlad? Do you live in downtown Nizhny Novgorod or a village near the city?"

Although my questions of Vlad were quite pointed, his answers were never direct. It was obvious that he was very adept at considering every question before providing a vague answer. In the end, I was uncertain if he lived in an apartment in downtown Nizhny Novgorod, the outskirts, or in a village near that city or elsewhere.

During those first twenty-four hours on the train bound for the city of Perm, I learned a lot about Russia, Siberia, the Gulag, and about Vlad. Despite the ease with which we discussed a number of topics, I had a sneaking suspicion that Vlad was much more than a civil engineer. Recalling my earlier trip to the Soviet Union, I found it best to suspect everyone of being a double-agent. If my suspicion should prove otherwise, fine. Either way, nothing is ever lost by being vigilant.

Yaroslavsky Vokzal (Railway Station) serves all points east on the Trans-Siberian Railway route. First built in 1862, it is the busiest of nine railway stations in Moscow.

A typical Trans-Siberian Railway train.

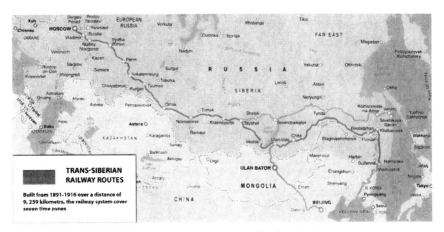

Map of Russia showing the Trans-Siberian Railway routes.

During that first night on the train, an inebriated passenger barged into our unlocked sleeper demanding a light for his cigarette. Later, he came back, quietly pushing open the unlocked door, and tried to make off with one piece of my luggage. To my surprise, it was Vlad who pushed him out of our compartment and then reported the incident to authorities. At a train stop early the next morning, I noticed through the window of our carriage that the same intruder was now in handcuffs being manhandled by police on the railway station platform. Although the arrest allayed many of my fears, it also re-affirmed my belief that one had to be on guard at all times. When we neared the city of Nizhny Novgorod, Vlad asked me the strangest question, *"Do you want me to join you and your family to your next stop in Perm?"*

For the longest time I thought about his question. What puzzled me was that Vlad had earlier told us that he had never heard of Perm-36. *How is that possible,* I thought, *to be unaware of Perm-36 when it is only one of two Gulag museums in all of Russia.* Here, presumably, is a person who lives relatively near the city of Perm and yet has never heard of the Gulag Museum? In contrast, even the university students I interviewed in Saint Petersburg were aware of its existence.

When Vlad left the sleeper for a visit to the toilet located at the end of our carriage (which is an experience in itself), I took a peek at a document in his briefcase. I am not an expert on the Russian language, but I can read words written in Cyrillic and know the definition of many of the basic Slavic words. What I saw was a document with the *Federation of Russia Seal* on it and the words *Federal Migration Service, Office for Passports and Visas.* One thing was certain—Vlad was not your ordinary electrical engineer. When Vlad returned to the sleeper, I was ready to respond to his offer to accompany us to Perm by saying, *"Thank you, Vlad, for offering to personally escort us to Perm. We appreciate it; however, we will be all right."*

"Da, da, I enjoyed meeting you. Perhaps we will meet again in Perm; maybe even in Tobolsk."

With those brief words, he was gone. I was thankful that we would have the sleeper compartment to ourselves. But, once again my elation was short lived. At the next major stop of Kirov, we were once again joined by another passenger. In a few moments, he secured the upper bunk next to the doorway and made himself at home. Much like Vlad did the previous day, he immediately introduced himself. However, unlike the talkative Vlad, Ivan spent very little time talking to me, he preferred to talk to Sharon and Nicole, constantly asking them questions about Canada and the purpose of our trip to Russia. By this time, both Sharon and Nicole were well aware that any passenger joining us in the sleeper might be a member of the federal police force. As a result, neither was willing to say much about the purpose of our trip other than to affirm that we were going to Siberia as tourists. Meanwhile, I made sure that the door remained locked throughout the night and especially while we slept.

From Ivan, I learned that Russia was coasting along on a wave of petrodollar profits and that growth was running at over seven percent per annum. According to him, since the breakup of the Soviet Union three-quarters of state enterprises had either been fully or partly privatized. Several of the towns through which we passed showed signs of renewal and perhaps even the emergence of a middle class. However, economic changes created new challenges. *"Russia no longer has the social safety net,"* explained Ivan, *"that we had under the Communist State. At least five million Russians are unemployed, resulting in an increase in corruption."*

"What about the increased policing by the KGB, is that not working in Russia?"

"The KGB is history," explained Ivan, *"but ordinary Russians still look over their shoulders for Putin's shadowy force of siloviki, an unholy alliance of authoritarian law enforcers and bureaucrats who, many believe, really run the country."*

"Siloviki? Who are they?"

"The siloviki are the people of force in Russia. They are the military police and the other uniformed agencies."

"What about Vladimir Putin? Does he continue to lead Russia?"

"Many Russians think that Putin is exploiting the recent wave of terrorist attacks to further curb civil liberties," explained Vlad.

"Why," I asked, *"do you continue to talk about Putin as though he were still the president of Russia? What about the current president, Dmitry Medvedev?"*

"Medvedev? Our third president? He was Putin's Chief of Presidential Staff. Putin backed him for the office of President. But, all Russians know that Putin is our main man."

"What about the break-up of the Soviet Union?" I asked Ivan, *"What impact has all of this had on Russia's leaders?"*

"Da," responded Ivan, *"the popular revolutions which recently swept across Ukraine and Kyrgyzstan led to nervousness in the Kremlin that similar events could happen in Russia. At the same time, our nation is united in its fight against terrorism, especially after the Beslan crisis of 2004."*

"The Beslan crisis? What is all that about?"

"The Beslan School hostage crisis," explained Ivan, *"was a three-day hostage-taking of over 1,100 people which ended in the death of over 300. It was a day in which a group of armed Inguish and Chechen militants took more than 770 school children hostage on September 1, 2004, in the town of Beslan. This tragedy lives with me as though it happened yesterday."*

"Where is this place Beslan?"

"The town of Beslan is in North Ossetia."

"How did the hostage-taking end?"

"On the third day of the standoff, Russian security forces stormed the building, using tanks, incendiary rockets, and heavy weapons. In the end, I believe that at least 334 hostages were killed, including 186 children."

There was a long silence in our sleeper when Ivan finished talking about the tragedy of Beslan. Deep in thought, I considered the emotion he showed when he talked about this event in contrast to the absence of emotion when ordinary Russians talked about the tragedy of the Gulag. Unlike other Russians I had met earlier during our journey, Ivan did not shy away from talking about the deportation of Russian citizens to Siberia as early as the 19th century, and especially since the time that Josef Stalin came into power.

"You know, Steven," he offered after a long silence, *"I am a descendant of a Russian family that was deported to Novosibirsk in the 1940s."*

"What is the impact of these deportations upon you and your family?"

"Like so many other deportees, most of those who ended up in a labour camp died within the first two years from hard work, hunger, and disease."

Although it may have been true that Ivan willingly talked about deportations to Siberia, I found it difficult to get him to admit that Josef Stalin had been an evil dictator. His attitude mirrored that of most Russians. They wanted to bury the past and talk of their victories in an often hostile environment. He especially wanted to talk about the upcoming Victory Day celebrations. In the end, I found that Ivan had revealed only so much of himself. He seemed much more successful in squeezing information out of his fellow travelers than we were at getting anything useful from him. I was thankful that we would soon reach our next stop.

Sharon and Nicole Kashuba at a Trans-Siberian Railway train stop.

Meadows of undulating steppe feather grass, a common sight in Siberia.

For some time I had been looking forward to visiting the city of Perm. Earlier, a guide in Moscow's Gulag Museum assured me that it would be here that I would find vivid reminders of Soviet repression. Somehow, I had envisioned Perm as a small city, not one with a population of over one million. Evidence of Perm's place in the Gulag and its military history were visible everywhere. However, of special interest to me was the Perm-36 Gulag Museum, which is located about one hundred kilometers east of Perm in a tiny village on the shores of a small lake.

For most of its history since 1946, Perm-36 was a labour camp for political prisoners. Today, it is preserved as a fascinating and moving memorial to the victims of political repression. The museum promotes democratic values and civil consciousness in contemporary Russian society. This is accomplished through the preservation of the last Soviet political labour camp as a vivid reminder of repression and an important historical and cultural monument.

Countless artists, scientists, and intellectuals spent years in the cold, damp cells, many in solitary confinement. A specially-constructed punishment cell had only sufficient room for a prisoner to stand up vertically for hours at a time. Prisoners worked at mundane and repetitive tasks, such as cutting and assembling fasteners for up to twenty-three hours each day, surviving on measly portions of bread and gruel. Much of the evidence of Perm-36's history was destroyed when the camp was closed in 1988, but museum staff is dedicated to re-creating the camp as it was. Windowless cells, floors made of half-round logs, and barbed wire are eerie reminders that the Gulag's history is not so distant. These stark exhibits make the reality of prison life all too clear.

Today, it is difficult to find a Russian family who has not been touched by the evils of totalitarianism. During Stalin's reign, most everyone knew that the sole source of economic might in the Soviet Union came from deportations, and Perm-36 was one of the most notorious of the camps. The maximum security area was created for repeat offenders in near complete isolation. Sadistic guards used the terrible winter as an instrument of torture to break their health and spirits. Those who died were buried nearby and their graves marked with just a number on a post, the ultimate power to render them invisible.

While visiting Perm-36, we walked the same paths as the former prisoners and felt the depressing atmosphere of isolation. Perhaps it is true that during Stalin's time there were so many labour camps throughout Siberia that they became an integral part of the landscape. Our Russian tour guide defined it this way: *"This museum is not only a symbol of the totalitarian past, but of resistance and the continuous and fearless struggle against the criminal essence of authority."*

Many have written and even sketched images about life in the Gulag. Varlam Shalamov, a citizen of Russia, spent 17 years in the Gulag during which time he expressed an anti-Stalin viewpoint and upon his release in 1953 wrote *Kolyma Tales*. Perhaps Shalamov captured the real impact of forced labour on each prisoner with these thoughts, *"A labour camp is a negative school of life, completely and absolutely. No one brings away anything useful, or necessary from there, neither the prisoner himself, nor his leader, nor his guard, nor the involuntary witnesses, engineers, geologists, doctors; neither the superiors nor the subordinates. Every minute in camp is a poisoned minute."*

Perm-36 was home to many prominent dissidents, among them Vasyl Stus, a Ukrainian poet who was nominated for the Nobel Prize in 1985. However, he died in the camp a month before the prize was awarded. Another *zek* (an inmate of a Soviet labour camp), Levko Lukyanenko, a lawyer who was sentenced to death when he created the underground organization *The Ukrainian Working Class and Peasants Union,* was given clemency and fifteen years in prison. Upon his release, Lukyanenko worked for the Helsinki Ukraine Group and in 1991 authored the law which gave Ukraine its independence.

What is troublesome to those released from the Gulag is that their rehabilitation documents state only that they have been rehabilitated. Their sentences have been erased as if they never happened. Most of the former prisoners dismissed any talk of bringing their former jailers before the international court. They say that there have been enough courts; enough blood. There was some solace and quiet pride in the mere fact that they emerged alive, if not unbroken. Still, the former prisoners would like wider recognition of how they were wronged. Even after Mikhail Gorbachev's *perestroika*, prisoners who survived the camps were treated as dangerous criminals on parole. The eventual formal recognition of their rehabilitation was often a letdown.

Perimeter guard fence at the Gulag
History Museum, Perm-36.
Source: Perm Gulag Museum.

Main barrack, Gulag History
Museum, Perm-36.
Source: Perm Gulag Museum.

During our visit to Perm-36, we had the good fortune to meet a family of tourists from The Netherlands who told us that they lost several members of their extended family to the Gulag. *"You know,"* expressed one member of the group, *"those damn Stalin murderers deported the Van Dyck family from the Polish border in 1940 and we never saw them again."*

"A Van Dyck family living in Poland, how did that come about?"

"Well, many Dutch names have a Germanic background. The Van Dyck family lived in a German settlement in Poland. That is how they came to be identified as being a potential problem to the Soviet Union should a war break out."

We had another surprise when a member of the Platonenko family visiting the museum from Tyumen overheard our conversation and told us that they, too, like so many other Russian families, had been touched by the tragedy of the Gulag. When I mentioned to them that we would be in Tyumen on May 9 for the Victory Day celebrations and that I met a Dr. Vasily Morozov in Edmonton, Lydia Platonenko proudly announced, *"Why, what a surprise! Our family doctor in Tyumen, until he was promoted to his current position, was a Dr. Morozov."*

For the longest time I thought about Lydia's statement that she remembered Dr. Morozov as their family doctor before the collapse of the Soviet Union in 1989. Even though the people of Edmonton and Tyumen may be separated by a great distance, I could not help but remark, *"Small world, isn't it?"* I was struck with a feeling that somehow we are all connected to each other in a circle that never ends. Even in the midst of the Perm-36 Gulag Museum, I felt compelled to accept that God is what happens when humanity is connected. We all owe every moment of our lives to countless people we will never meet. Soldiers give us freedom when they fight for our country and the surgeons give us the cures that keep us alive. Bringing my thoughts back to the present, I asked Lydia, *"Have you heard of the family name Kozlov?"*

"The family name Kozlov? Da, Kozlov is a common family name in Tyumen. Our Governor for the Oblast of Tyumen is Vladimir Yakushev. His office has 34 deputies who are elected by the citizens of the oblast for a period of five years. I do recall that a person by the name of Eduard Kozlov was involved with the Governor's office."

"What do you know about Eduard Kozlov?" I asked Lydia. Not surprisingly, my question brought very little information other than the observation that he was a community-minded individual. Just as was my experience with so many other Russians whom I had interviewed, this family knew the difference between idle conversation and a leading question from a complete stranger that might well have its consequences, even so many years after Stalin's Reign of Terror.

When we returned to Perm and our mini-hotel, the granddaughter of the owner, Karenina, told me that she was not only practicing her English but also her musical talents. *"Pan Kashuba,"* she asked, *"would you like to listen to one or two Russian love songs?"*

"Surely," I responded, *"these love songs are not aimed at me."*

"Nyet, these love songs will be sung for a special guest."

"Love songs for a special guest? He must be a very special and lucky guest!"

"Da, our hotel caters to Italian bachelors looking for Russian brides. An Italian gentleman is making his second trip to Perm tomorrow."

"So, you are a match-maker, eh?"

"I think that this particular Italian really likes one of the girls he met on his first trip to our hotel. I want to sing a couple of Russian love songs for the two of them. Maybe the romance will lead to a marriage. Who knows? Besides, I want to practice strumming my guitar."

"How can I possibly refuse?" I asked her. Fully relaxed in the lobby of the hotel and now in a dream world of my own, I listened to the lyrics of her love songs. I had to admit that the moment was in stark contrast to my earlier experience in Perm-36. *How is it possible,* I asked myself, *for wealthy, attractive young bachelors from Italy to find love in Siberia?* And, even though I did not completely understand all of the Russian lyrics, I could see that an Italian male, bent on a journey of love, could be smitten by her love songs.

At first, I thought that she would perform at least one or two songs in English. Not so! She kept me entertained with those Russian love songs until midnight. I hoped that Sharon might rescue me. No such luck. Both Sharon and Nicole had departed earlier and were fast asleep in our hotel room in preparation for the next day's journey.

Having completed our enquiries and interviews about the history of slave labour in the city of Perm and in Perm-36, we took the Trans-Siberian Railway to the historic Siberian city of Tobolsk, a city that played a significant role during the time of Stalin's deportations. The Kremlin is located on a plateau overlooking the intriguing old town that lies on the Irtysh River flood plain below. It is here that that we found the attractive, well-proportioned and imposing appearance of their Kremlin, standing majestically overlooking a charming but decrepit old town full of collapsing old wooden buildings and churches.

Tobolsk became the seat of Siberia's first bishopric in 1620 as Christianity tried to stamp out incest, wife-renting, and spouse-stealing by sexually frustrated Cossacks. Especially after the Bolshevik Revolution, the Cossacks continued to embrace democratic principles and supported the Russian White Army in opposition to the Russian Red Army. From 1708, the city of Tobolsk became the region's politico-military hub. Unfortunately, its strategic importance started to wane as early as the

1780s when it was bypassed by the new Great Siberian Trakt, now known as the Trans-Siberian Railway system.

The historic city of Tobolsk, however, does have a dark side. Involuntary guests included many Decembrists and Tsar Nicholas II and his family who spent several doomed months in Tobolsk in 1917.

Historically, ever since the first days of the Bolshevik Revolution of 1917, the Royal House had been the field of persistent battle between those who wanted to preserve the Romanov dynasty and those who wished to annihilate it. These discussions went on while the Romanovs were interned in their usual residence of Tsarskoye-Selo, close to the capital of Saint Petersburg. After the riots of July, 1917, the Kerensky Cabinet exiled the Imperial family to Tobolsk. The Romanov family, which included Nicholas II, his wife and children, his retinue of five courtiers, and thirty-five servants left Tsarskoye-Selo in Saint Petersburg in August in a special train. Upon their arrival in Tobolsk, they were lodged in the Governor General's mansion.

While the civil war raged across the country, the Romanovs spent the winter in Tobolsk. However, from among the soldiers guarding the Royal Party, a group came together swearing that they would never allow the Romanovs to escape alive. The Ural Regional Soviet demanded that the royal captives be transferred to Yekaterinburg. In Yekaterinburg, a decision was taken to execute the Romanovs and destroy their remains so that no relics might be left for future use.

The tragedy of the Romanov family. Left to right are Olga, Maria, Nicholas II, Alexandra, Anastasia, Alexei, and Tatiana.

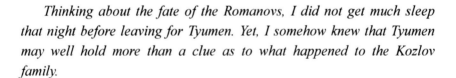

Thinking about the fate of the Romanovs, I did not get much sleep that night before leaving for Tyumen. Yet, I somehow knew that Tyumen may well hold more than a clue as to what happened to the Kozlov family.

Chapter 4

MY NAME IS KOZLOV, EDUARD KOZLOV

The frozen silence of the Gulag begins to melt

As the Trans-Siberian passenger train wound its way into the capital city of the vast oblast of Tyumen, which stretches all the way from the border of Kazakhstan to the Arctic Circle, one could sense the growing prosperity of a metropolis that exudes no shortage of confidence. The taxi driver who would take us to Hotel Vostok spoke English and, like many taxi drivers in Russian cities, he did not shy away from talking. In response to a question about Tyumen, he proudly declared, *"The strength of Russia rests in Siberia!"*

Founded in 1586, the city of Tyumen was the first Russian fort in Siberia. As testimony to the importance of the city, our taxi driver described it this way, *"This city is recognized for its leadership in politics and in culture. Do you see the river over there? It is the Tura River, our waterway to the outside world!"*

Looking at the landmarks, Tyumen reflected a business-like atmosphere with a youthful bustle. With tree-lined streets, a few older buildings amid all the new construction, it could have passed for any city in Western Canada. Even more impressive, the city's population was quickly approaching the one million mark.

"Where are you from?" was his first question.

"We're from the city of Edmonton, the heart of hockey in Canada!"

"Edmonton? Hmm, is that anywhere near Calgary?'

"Yes, of course. Why do you ask?"

"Tyumen is an oil and gas center. So is Calgary. Our city is twinned with Calgary."

"That," I replied, *"is news to me. It is too bad that Tyumen is not twinned with Edmonton, the real oil capital of Canada. What about your city? What is it important for?"*

"We are over 2,000 kilometers east of Moscow. This city is two time zones ahead of Moscow. Tyumen is the transportation center for all of the oblast. Not only that, but Tyumen is a center for higher education."

"Transportation center for goods, services, and people?"

"Da, da, for people and for freight," the taxi driver replied with a sense of satisfaction. *"We move over 10 million passengers each year. Our rail station has four platforms, nine railway tracks, and eleven ticket windows."*

"So, Tyumen is the among the most prosperous oblasts in Russia?"

"Da, that's what the Governor of the Oblast likes to brag about. Our Oblast is big, very big. It consists of two autonomous okrugs within its boundaries, Khantia-Mansia and Yamalia."

"Autonomous? Why are they autonomous? In what way?"

"They were declared autonomous districts in 1990 by the Russian Federation to recognize the indigenous peoples of the north. The two

autonomous districts report directly to the Russian Soviet Federative Socialist Republic in Moscow."

As we were being dropped off at Hotel Vostok, I had one more question for our taxi driver, *"Has Tyumen been influenced by the presence of labour camps? The Gulag?"*

"Da, yeta verno (yes, that is true). All of Siberia has been influenced by the influx of labourers. Stalin made sure of that."

"Are there any Tyumen residents whose ancestors came here from Ukraine or Poland, residents who can trace their family roots to Europe?"

"Ukrainians and Poles, they're everywhere, especially the Ukrainians."

When we arrived at Hotel Vostok, we checked our itinerary and discovered that we were one day ahead of our schedule. We quickly learned that the slightest of changes in our travel plans caused enormous problems for the hotel and for us. It took considerable time and a meeting with the manager to accommodate our needs. This included a call to our Russian travel agent in London so that the changes in our itinerary could be officially recorded. The price for the night we had originally reserved had to be refunded and new and additional charges calculated. As might be expected, the additional costs were inordinately high and had to be paid directly to the hotel.

In initiating a search for family in a foreign country, one should never underestimate the power of evolving technologies. Before leaving Edmonton, I had undertaken a search of the Internet with the hope of finding the name of Kozlov listed in one of the towns or cities in the oblast of Tyumen. I reasoned that the name might appear in a region of Siberia that would have been the destination for Ukrainian deportees in the 1930s. Of the heavily populated regions of Tyumen, Omsk, Tomsk, and Karaganda in Kazakhstan, only Tyumen showed several positive results. This result was also consistent with Russian statistics which show that Ukrainian is frequently spoken in Tyumen.

Much like any major city in Russia, Tyumen did have a telephone directory and this is where I began my search. My hope was that one of the several Kozlovs listed in the telephone directory would be a descendant of Alexei Kozlov. I recalled that an earlier search for relatives living in the region of Lviv, Ukraine, I used a similar technique with positive results. My first telephone call was made to the first Kozlov family name listed in the telephone directory.

"Hello, is this the residence of the Kozlov family?" Knowing that my command of the Russian language was minimal, I hoped that whoever answered the telephone would not hang up on me immediately, as typically happens. Still, as I spoke slowly in Ukrainian, the listener at the other end of the telephone seemed to be able to quickly grasp the gist of my question.

"Da, this is the Kozlov residence. Who are you? What do you want?"

Unfortunately, it seemed to me that in each case when a Russian family did not recognize the caller, they would become suspicious and hang up. Perhaps they thought, *this must be the police, maybe a foreign operative. Have I done something wrong? Why would this stranger with a foreign accent be calling?* After making no fewer than two dozen telephone calls, I was successful when the person on the other end of the telephone line said, *"Da, my name is Kozlov, Eduard Kozlov. What do you want?"*

"My family name is Kashuba. I am searching for a member of my family. I am from Canada."

As I struggled to communicate with Kozlov, mixing my limited knowledge of Russian with a few words of Ukrainian and English, I was relieved to note that he did not terminate our telephone conversation. *"I am from the City of Edmonton,"* I explained to him, trying hard to contain my excitement while at the same time hoping to get a response from Kozlov. *"My father was born in Austrian Galicia. Did you ever have family living in Soviet Ukraine who might have been deported to Siberia?"*

There was a long silence on the telephone before Kozlov responded, *"Perhaps I did. But, that would not be unusual."* From the seeming reluctance with which he shared this information, I could tell that he was not overly anxious to discuss the matter over the telephone.

"Is it possible," I asked Kozlov, *"for us to meet at our hotel?"* After a brief discussion, he agreed to meet us that evening at Hotel Vostok.

From the moment that Eduard Kozlov appeared in the lobby of the hotel, I could tell from his facial features, his height, and his stocky build that he could well be related to the Kashuba clan. The generic facial features of the eyes, nose, mouth, and chin reminded me of my father's facial features. I suspected this because I had spent a considerable amount of time searching for family in Poland and Ukraine and found facial resemblance to be one of the potential cues in individuals that establish family ties. In turn, recognition does engender trust. Meanwhile, I hoped that in me Eduard might see some similarity to his own physical features.

In order to have a confidential discussion with Kozlov, I knew that trust would be an important consideration for him. After all, individuals do respond to facial resemblance in ways consistent with inclusiveness. Since Kozlov greeted me with a warm Russian hug, I concluded that this was another clue that he was at ease with me. As we sat in the hotel's foyer, I told Eduard Kozlov about my family and the purpose of our journey to Siberia.

"A long time ago," I explained to Eduard, *"my father told me about his cousin's family by the name of Kozlov. Before the outbreak of World War II, the family lived in Horodok, Soviet Ukraine. According to my father, the Kozlov family was deported to Siberia. I am searching for*

any descendants of Alexei Kozlov. Does the name of Alexei Kozlov mean anything to you?"

"Alexei Kozlov? Da, it could be. My father's name was Konstantin Kozlov and my grandfather's name was Aleksandr Kozlov. But, there are many Kozlov families. My parents and grandparents are no longer living."

I had a great deal of difficulty containing my excitement when Eduard mentioned that his grandfather's name was Aleksandr Kozlov. After all, it is common to abbreviate Aleksandr to Alexei. *"I am sorry about the loss of your parents. But, I am so happy to have found you. I do believe that you are the person that I have been searching for."*

Even as I made this observation, I was mindful of the comments from the Russian Consulate officials in Toronto who looked dimly upon granting a visa to Canadians undertaking family searches. *"I would like,"* I continued, *"to learn more about your family."* Even as I shared a few thoughts with Eduard, the tone of his voice told me a lot. Over the years, Russian citizens were made aware that an innocent or careless remark could have been one's ticket to a labour camp. *"I am not,"* I added, *"a spy, an informant, a police officer, or a researcher. I am searching for members of my family. It could well be that we are related."*

"I understand," was Eduard's response.

"Listen, Eduard, my wife and daughter are also here. Would you like to meet my family tomorrow?"

The next evening we greeted Eduard, his wife Lara, and his son Vladislav in the lobby of our hotel. With the importance attached to the meeting, I wondered if I should use the familiar form of you, *ty,* when addressing Eduard and his wife, or the more formal *vy* form. The use of *ty* or *vy* in a Slavic language, including Russia, is a very important consideration. Although both can be translated as *you,* a distinction

59

is made. The form *ty* is traditionally used between friends to reflect familiarity, while *vy* is the more formal version of *you*.

As we were being introduced, I noted that Eduard used the first name as well as the *otchestov* or patronymic name of his wife and his son to reflect the *son of* or *daughter of* suffix. During the Soviet Union era, it was obligatory to list a person's middle name in the patronymic format. This meant that a child's middle name would always be the derivative of the father's first name. Once the formal introductions were over, Eduard reverted to the use of the diminutives by referring to his wife as *Larushka* and his son as *Vladya*. Traditionally, Russians shake hands with strangers when they greet and when they part. At first, they rarely if ever smile because to them it could be seen as a sign of stupidity or foolishness.

However, despite some of these traditions, I got my second bear hug from Eduard, while Sharon and Nicole got those two kisses, one on each cheek. Unlike Canadians, I noted that Eduard wore his wedding band on his right hand and that each member showed immediate respect for Sharon and me because, of course, we were older. Even though I spoke to them in Ukrainian, they answered me in Russian, appearing to be very grateful that at least I made every effort to speak Russian. In response, both Eduard and Vladya made an attempt to speak a few words of English to Sharon and Nicole.

During our conversation, I recalled that the Russian customs of sharing space and touching were positive values. With members of their own sex, the Russians will hug, stroll arm in arm, touch each others' hands and arms, and occasionally kiss on the lips when talking. Women tend to sit while talking to each other. Lack of physical contact is considered a sign that there is something wrong between the two speakers. Although smiles are a sign of approval, they are not given freely. Thinking about this, I realized that Sharon spoke only a few words of Russian and liked to smile a lot.

When we presented a bouquet of flowers to Lara, we made certain that there was an odd number of flowers because even numbers are given only in times of the occurrence of a sad event. I also recalled that you never call a Russian *comrade,* unless you were close friends or associates in the military. In the eyes of a Russian, the use of such terminology reflects ignorance, greed, and the absence of good taste.

True to Russian tradition, Eduard presented each of us with a gift of an intricately carved whale. In accepting the gifts, I thanked Eduard remembering not to gush over the gifts as that is considered to be rude. Had we gone to their home, I am certain that we would have been greeted at the front door with the Russian tradition of bread and salt.

In contrast to what we were wearing, the Kozlovs wore more somber colours. Perhaps the Russians are of the mind that light or bright colours make one appear lazy and unreliable. When we sat down in the restaurant to have a snack, Eduard told me that in Russia it is not considered that you have eaten unless meat is included. Unlike Canadians who like to add ice to their alcoholic drinks, the Russians don't. They prefer to drink their beverages at room temperature. To them, cold liquids are thought to cause throat illnesses.

I wondered why the Kozlovs did not start drinking, until Eduard reminded me that Russians do not start drinking until a toast is made. As the evening progressed, the toasts became lengthier and occasionally humorous. Always clinking our glasses, there were toasts to peace, family, friendships, to the beautiful city of Tyumen, and to the beauty of Siberia. Of course, the clinking of glasses is essential unless you are toasting the dead. If you do not drink a toast to the bottom, you are considered to be excusing yourself from the toast, which is extremely rude.

Only after all of these formalities were out of the way were the Kozlovs ready to talk about family. We had a lot to talk about. During the evening we learned that Eduard Kozlov was employed by Trans-Siberian Railways. Since his father was employed by Trans-Siberian before him,

Eduard was able to attend a local university where he majored in railway economics.

"My work," explained Eduard, *"has to do with the development and maintenance of high level relationships with travel agents and freight companies."*

Looking at his greying hair, I couldn't help but ask, *"Are you nearing retirement?"*

"Da. It is interesting that you should ask. I will be retiring from my position next year."

Their son, Vladya, was also a graduate of the local university, the Tyumen State Oil and Gas University. According to Vlad, the university was the only one of its kind in Siberia. With an enrolment in excess of 70,000, it boasted four major departments, one of which was the Institute of Transport, Vlad's Alma Mater. Unlike his father who was involved in the movement of people and freight on the Trans-Siberian Railway, Vlad was involved in the transport of gas and oil. Married to Karina, they had one son, Dmitry, who was born in 2004.

"Vlad," I ventured to ask, *"are you involved in any way in the transmission of natural gas to Europe? The transport of natural gas through Ukraine?"*

"Da, unfortunately, Gasprom does have some disputes with the Ukrainian oil and gas company, Naftogas. These problems have to do with gas supplies, prices, and debts."

"Are these problems serious?"

"Da, very serious. The disputes started in 2005 and, to date, have not been resolved."

From Vlad, I learned that 80 percent of Russian gas exports to the European Union were made through Ukraine and that two-thirds of Gasprom's revenue came from the sale of gas that crossed Ukraine. *Little wonder,* I thought, *that the transmission of natural gas to European Union countries through Ukraine continues to be a question of economics as well as a hot election issue in Russia and in Ukraine.*

We spent the remainder of the evening talking about the deportation of Eduard's grandfather and his family to Omsk, Siberia. What surprised me was how the events surrounding that deportation were indelibly etched into Eduard's memory. With a couple of notable exceptions, he seemed to know all of the small details about the circumstances associated with the destination of his grandparents. To me, this meant that Eduard's father must have been an effective communicator.

"To tell you the truth, Steven," was Eduard's assessment, *"the deportation of my grandfather's family from Ukraine to Siberia broke up the family. We are just now building our own family, not in Ukraine but in Russia."*

At midnight we were in the process of saying our goodbyes when Eduard asked, *"Would you like to attend the Victory Day Celebrations with our family tomorrow?"*

The Kozlov family arrived at Hotel Vostok at ten o'clock on the morning of May 9. When I invited them to a light mid-morning meal, they politely declined saying that they already had a full breakfast of kasha and coffee. However, they accepted to have a drink of kvass, a non-alcoholic fermented drink made from rye bread available in the hotel. As we chatted over our drinks, Eduard provided us with a list of the formal activities scheduled for the Victory Day celebrations. As I listened to Eduard telling us about Tyumen, I realized the pride he had in his family and in Russia. *"Foreigners see Siberia as a prisoner of peoples during the reign of Josef Stalin. At the present time,"* explained Eduard, *"we are doing our very utmost to raise the level of our democratic and socialist consciousness. One century ago, we were a nation of serfs, from top to bottom—all slaves. We have come a long way since that time."*

Thinking about Eduard's reflection about his love for Russia, I reminded him that many foreigners look upon Russia as being a nation that proved capable of providing mankind with models in the struggle for freedom and socialism, but also with questionable pogroms, rows of gallows, dungeons, famines and servility to priests, tsars, landowners, and capitalists. Somewhat startled by my comments, he asked me if that was the way I felt about Russia.

"No, Eduard, this is not my view. It is a view held by many Westerners. I have a great admiration for the people of Russia. When I served in the Canadian Air Force in Germany, I saw the movie Dr. Zhivago at least four times! That movie told me a lot about the Russian soul."

As the morning wore on, we switched from drinking kvass to drinking compot (made by boiling fruit in hot water) and having a snack of chocolate cake. In the process of completing our mid-morning get-together with the traditional loose black Russian Caravan tea, my curiosity was piqued when Eduard said, *"My father had several very close military friends here in Tyumen. I want you to meet three of them at eleven o'clock this morning."*

As evidenced by the multitudes of people taking in the festivities, May 9 Victory Day celebrations were Russia's biggest national holiday. As we made our way to the heart of the patriotic activities, Eduard, Lara, Vladislav, Karina, and Dmitry all seemed to be as proud as peacocks. Each wore the traditional commemorative Ribbon of Saint George, a symbol of the nation's highest award for military valour. When we arrived in the central park, home to all of those patriotic songs and Russian ballads being piped over outdoor speakers, the enthusiasm for the Victory Day celebrations seemed to be contagious. Eduard escorted us to a section reserved for dignitaries and introduced us to three World War II Russian war veterans who survived the war's largest tank battle, the Battle of Kursk. *"These three veterans,"* explained Eduard, *"were close friends of my late father, Konstantin Kozlov."*

"So, your father served in the Soviet military with these three veterans?"

"Da, my father did serve with them. You know, Steven," Eduard explained proudly, *"Kapitan Igor Gyskov operated one of those famous Russian T-34 Tanks. Try to imagine surviving that ferocious tank battle!"*

Kapitan Igor Gyskov, in describing the horrors of the war, showed us, with pride, some of his physical scars that were souvenirs of that tank battle in the summer of 1943. With a big grin, proudly showing a row of gold-capped molars, he recalled how the German forces included a total of 50 divisions, composed of 17 armoured and mechanized divisions.

"Thanks to the Soviet spy network named Lucy, which operated out of Switzerland," Gyskov explained, *"the Russians received full details of the German plan."* Adding as an afterthought, *"We had a total of 1,300,000 soldiers, 3,600 tanks, 20,000 guns, and 2,400 aircraft. We eventually overpowered those stupid murdering Nazi thugs."*

I could not help but be impressed with the Kapitan's recollection of the Soviet fire-power. During one of our conversations, Kapitan Gyskov turned to me asking, *"Comrade, did you serve in the Canadian military?"*

"Nyet, no, sir, I did not. The closest I came to serving in the military was my time in Germany with the Canadian Air Force as a civilian."

As I reflected on that conversation, I am certain that Kapitan Gyskov misunderstood me. Much like the KGB agents during my time in the Soviet Union in 1967, he immediately took me to be a civilian in the Canadian Air Force under special assignment. Not wanting to argue with him, I let his belief slide. As we observed the morning festivities, Kapitan Gyskov asked, *"Will you be here at two o'clock this afternoon?"*

"Da," I responded, *"we will be here at that time."*

"In that case, our veterans will be passing this point in the parade at about two o'clock. I would be honoured if you would take our salute."

Not ever having been accorded such an honour before, I was at loss for words. All I could do was to nod my head in the affirmative.

The parade of veteran soldiers, military vehicles, public servants, youth groups, and emergency vehicles seemed to go on forever. Sure enough, just before two o'clock, Eduard and I spotted an open-air military vehicle approaching us with the three war veterans in it. When the vehicle was directly opposite our position, the three veterans stood up and saluted us. Standing at attention, I felt honoured to take their salute. Just for the moment, I put aside all of those negative feelings that I might have harboured about Josef Stalin. Instead, I remembered that Russia participated in the war on the side of the Allies. The three veterans stood ramrod straight as they held their salute until I completely acknowledged them.

Center-piece of the Victory Day Celebrations, Tyumen, Russia, 2010.

Victory Day Celebrations, Tyumen, 2010. Steven Kashuba with two Russian Military Guides.

Two veterans of the Great Patriotic War, Tyumen, 2010.

Victory Day Celebrations in Moscow, 2010. Russian Prime Minister Vladimir Putin in the center and President Dmitry Medvedev at the right.

I recalled the exuberance of the celebrations in Edmonton when the Edmonton Oilers won their first Stanley Cup, but I had to admit that those celebrations paled in comparison to the Victory Day celebrations in Tyumen. Starting during mid-morning, the traditional ceremonial military parades lasted the better part of the afternoon in front of crowds in excess of one-half million. We spent the afternoon with Eduard and his family, trying to get caught up on the checkered history of his family. That evening, Sharon, Nicole and I watched the celebrations from our hotel. With car horns blaring, flags waving, patriotic music, and loud shouts bordering on ecstasy, the revelry went on deep into the cloudless and warm night. Finally, at the precise hour of midnight, a quiet descended upon the city as we settled in for the night. Tomorrow would bring the last leg of our Trans-Siberian journey.

On the morning of our departure for Yekaterinburg, the Kozlov family joined us for breakfast. Before our train left for Yekaterinburg, I had one specific question for Eduard, *"Did your father ever receive a letter in 1963 which explained something important about what happened to his brother, your uncle Pyotr?"*

Looking at Eduard, I could see that my question caught him off guard. It took him several moments to get his composure back before asking me a question.

"Good Lord, Steven, what are you, a psychic? Do you have some magical powers?"

"No, this is not a case of magic. It is a case of good luck and being in the right place at the right time."

"Da, I do have a letter that my father received from someone in the Soviet Air Force."

"What happened to that letter?"

"That letter is in our home along with my father's other personal belongings. I also have the letter that my father wrote to the sender of that letter."

"You have the letter that your father wrote to this person? How is that?"

"My father wrote a letter of thanks to the sender. But, the letter was returned."

"The person who wrote the letter, was his name Commander Korab?"

Eduard looked as though he had been struck by a bolt of lightning. Finally, after the longest pause, *"How in the world did you ever come up with that information?"*

"That," I assured Eduard, *"is quite a story in itself."*

"Amazing, simply amazing! All this time my father thought that the letter was some kind of a cruel hoax. I am at a loss for words!"

Since the Trans-Siberian passenger train was not leaving until later in the day, Eduard granted my wish, went back to his home, and got a photocopy of that letter for me. As he handed me a copy of the letter, I could see that curiosity was getting the best of him.

"Trust me, Eduard, you will soon learn why these letters are so important. Meanwhile, I have a promise to keep in Lviv."

The final leg of our Trans-Siberian journey took us west from Tyumen to Yekaterinburg (Sverdlovsk from 1924-1991), a distance of about 350 kilometers. Yekaterinburg, a city founded as a factory-fort in 1723, was a part of Peter the Great's push to exploit the Ural region's mineral riches. Unfortunately, Yekaterinburg is known for an incident that has nothing to do with the region's economy.

It was here, on a night in mid-July of 1918, that Tsar Nicholas II (56), Tsarina Alexandra (46), Tsarevich Alexei (13), and the four young Grand Duchesses Olga (23), Tatiana (21), Maria (19), and Anastasia (17), were asked to assemble in a ground-floor room. As they stood in a row facing a group of armed men, they expected to be transferred somewhere else once again. Instead, to their surprise, the sentence of death was read out to them in the name of the Regional Soviet. Moments later, the Romanovs were no more than a heap of bloodied corpses hurled against a bullet-pitted wall. Their remains, rolled in bedclothes, were taken to an abandoned mine outside the city, their clothing meticulously searched, valuables removed, their bodies burned, and the ashes buried in a nearby swamp.

Above all else, it seems that Yekaterinburg is remembered for this dastardly event. However, Yekaterinburg is famous for other reasons. World War II turned Sverdlovsk (Yekaterinburg) into a major industrial center as hundreds of factories were transferred there from vulnerable areas west of the Urals. Because of the many defense plants, the city was closed to foreigners until after 1990. Remnants of this era still litter the city. Fighter planes are proudly displayed in schoolyards and missiles are housed in the city's Military History Museum.

Yekaterinburg, with a population approaching 1.5 million citizens, is famous as a transportation center. It is a major rail junction with connections to all stops on the railway system and, dating from 1881, the Railway Museum is housed in the old train station. Exhibits highlight the history of the railroad in the Urals, including a re-creation of the office of the Stalin-era railway director. It is the economic and cultural capital of the Urals' region, offering tourists more than a dramatic history. The wealth of the Urals is on display in the city's many museums and the ongoing economic boom is evident in the crowded cafes and clubs.

A modern freeway took us from our hotel to Yekaterinburg's Koltsovo Airport for our flight to Frankfurt, Germany.

On our flight from Frankfurt to Edmonton, I reflected upon the meaning of *Diaspora*. It occurred to me that it was the scattering of family like the scattering of seeds. Countless members of my family have become citizens of other countries, adopting that country's mores and culture. To them, homeland is a concept of the territory to which one belongs. There are synonyms with varying connotations: fatherland, motherland, mother country, country of origin, and native land. All are a reflection of the concept that the land does not belong to us. We belong to the land.

No matter. Josef Stalin had little regard for definitions. Deportations were taken in the absence of any such nuances. Stalin treated everyone the same—equally bad.

Singled out as belonging to the class of kulaks, what follows is the story of the deportation of the Kozlov family to Siberia.

PART 2

DEPORTATION

Chapter 5

YOU HAVE TWO HOURS TO PACK

*Take all that you can carry on your back in preparation
for a long journey*

When Alexei Kozlov heard the words, *"Attention, you kulak ublyudok (bastard). I am Commander Getnikov,"* he stood there for what seemed like an eternity, frozen to the spot, unable to move or utter a word. Confused and dumbfounded with his heart pounding, his whole life flashed before his very eyes. Barely able to look up at the tall Commander and his Brigade, Alexei suddenly realized that the rumours floating about in the community were true.

World War I had been over for twelve years and the memory of the Bolshevik Revolution was receding in the memory of Aleksandr Mikhailovych Kozlov. In the bustling village of Horodok, Soviet Ukraine, located near the Polish border and southeast of Tarnopol, Poland, life seemed to be unfolding the way it should. Although Horodok was home to three ethnic groups, Ukrainians, Poles, and Jews, there was little evidence of any open hostility among the groups. In fact, most local residents thought that the village was appropriately named—Horodok, a small and peaceful little garden. Unfortunately, the village had a secret; it portrayed a high degree of anti-Bolshevik sentiment. That would prove to have unintended consequences.

The year was 1930 and the fall harvest was about to be taken in by the Kozlov family. As Alexei surveyed his farm buildings that he helped his father-in-law construct, he had an uneasy feeling and for good reason.

It was late September, a time when the villagers customarily took in their gardens for storage in a root cellar in advance of the cold winter months. Perhaps as a harbinger of things to come, there were rumours of increasing food shortages. It was also a time when many peasants recalled the words of Vladimir Lenin, the communist revolutionary when on April 3, 1917, he promised the people *peace, bread, and land*. Most were hopeful that Lenin's promise would come true even though Russia was now firmly under Stalin's control.

Lenin's message had truly resonated with the peasants and provided them with hope for a healthy economic future. However, the dark clouds of Marxist-Leninist ideals would soon cast a long dark shadow upon the concept of peace, bread, and land. Marxist principles embodied the belief that a revolutionary proletarian class would not emerge automatically from capitalism. Instead, there was a need for a professional revolutionary vanguard party to lead the working class to a violent overthrow of capitalism followed by a dictatorship as the first stage to moving from Bolshevism to Communism.

Before the outbreak of World War I and following the war, Bolshevik leaders wanted to determine the reliability, or unreliability, of groups of peoples of Slavic origin living in the border region separating Poland and Soviet Ukraine. It was no surprise when the report from the statisticians concluded that the degree of loyalty to the principles of Marxism of groups of people was directly related to the geographic region in which they lived. The report concluded that the degree of reliability and support for the Bolshevik political cause decreased the further you looked for support from the center of Russia to the outskirts of the Russian Empire. In particular, they singled out the Poles and Ukrainians living in Russia's border region as being the least reliable in a time of crisis.

The future officers and commanders of the Tsarist, White, and Red Armies listened to this, studied it, and definitely took note. Since the village of Horodok was relatively close to the Polish border, its residents and the residents of the region quickly came under suspicion—especially the *kulaks* who had become prosperous peasants as evidenced by the amount of land and farm animals they owned, and their ability to hire workers. Lenin described the kulaks as exploiters and profiteers who used their surplus grain to enrich themselves at the expense of the starving non-agricultural parts of Russia. Worse luck for the kulaks, the village of Horodok was located near an efficient railway system that would soon play a pivotal role for the Bolsheviks.

Such military statistics were not limited to mere assessment and speculation. They were used to support an active and evolving policy that dealt with the reliability differentiation among Russian territories. As a result, regions with a highly concentrated unreliable population were registered and kept under control. In war zones, the strategy extended to taking civilian hostages, confiscating land, liquidating property and cattle, and deporting certain ethnic groups based on their national membership or group affiliation. As a result of this doctrine, special punitive military units were created and schooled in the use of systematic cruelty in stamping out any minor manifestations of discontent or rebellion against the Russian colonization of the Empire.

Just before the outbreak of World War I, Russia was aware of the dangers from within its borders from its own citizens and promptly launched arrests and deportations of German and Austro-Hungarian nationals in the regions of Saint Petersburg, Odessa, and Volyn. At first, the destination for these deportees was the Vologda Guberniyas (Northwestern Russia bordering the oblast of Arkhangelsk), but later shifted to Siberia. Not only were those suspected of espionage subjected to deportations, but also all men of conscription age as a preventive measure against their joining the armies of the enemy. In particular, the ethnic Germans living in the province of Volyn, Ukraine received exceptionally cruel treatment. In most cases, the Germans were required to pay their own deportation expenses. If they did not have sufficient means for their own relocation, they were transported to their destination as prisoners.

Map of Inter-War Poland, 1919-1939. The villages of Horodok and Lisovody
were situated in Soviet Ukraine, near the Polish border.

In the 1920s the Bolsheviks began to lean toward the idea of
collective agriculture. However, to their surprise they discovered that the
pre-existing communes which redistributed land periodically did little
to encourage improvements to the land. They formed a source of power
beyond the control of the Soviet government. As a result, the Bolsheviks
began to take aim at the kulaks, who in their view were beginning to
embrace capitalistic ideas. If some of the villagers in Horodok did not
know the definition of kulaks, they were about to find out.

Looking up at the azure blue sky, Alexei thought back to World War I and how he had, by virtue of living near Rava Ruska, served in the Red Army. How lucky he must have felt just to survive the conflict. Unlike his cousin, Andrij Kashuba, who served in the Austrian Army, the circumstance was far different and far more complex for Alexei. After the war, the Galician region, where the extended Kashuba family lived for so many years, was ceded to Poland. Not able to hide his disappointment, Andrij immigrated to Canada. However, Alexei did not want to entertain the idea of living in Poland, nor did he want to immigrate to another land far removed from his ancestral homeland. In contrast to the journey of no return that Andrij took, Alexei had earlier elected to move a short distance east of the Polish border to Soviet Ukraine and take up residence in the village of Horodok, nearer the family of his wife.

But, life in the new village of Horodok was not that easy. The demand for more grain by the Bolsheviks in 1928 resulted in the reintroduction of requisitioning. This initiative was resisted by peasants in rural areas. In turn, Stalin claimed that grain was being hoarded by the kulaks. The seizures of grain by the Bolshevik regime discouraged the peasants from producing more grain. Contrary to Stalin's directive to kulaks to increase grain production, the opposite result was achieved when authorities discovered that less grain, not more, was produced.

Resistance to seizures of grain led to some violent incidents and resulted in massive hoarding. The most common practice was that of burying the grain. If the peasants could not hide or otherwise dispose of their entire crops, many would harvest the crop as hay while others would burn it or throw it into the river. The Bolsheviks promptly concluded that unless they took drastic steps, economic terror would soon become rampant in the region.

Russian intelligentsia had contradictory views of the peasants. Many Bolshevik leaders believed that the peasants were the soul of Russia—sincere, patient and enduring, all the while being free of the falsities brought on by wealth. However, as events unfolded, the peasants developed a mutual antagonism toward the Bolshevik leaders. As a result, Bolshevik revolutionaries began to have doubts about the peasants. Even before the war, Bolshevik revolutionaries tried to stir up the *narodnikis* (village people) but without success. The founder of Russian Marxism, Georgi Plekhanov, described the peasants as *barbarian tillers of the soil, cruel and merciless, beasts of burden whose life provided no opportunity for the luxury of thought.*

The Bolsheviks felt that the poorer peasants could be herded into collective farms. However, all too soon the more enterprising of the peasants gained more and more land and even employed others to help them with the farming enterprise. Unfortunately, the sudden appearance of these kulaks presented a perceived opposition to the advancement of the Bolshevik ideal. In the eyes of Lenin (and later supported by Stalin), they had become a class enemy that had to be destroyed, either by deportation or death. In reality, most of the kulaks had only a few cows and horses and only one in a hundred farms had more than one hired worker. The average kulak's income continued to be lower than that of the average rural official persecuting them. Suddenly, any peasant, whosoever, was liable to the policy of *dekulakization.*

Josef Stalin embraced many of the political ideas of his predecessor Vladimir Lenin, the leading political figure in the 20th century who masterminded the Bolshevik takeover of Russia. Stalin spent fifteen years as an activist in Siberia which prepared him well for the office of General Secretary of the Communist Party in 1922. When Lenin died in 1924, Stalin promoted himself as political heir. By the late 1920s, he became the dictator of the Soviet Union. To his dismay he discovered that the stubborn Ukrainians went on struggling to assert their linguistic and cultural separation from Russia. This, in the view of Stalin, was contrary to one of the central tenets of Marxism-Leninism which stated that the proletariat has no country. Nationhood was a characteristic of capitalism whereas the aim of socialism was to merge nations, eliminate classes, and develop an international perspective. All of this was to be accomplished in the absence of a private conscience, private value, without property, and without a spiritual dimension.

On December 29, 1929, Stalin announced in the newspaper *Pravda* that, *"We have gone over from a policy of limiting the exploiting tendencies of the kulak to a policy of liquidating the kulaks as a class."* To accelerate collectivization, the Bolsheviks decided to send 25,000 socially conscious industry workers to the countryside from 1929-1933. These workers became known as the *Twenty-five-thousanders.* Stalin used shock brigades to force reluctant peasants into joining the collective farms and removed those who were declared kulaks and kulak helpers. Collectivization sought to modernize Soviet agriculture, consolidating the land into parcels that could be farmed by modern equipment using the latest scientific methods of agriculture.

The dekulakization program could not be carried out in a vacuum. When the Bolshevik regime first laid out its program in 1917, they created the Cheka or the All-Russian Extraordinary Committee to Combat Counter-Revolution and Sabotage. In 1922, Cheka morphed into the NKVD or the People's Commissariat for Internal Affairs. Proudly wearing special uniforms, their main role was one of acting as an internal security and a prisons' guard force responsible for maintaining the regime in Russia's labour camps and undertaking the mass deportation of Ukrainian kulaks.

Commander Getnikov's unit, now confronting a dumbfounded Alexei, consisted of five officers. Their task was to receive orders from the NKVD headquarters in Moscow, and to identify and collect those kulaks earlier identified by a Communist Troika for deportation to Siberia. Unlike other NKVD units, Getnikov's unit did not contain any volunteers; they were all professional military personnel ready to do Stalin's bidding.

The assignment on this day was to arrest a specific kulak family, collect their internal passports, give the family two hours to pack their belongings, and transport them to a Khmelnitsky railway station, a distance of 40 kilometers. Once delivered to the railway siding outside of the city limits, the task of guarding the train while it was en route to a destination somewhere in Siberia would be left to another NKVD unit.

The Commander's unit prepared well for its duties. In their possession the unit had the names of the families they would be arresting and deporting over the next month. There were other NKVD units operating in the same region; however, that was of no concern to Getnikov. Looking around at his heavily-armed unit and the dark green truck equipped to transport prisoners but camouflaged as a vehicle to deliver bread, he felt confident that nothing would stand in the way of success. He already knew that the kulaks were most unlikely to offer any armed resistance to their arrest. If they did, his unit had a very good remedy for that.

When Alexei heard the truck approaching the family residence, he had prayed that it was some sort of a mistake. Earlier in the day he had heard rumours about the NKVD units operating in the oblast. However, he was reluctant to accept that Stalin would put into operation a plan to rid the countryside of the most effective small property owners. As the truck approached the farm house, there was no mistaking their affiliation. Noticing only two men in the cab of the truck, his first impulse was to shoot them both. Unfortunately, he also knew that to confront them was completely out of the question.

As the truck came to an abrupt halt in front of house, the driver of the truck and his assistant got out slowly and deliberately, approached the rear of the truck, opened the doors and motioned three more soldiers to get out. Then, looking directly at Alexei, he declared, "*Attention, you kulak bastard. I am Commander Getnikov. Is your name Aleksandr Kozlov?"*

The question sent chills through Alexei's body. For just a moment he could not find the words to respond. Finally, in a shaky voice, *"Tak, it is."*

"You are no more than a common thief stealing from the common worker. I command you to bring all members of your family into the front yard. Na kaleni, subaka (on your knees, you dog), when I give my orders!"

While on his knees, Alexei suddenly got enough courage to ask, *"Why do you want all members of my family?"*

"Don't ask me stupid questions. Get up off your knees and get them out here immediately. You will soon know your fate. Snap to it or we will bury you right here."

Quickly getting to his feet, Alexei had no choice but to hustle all members of his family out of doors. His father-in-law, Mikhailo Luzinsky, now in his late 60s looked as though he were about to have a heart attack when he saw what was unfolding before him. Alexei's mother-in-law, Maria Luzinska, several years younger than her husband, took the shock of the moment considerably better. She had to be restrained while Alexei's three teenage children seemed to show more curiosity than fear. Once assembled in the yard, the Commander bellowed, *"I need all of your passports."*

Commander Getnikov, a fervent disciple of all things Bolshevik and now a member of the feared NKVD, wasted no time in establishing his authority over Alexei Kozlov and his family, declaring, *"Any sookin syn (son of a bitch) who does not follow my commands will be shot. The document I have from NKVD headquarters indicates that your family consists of six members, not including your wife's parents. I want the passport of each member of your family! Get them immediately, you durak (stupid person)!"*

Alexei knew where he kept all of his important documents. With shaking hands and tears welling up in his eyes, he retreated into the bedroom of the family home frantically searching for the passports. When he located them in the bottom drawer of the wooden cabinet, he also saw his bolt action Austro-Hungarian World War I Ruck-Zuck rifle neatly wrapped and tucked away in the rear of a drawer. *I wonder,* he thought to himself, *if I should grab my rifle and shoot all those damn Bolsheviks.* But, just as quickly he nixed the idea knowing full well that his whole family would likely perish in a pitched gun battle. As Alexei put the passports together, he was fully aware that the NKVD would realize that their eight-year-old son, Pyotr, was not at home.

"Here are the passports of my family, Commander."

As Commander Getnikov scrutinized each passport, he asked the obvious question, *"Where is Pyotr? Is he not at home?"*

"Nyet, Pyotr is in another village visiting his aunt and uncle."

"You say that he is visiting his aunt and uncle? In what village?"

Despite the confusion of the moment, Alexei immediately made a decision to declare, *"Our son is in the village of Balyn. He is with his aunt for a couple of weeks."*

"Balyn? Where the hell is Balyn. I have never heard of the village."

"Balyn," explained Alexei, *"is a small village about thirty kilometers from here."*

Alexei reasoned that were he to tell the truth that Pyotr was in the nearby village of Lisovody, only five kilometers from Horodok, Commander Getnikov's henchmen might set out in search of him. However, to his relief, Getnikov neither questioned the name of Pyotr's aunt nor did he show much interest in setting out in search of their youngest son. At that point Getnikov ordered two of his lieutenants to search the house and the farm buildings. Finding no sign of Pyotr, Getnikov accepted Alexei's explanation. After a few moments of thought, the Commander declared, *"In that case, we shall leave without Pyotr. We can look after that little pasek (puppy) at another time."*

Alexei didn't know what to make of the decision. In a way, he was thankful that at least one member of the family would be spared the calamity awaiting each one of them while on the other hand he was most reluctant to split up his family. Commander Getnikov once again examined the passports of 39-year-old Alexei, 36-year-old Luba, and their children, 16-year-old Konstantin, 15-year-old Katusha, and 12-year-old Nikolashya. Once satisfied that the passports were in good order, he turned them over to his lieutenant. Following a brief discussion with his lieutenant, Commander Getnikov announced that the Luzinskys would not be joining the family for the journey. *"My instructions,"* he paused to tell his brigade, *"are to get this no-good kulak family to the train on time for their journey. That's all!"*

The physical appearance of Alexei, a stocky and solidly-built farmer of medium height, was in sharp contrast to a tall and slender Konstantin. With unruly blond hair and sky-blue eyes, Konstantin was a star soccer player on his school's soccer team and the heartthrob of several girls. Katusha, a mature fifteen-year old, reflected the appearance of her mother, an attractive middle-aged woman of slender build and blue eyes. In contrast, brown-eyed Nikolashya was a bit of a tomboy. She loved animals, especially her pet cat Musha.

As the family hurriedly prepared for the journey, it was clear that this particular NKVD Commander had some discretion in his decision-making capacity. Otherwise, why would he not pursue further the matter of the absence of Pyotr? And, why did he suddenly announce, even to the surprise of his unit, that they would be leaving without the Luzinskys? Didn't Commander Getnikov know that the unit could eliminate the Luzinskys and burn to the ground the family home? Obviously, Getnikov did not have to rationalize his actions.

A kulak family being arrested by the NKVD and then deported to Siberia.
Source: Gulag History Museum, Moscow.

A truck disguised as a bread delivery van used for the transport of kulaks to a railway siding. Source: Gulag History Museum, Moscow.

Railway cattle cars were used for transporting deportees to Siberia.

When it came to the question of packing, Commander Getnikov was very clear, saying to Alexei, *"Your family can take warm clothing, underwear, footwear, bedding, kitchen and dining utensils, one month's supply of food for the family, small agricultural and domestic implements, personal valuables, and money without limit. That is all."*

Still in a state of shock, Alexei ventured, *"Is there a limit to how many kilograms we can take for the journey?"*

"Tak, there is a limit of 500 kilograms for the family. This is about all you would be able to carry on your backs."

"What will become of my wife's parents and the land?"

"After our departure, your land will be turned over to the local authority. As for your wife's parents, the NKVD authorities will allow them to continue to live in the family home."

A thousand thoughts raced through Alexei's mind. It seemed as though his whole life was coming undone. Somehow, he knew something terrible was taking place. Whatever it was, he did not want to think about it. In fact, he had to pinch himself to confirm that this was actually happening to him and his family.

All too soon Alexei would learn of the family's destination, a fate worse than death.

Chapter 6

SIBERIA!

*You are traveling a long way and there you will not eat
from spoons*

Without specific information about their destination, the Kozlovs had to quickly decide on what to take for the journey and what to leave behind. The process, to say the least, was heart wrenching. Whatever they considered for the journey, there was no shortage of memories associated with each possession. After a brief discussion, they had to rely upon the rumours of others who had recently been deported from the region. *"Luba,"* was Alexei's final decision, *"I think it best that we take a supply of warm winter clothing. Surely Siberia is our destination and Siberia is a very cold country. We had better take all the food we can carry, a few kitchen utensils, and some basic gardening and carpentry tools."*

"I think, Alexei, that each of us should dress with at least two, even three, layers of clothing. Maybe I should take my sewing machine. I know that it will come in handy when we need to mend our clothes. I shall also take the family bible," ventured a determined Luba.

In less than two hours and always under the watchful eyes of the NKVD, the family packed all that they could into five cotton sacks—bedding, clothing, and items of personal belongings, basic gardening tools, and food. Fearing that they would be shot if they screamed or sobbed at any time during the ordeal, Luba's parents kept to themselves, too bewildered and frightened to do otherwise. Alexei was kept under constant armed guard, leaving Luba and the children to do the packing. To expedite matters, one of the NKVD guards assisted with the packing, making sure that plenty of warm clothing was included. When Luba asked about the small sewing machine, the guard nodded affirmatively without saying a word, cautioning her, *"You are travelling a long way and there you will not eat honey from spoons. In truth, you may not be eating very much at all."*

As the family placed their belongings onto the dark green truck, they noticed that it was camouflaged as a delivery truck with the words *bread* printed on each side in Ukrainian and Russian. *"This truck,"* Commander Getnikov was heard to say, *"is being provided for your family's transport. You may want to take some utensils that will be of use to you in the future."*

"You mean like gardening tools?"

"Stop asking stupid questions, you dumb kulak. Others arrested in this village and surrounding area will be transported by horse-drawn wagons or ordered to walk to the railway station. They will take only those things with them that they can carry on their backs."

The head of the NKVD in the district had at his disposal a large number of confidential party workers, the district militia, and local activists. The act of evicting hundreds of kulak families in the district was supervised by units of NKVD Troikas. The Troikas were commissions of three people employed as an additional instrument of extrajudicial punishment introduced to circumvent the legal system with a means for quick execution or imprisonment of anti-Soviet elements. Over the years, the Soviet Troikas would be credited with the murder or exile of over 600,000 citizens. However, during the initial stages of Stalin's plan to deport kulaks, evictions were supervised by militia units composed of five military personnel. For reasons known only to the head of the NKVD in the district, the Kozlov family qualified for escort by a military unit.

On its journey to Siberia, the train would not take the usual route through the Ukrainian capital city of Kyiv but rather swing north and east to stay away from major centers. The NKVD wanted to minimize any potential problems along the route to Moscow before continuing its eastward journey. Once the deportation train reached Moscow and entered the Trans-Siberian Railway system, the NKVD felt confident that the chances of any kind of disruption from deportees or residents along the route would be considerably lessened.

Commander Getnikov was aware that most of the arrests of anti-Soviet categories of population, often classified as *enemies of workers*, were being undertaken in the middle of the night. The scheduling of night action was taken to ensure the element of surprise and to make certain that those about to be arrested and deported would not escape. However, that was not the case with the arrest of the Kozlov family. Since this was the initial stage of dekulakization, NKVD headquarters in Moscow wanted a high profile arrest conducted in the late afternoon to have the maximum impact upon the neighbours and those living in nearby villages. The Kozlov family was among the first of the kulak group to be earmarked for immediate deportation.

At the same time that the kulaks were targeted for deportation, there was a renewed assault on religion when numerous priests were deported or shot. Churches were closed and turned into workers' clubs, cultural institutes, and granaries. Church bells were sent to scrap. By the end of 1930, four-fifths of the churches in Western Ukraine were closed. Luba was fortunate that the NKVD was not aware that she had packed a bible for the journey. In referring to the deportation of kulaks, Stalin was heard to muse, *"Not one of the kulaks is guilty of anything, but they belong to a class that is guilty of everything."*

As the family's home receded in the distance, Luba broke into tears. The pain of leaving behind the village that was witness to her marriage, the birth their four children, and the family's search for economic security was unbearable. Most of all, she had a special place in her heart for the Ukrainian Orthodox Church her family helped construct and where she and Alexei were married, and their children baptized. The best she could do was close her eyes to the unimaginable pain of it all. Perhaps even individual members of the NKVD unit felt a tinge of remorse as they watched the family being driven to the railway station. After all, many of them had families of their own. They, too, might soon meet a fate similar to that of the Kozlovs.

As the truck passed through the village of Horodok, it was as if each resident wanted to know which family was being singled out for deportation. Of course, none wanted to make their curiosity too obvious for fear that they, too, might be on the list. Worse yet, no one seemed to know with any certainty the criteria that the Bolsheviks used to define a kulak. Each perhaps asked, *"Will I be the next person to be deported?"*

Under the ever watchful eye of the armed guards, each member of the family cried quietly and uncontrollably. With tears streaming down their faces, each member had to deal with their own pain. With the village receding in the background, Alexei had to admit that his family was getting special attention. En route, they passed three horse-drawn wagons and several armed units, all marching their prey in the direction of the small city of Khmelnitsky. Those on foot carried nothing more than their meager belongings on their backs.

Even at the earliest stages of the dekulakization campaign during 1930-1931, the NKVD would deport tens of thousands of kulaks from

Ukraine to labour settlements in sparsely populated regions of Siberia and Soviet Central Asia. During those fateful years from 1930-1932 when nearly two million kulaks were deported, the average kulak family consisted of 5.5 persons. Tens of thousands of criminals, petty thieves, prostitutes, and political activists were deported to labour camps where the survival rate was very low. Of the nearly two million deported during those two years, 400,000 perished during their unrelenting journey to Siberia.

During the initial stages of the deportation of kulaks, many of the sophisticated techniques of arrest and sentencing were not yet in place. Through trial and error, the process of removing kulaks from Ukraine was constantly upgraded and improved. In cases where one or more of the children were not at home during the arrest, they were located soon after or even weeks later and deported to places different from that of the family. However, the deportation of a child left behind was not a priority of the NKVD.

Her heart breaking, Luba could not put her family's misfortune out of her mind. *Why our family? Did someone report us to the NKVD as cultivating more land than would a small farmer? Is it because our family has been successful while others have failed? Why the special treatment from the NKVD guards? Is it as a result of an order from a ranking Bolshevik or from Stalin himself? Or, is it a decision that Commander Getnikov made?*

Luba could imagine the attitude of some of the zealous neighbours towards the family's deportation. Outside the limits of Horodok she observed a group of teenage boys from the nearby village through a small window in the rear of the van. One of them assisted the Kozlov family with the previous year's harvest, now waiting perhaps for an opportunity to plunder their property. It was not unusual for the military units to receive assistance from locals in the form of transport to a collection point. As working peasants, they knew that the possibility of their own deportation was slim. After all, the NKVD Troikas were aware that the deportations were aimed at kulaks, an identifiable group which did not embrace the ideals of Bolshevism.

By late afternoon, the bread truck arrived at a point near the town of Khmelnitsky. In order to keep the deportation away from prying eyes, the deportees were immediately loaded onto a cattle transport train at a railway siding away from the main station. The warm temperatures and the beauty of the surroundings belied the gravity of the situation.

It seemed as though Katusha, Konstantin, and Nikolashya had mixed feelings about their plight. As teenagers, how were they to know otherwise? In contrast, their parents knew full well their circumstance. To Luba and Alexei, it was as if they had received a death sentence.

The Kozlovs discovered that the train was especially prepared for the transport of prisoners. Two of the 55 cars were set aside for NKVD guards and a first-aid station, while all other carriages were earmarked for the transport of prisoners. Each railway cattle car, bolted securely from the outside, was able to accommodate up to 60 deportees and their belongings.

According to Bolshevik records, medical care was to have been provided by a medical orderly and two nurses. Unfortunately, what Bolshevik officials envisioned for this or any other journey and what really happened was strangely disconnected. It seemed as though there were as many militia as deportees at the railway siding. In order to hasten the loading operation, there was no shortage of shouts and orders from guards, all to the sound of moans and wails emanating from young and old. The Kozlov family felt very much alone. Even if they could, there was no one they could embrace or to whom they might say *good bye*.

Whether on foot, by wagon, or by truck, prisoners eventually reached the train station. In this case, the station was a piece of land enclosed by barbed wire. Looking around, Alexei noticed that the prisoners were subjected to a series of special rituals before they were allowed to board. For whatever reason, the prisoners were counted by an NKVD guard who swung his revolver through the air while shouting at them, *"Get on your knees, you dogs!"* Each was then counted and re-counted while the train waited. The most potentially explosive time occurred during the loading of the transport carriages when someone would start running only to be stopped by the butt end of a rifle. To better control those being loaded, everyone had to kneel before receiving permission to load. To get up too quickly could mean a bullet in the back of the head from a trigger happy guard.

An official checked off the name of each family member as they were loaded onto Car 34. The list contained the names of six members of the Kozlov family. Looking at Kozlov, a guard barked, *"Are you the head of this family?"*

"Tak, I am the head of this family," was a meek and frightened response from Alexei.

"I have checked off five members of your family. Where is the sixth member?"

"That missing name," replied Alexei in fear of what might happen next, *"is the name of my son Pyotr. He was away from home visiting his aunt. The NKVD left him behind."*

As the prisoners were being loaded into Car 34, an official checked with Commander Getnikov to confirm the accuracy of the information provided. Once confirmed, the family was ordered to board the carriage and to take all of their personal belongings with them.

The inside of the car was dark, the only source of light coming from the small openings near the ceiling. Most seats were taken when they boarded, so they elected to lay claim to a couple of bunk beds and use these for seating. Later, they would learn that the train was a mixture of passenger and cattle cars and that Car 34 was known as a *Russian hard car* with pairs of hardwood double seats facing each other. That evening, they would discover that they made a good choice. Even before the train was fully loaded, the smell of humans crowded into a relatively small space signaled a harbinger of things to come. Each of the 60 passengers in the car was about to take the journey without the benefit of a change of clothing or a bath.

From the outside, all the train cars looked perfectly ordinary—except that some were better protected than were others. Several of the carriages exhibiting a great many iron bars and grillwork were regular third-class carriage cars modified specifically for the transport of prisoners with criminal records. Known as the *Stolypinki*, each of these had two compartments, one for passengers and one for cattle. In this particular case, the passenger sections were set aside for guards while the cattle sections were used for the transport of prisoners. The windows in all the carriages were barred and individual compartments were separated by steel nettings instead of walls, giving them the appearance of cages. A long iron net separated the compartments from the corridor. This arrangement enabled the guards to constantly keep an eye on all prisoners in the cars.

Even though conversations were discouraged, the Kozlovs soon learned that there would be no hot meals during the journey to an unknown destination. At first, the NKVD commented that each person would get 800 grams of bread each day. This would have translated into about 28 ounces of bread. However, this turned out to be no more than wishful thinking. In reality, there were days when the guards did not open the cars and the food supply was limited to hot water and the odd loaf of bread supplemented by a pot of watery soup which had to last for a few days for everyone in the car. The cast iron coal-burning stove located in the middle of the car did not give off much heat, making it difficult to keep the occupants warm.

During the first two days of the journey, the train stopped at several locations to pick up additional passengers until, according to rumours, all 55 cars of the transport train had reached capacity. When the train reached Moscow, it connected with the Trans-Siberian Railway locomotive with over 3,000 deportees on board. Upon hearing that they were now on a world famous railway, the deportees in Car 34 promptly broke into the singing of patriotic songs, the most popular of which seemed to be *We Will Not Forsake Our Land*. At other times, it was not unusual to have the family kneel and intone, *Our Father* and *Hail Mary* prayers followed by the singing of the traditional hymn, *At dawn all lands and seas sing praises for Thee, God Almighty.*

In these conditions, deportees got sick, several died, and two children were born during the journey. Rumours circulated that any child born during the journey, as well as the bodies of the dead, would be dumped along lonely stretches of the railway. An opening in the wagon floor served as a toilet which, to keep up appearances, was screened with a blanket. The strong iron ring around the hole in the floor of the carriage prevented prisoners from enlarging the hole and dropping down onto the track. On occasion, the hole was also used during stops for trade and barter with locals for a piece of black bread or some tobacco. There were no washing facilities, no illumination, and it was not uncommon to share the same space with rats and other vermin.

The length of the train was illuminated by spotlights mounted on the leading carriages. Iron spikes were fastened underneath the carriages so that any prisoner trying to escape under a carriage would be scooped up by the spikes. The outside of the carriages were marked with the words *special equipment*, which explained the presence of armed guards with automatic weapons on the roofs of the cars. Deportees were not visible to an outside observer. Stopping only in deserted areas for inspection twice each day, all prisoners were herded to one end of the carriage and then counted as they moved back to the other end. Sometimes, a prisoner would be struck by a guard wielding a hammer just to keep law and order or just for the hell of it. At other times, the hammer was used for testing the soundness of the walls, ceilings, and floors.

At night, the Kozlov family, joined by others, would sing the songs they learned as children at home or in school. There were popular folk songs and army marching songs, some of the songs going back to the 17th century. As the sun began to set, the mood of the deportees mellowed and the lyrics reflected wistful songs of love and heartbreak. From the control car, NKVD officials sent reports to headquarters every few hours, reports that were promptly transmitted directly to the office of Josef Stalin.

Ever eastward, the train relentlessly sped along. Guards moved up and down the train at regular intervals beating on the walls of the cars with rifles to ensure that no planks were missing or broken. Since most of the deportees on this particular train were kulaks or political prisoners, the NKVD felt that not every car needed a guard. In the evening when the train stopped at some lonely station or railway siding, the door bolts were removed and from each carriage a few men with buckets went off to collect water. It was not unusual to seek out several young male deportees to assist with the water brigade, always under the watchful eye of heavily-armed NKVD officials. Perhaps the biggest challenge for many families was to protect their own food supply from those around them. This was not a problem for Alexei in that he felt comfortable with the vigilance and assistance of his closely-knit family.

Rations for all prisoners transported by rail were very similar—bread every two or three days and salted herring that did little else but cause a severe thirst. As a result, the biggest need for Alexei's family was that of an adequate supply of water. In all, the journey to the appointed destination lasted nearly three weeks during which time just about everyone was in a state of exhaustion, mentally and physically.

Even at this stage in the history of the development of a comprehensive railway system in Russia, the Trans-Siberian Railway, starting in Moscow, was the world's longest and most famous train route. Passing through European Russia, the railway wound its way through the Ural Mountains which separate Europe from Asia, and continued into Siberia's taiga and steppes ending in Vladivostok on Russia's Far East coast on the Pacific Ocean. Along more than 9,000 kilometers of its length, one would witness a myriad of landscapes. It was the only overland route through the whole country, thus giving it a unique status.

Constructed from 1891-1916 to protect Russian Pacific Ocean territories, the Trans-Siberian Railway was critical to Russia's sovereignty over the vast region. It boasted some unique features, among them the 2,612 meter bridge over the Amur River and the two kilometer tunnel through a mountain. It served numerous cities and towns along the route, crossed 10 time zones, and 16 large rivers. Little wonder that the vast region needed an influx of new immigrants and slave labour to develop and sustain its industry.

During the journey, very little of this information was made available to the deportees. Even at that, much of this information did manage to filter down to each passenger car. Yet, and even though the cars had no windows, the small openings secured by iron bars were left open and the changing landscapes were visible to all those interested in taking a peek by standing on a bunk. Even during the evening and night hours, the landscape, especially under a starlit sky, was very visible and often breathtaking.

Leaving Moscow behind, the train made its way in a northward direction through Yaroslavl before swinging south to the first major stop in Nizhny Novgorod, 560 kilometers east of Moscow. As the deportation train traveled farther into the Russian hinterland, more and more freedom of movement was allowed by the guards. Perhaps the guards were aware that the likelihood of escape decreased with every passing kilometer. Upon reaching Nizhny Novgorod, a guard informed those in Car 34 that this city marked the end of the Nizhegorodskaya Oblast region and the start of the Kirov region. The provision of this information helped ease the tension and led Luba to remark to Alexei, *"Could it be that this Bolshevik is a human being?"*

The stop in the small industrial northern city of Kirov was long enough to give the deportees time to get off the train and under the watchful eyes of the guards stretch their legs. The guards watched the prisoners at all times and were therefore able to control what prisoners ate, to listen to their conversations, and to decide when and where they would be able to relieve themselves. Virtually everyone had to face the horrors of urination and defecation either through the hole in the center of the railway car or in the great out-of-doors, always within view of the guards. Privacy was now a thing of the past. Those prisoners with stomach ailments, or other medical problems, were in a much worse position. Some would foul their clothes and often the prisoners sitting next to them. Even in the community of hardship, it was difficult for some prisoners not to hate those who did this. To add to this problem, the two young mothers, each with an infant child, experienced problems in keeping their infants clean and quiet. There was no water with which to wash the diapers, all of which added to the stench in the cattle car.

As the train passed through villages, there was no shortage of *babushkas* and *dedushkas* (*grandmothers* and *grandfathers*) standing on the railway siding with the hope of selling some homemade food, such as baked potatoes, fresh vegetables, flour, dried fish, meat, and desserts. Unfortunately, the deportation train did not stop in any of these villages.

As time passed, the lonely NKVD guard in Car 34 seemed determined to talk to somebody. At one point he went so far as to give

Luba a copy of *Nasha Rodina* (*Our Motherland*). The short publication contained a map marked with a red pencil indicating the family's final destination. When Luba thanked him, he cautioned her that divulging this kind of information was strictly forbidden.

When the train resumed its journey, the Ural Mountains came into view. They looked particularly inviting and serene to those able to catch a glimpse of them through the small openings in the top of the carriage. The next stop of any length did not happen until the train had traversed the Urals and pulled into the polluted city of Sverdlovsk (Yekaterinburg). At a railway siding outside the city, the guards allowed a small number of deportees to disembark and get some exercise. One carload containing 70 prisoners was uncoupled from the train under heavy guard and shuttled to another train. No one knew the final destination of that carriage. Meanwhile, a freight car loaded with merchandise was added to the deportation train.

In times of great stress, it was not unusual for someone in Car 34 to poke a bit of fun at their dire circumstances. One particular kulak, having a penchant for humour, was heard to remark that he hardly noticed that their train had passed through the Urals. Instead of awe-inspiring high mountains dividing Europe from Asia, he presented a strange point of view, *"All I saw were some snowy hillocks crowned by anemic-looking spruce trees."* To punctuate his observation, he added that, *"Comrades, I just had a crap in Asia and it is no different from the one I took in Lviv!"* By this time, there were all kinds of rumours as to which freight car with its prisoners, if any, would be left behind in Tyumen. However, after a brief stop, the train continued on its eastward journey.

The next major city on the Trans-Siberian Railway was Omsk, 2,700 kilometers (three time zones) east of Moscow. By the flurry of activity and anticipation, it now seemed certain that many of the deportees were actually destined for this region of Siberia. Despite the few weeks of planning the resettlement procedure, the release of prisoners in Omsk was anything but smooth. The stench from the open hole in the floor which served as a latrine, and the close quarters of deportees crammed together without the benefit of a shower or bath, was intense. Included in the transport lists were several deportees with physical handicaps or illnesses who should never have been subjected to this sort of punishment.

As the prisoners disembarked, it became clear that specific guidelines for this activity were never fully developed. Mistakes were made. When authorities reviewed the list of prisoners in the cars, there was the case of a military settler from Volhynia, Ukraine, a decorated World War I hero, whose personal questionnaire had a special note on it, *'Do Not Deport.'* Unfortunately, he found himself in Siberia in the company of kulaks.

As Alexei looked around, he was shocked to notice the composition of the group. From outward appearances, it looked as though some were criminals of the roughest kind—men who resembled beasts rather than human beings, rough and brawny enough to withstand the muscular wear and tear and the horrible agony of cold and frozen limbs during the journey. Others exhibited refined faces and comparatively slight physiques.

Also in the group being emptied into the vastness of Siberia were women convicted of various criminal acts and anti-soviet tendencies along with a vulgar and brutal crowd of convicts from low dens and vile brothels. Sandwiched among these dirty, foul-mouthed women were several young girls. They were brought up in refined homes, gently nurtured and reared in luxury, but who had been arrested and convicted of sympathy for the anti-soviets. Under guard by armed soldiers astride their horses, each deportee waited with fearful anticipation for what was to happen next. Their fear was not so much from the end of a rifle, but from the fierce-looking guard dogs.

"Listen up, you dumb kulaks, criminals, suki (bitches), and political saboteurs. My name is Commander Federko. You are now under the control of our Red Army Brigade. There are four destinations from here and I will read the names of those assigned to each group. From here, you will carry your belongings and walk to your destination. Do not try anything stupid or a bullet in the back of your head will put you to sleep forever."

The names of 65 deportees were read out, their credentials checked, and assigned to Group One. Under the direction of two heavily armed Red Army soldiers and one guard dog, they trudged off in a northerly direction. Two other groups of similar size were sent in an easterly direction, and the final group of 60 deportees, composed of kulaks and their families, was assigned to Group Four. Weary, hungry, tired, and completely disillusioned, the Kozlov family had their internal passports verified by NKVD officials. With that, the family was now ready for the final leg of their journey to begin to " . . . *pay their debt to society and make themselves useful by not contaminating others with their ideas or their criminal acts."*

In all, five railway cars were shunted to a railway siding for deployment to work camps in the Omsk region. The remaining cars continued their journey to the next region of Novosibirsk. As Car 34 was being unloaded, Alexei counted the number of deportees that survived the journey from Ukraine. Initially, there were 60 passengers in Car 34, but now only 55 remained. Of the 300 deportees who should have been disembarking from five cattle cars, 25 were missing. It was becoming abundantly clear that the Gulag was already taking its toll long before the end of the journey. The future was looking anything but bright.

The history of Russian exile goes back to Russian law of 1649. At the time, exile was considered to be a new, more humane form of criminal punishment—far preferable to the death penalty, branding, or mutilation. The kulaks being dropped off at the railway siding were not guilty of any crime, but in the opinion of the NKVD, their economic status or presence in a particular place was " . . . *contrary to the ideals of Bolshevism and prejudicial to public order and incompatible with public tranquility.* "

In the early days of the Gulag, the locations for the camps were chosen primarily for the purpose of isolating prisoners as well as providing labour for the building of Russia. Remote monasteries, in particular, were frequently re-used as sites for new camps. These camps were being presented to the world as an example of the new Soviet way of re-education of class enemies and re-integrating them through labour into the Soviet society.

With the new emphasis on the Gulag as a means of concentrating cheap labour, new camps were constructed throughout the Soviet Union, wherever the economic task at hand dictated their existence. The majority of Gulag camps were positioned in extremely remote areas of northeastern Siberia along the Kolyma River and in the southeastern parts of the Soviet Union, mainly in the steppes of Kazakhstan. These were vast and sparsely inhabited areas with no roads. Camps were spread throughout the entire Soviet Union, including the European parts of Russia, Belarus, and Ukraine.

Prisoners in the first three groups had been charged with a variety of petty and political crimes and considered to be criminals. As a result, they would be held from two weeks to two years in a concentration or labour camp doing hard labour before evaluation. Then, they would be transferred to another labour camp within the limits of the empire where they would be put under police surveillance for another period of one to ten years. Most would not survive the treatment that awaited them.

After three or four years of hard labour, the chance of survival for any additional length of time diminished with each passing month.

Before departing, Group Four was addressed by an NKVD official, *"You useless scoundrels are now ready for your new lives. Take your belongings and follow the lead horse. I will follow you mydaks (assholes). Anyone not able to keep up will be punished."* To emphasize the seriousness of his command, the NKVD official fired one round from his rifle into the air. As the Kozlov family readied for their march to the work camp, they suddenly realized that carrying nearly 500 kilograms of clothing, kitchen utensils, gardening tools, and a sewing machine was no easy task. Luckily, those with a lighter load of personal belongings in the group offered to help. *"Let's go, you lazy no-good saboteurs,"* was the command from the lead guard.

Alexei couldn't think of anything to say that would take away the pain. Each member of the family remained silent with their own thoughts. Luba thought about Sunday Mass and the regular family dinners which followed. Konstantin, a *gymnasium* (secondary school) soccer star, thought about a soccer match he missed the previous week. Katusha thought about the boy who played on that very same soccer team, the secret love of her young life, and Nikolashya harboured images of her closest friends and her pet kitten Musha. Looking at the heavens above, Alexei was moved to ask of no one in particular, *"What is to become of us? What will become of Pyotr? Is it possible for God's creatures to carry out this terrible plan?"*

"These," replied Luba, *"are not God's creatures. This is the work of the devil."*

Answers to these questions were not forthcoming. Silence enveloped the Kozlovs as they trudged along to an unknown destination.

Chapter 7

THE SHOCK OF SIBERIA

Survival in a harsh and hostile environment

As the fourth group of deportees set out for a labour camp, Luba took note of the wild looks of those around her. Sobbing and rocking back and forth, their faces pale and drawn, they marched along the trail under the watchful eyes of two Red Army soldiers. Their very deportment told of their mental agony as they suffered through their physical pain, perhaps some dreaming and even praying for death, which would mercifully come to many of them before long. In particular, the sympathy from the physically strong for the younger children in the group was palpable. Throughout the march, there was no shortage of moans, sobs, and wild cries for pity and mercy. Perhaps the religious in the group wondered why their prayers to God were not being answered.

Most had prepared well for the journey, wearing at least two shirts, two pairs of trousers, and instead of socks, pieces of linen wrapped around each foot. Many wore a large heavy woolen overcoat. When a woman in the group asked for a brief moment to relieve herself, the response from the soldier in the rear was immediate, *"Take a moment only, you bitch, and catch up to the group."* Right there at the side of the trail the frightened woman squatted, relieved herself, and immediately resumed the march without the benefit of even wiping herself.

It was not unusual for a laggard in the group to receive a swift kick in the rump or the back of the head from the mounted soldier.

After marching for five hours with constant shouts to keep moving, the progress slowed. Several were afflicted with swollen limbs as a result of walking on a muddy trail with wet feet, constantly crying out in pain for help. Mercifully, the NKVD guards called for a rest period as darkness began to envelop the group. However, the rest period was woefully short. Some terrible scenes developed and Alexei felt that it was a wonder that some of the wretched marchers did not murder one another or one of the guards. Such were the indescribable horrors endured by the marchers. Unfortunately, most knew that this was just the beginning of their suffering.

After about five minutes of rest, a command from an NKVD guard got the attention of the group, *"Let's go, you no good lazy dogs."* With the weight of their belongings, several in the group had difficulty in getting back on their feet. In such cases, Konstantin and Alexei reached out to provide assistance before resuming their own march.

The group's struggles reached a merciful end when, under a full moon, the group arrived at the work camp. Even though the hour was near midnight, four barracks were visible in the large opening in the forest. In addition to the barracks, two smaller log buildings were visible, one for the use of camp administration and one shell of a building for the use and care of work horses. Before being assigned to a barrack, each of the deportees was searched once again by camp guards for any articles of food or money that they still might have in their possession. These were confiscated by the guards for their own benefit, following which the process of sorting out the prisoners continued. Luba was thankful that the family bible was not confiscated by the guards. It appeared as though the guards had no interest in religion.

Marching deportees to a labour camp. Source: Gulag History Museum, Moscow.

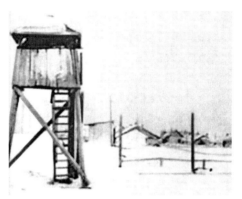

A guard tower in a Siberian labour camp.

Russian Black Terriers and Siberian Huskies were commonly used by the
NKVD as camp-guard dogs.

A dimly-lit barrack awaited the kulaks and their families. In the center of the large earthen-floor room was a narrow table on which were located two coal-oil lamps. On the perimeter of the room were two tiers of narrow plank beds nailed against the wall. At both ends of the barrack were piles of straw meant to be made up by the kulaks as mattresses for beds. Sore and bruised, many would have difficulty climbing into the upper bunk bed.

Before retiring for the night, each family was served a small amount of bread and water. Somewhat energized, they wanted to mingle and talk about their personal ordeals. Alexei noted that Barrack One was filled to capacity with several families and their children. The other three barracks were either assigned to newcomers or left vacant until the arrival of the next exiles. The lingering smell of the interior of the barrack left the impression that it had been recently occupied. *"Alexei,"* enquired Luba, *"I wonder who occupied this barrack previously? Where are they now?"*

In response, Alexei simply shrugged his shoulders. He did not even want to entertain a thought as to what might have happened to them. In taking a count of those in the barrack, Alexei determined that there were 29 adults, 10 teenagers, and 11 children ranging in age from infancy to twelve, for a total of 50 occupants. Exhausted and tired, the deportees were not angered by the words from an NKVD official who poked his nose into the dimly-lit barrack, shouting, *"You bourgeoisie dogs are now in Labour Camp 27. Make your own beds and then its lights out. Everyone to bed within one hour."*

It might have been a journey to hell, yet aside from the fact that the family was a virtual prisoner of the Bolsheviks, the setting belied the seriousness of their predicament. Even the beauty of the surrounding forest had a silver lining. It would soon provide the barrack with a ready source of firewood. Since the barrack did not have the luxury of manufactured mattresses, the deportees were required to make their own from two piles of straw. In addition, there was a small pile of cotton wool in one corner of the barrack which could be used in making pillows.

Barracks in a Siberian logging camp.
Source: Gulag History Museum, Moscow.

The Kozlov family chose a location in the center of the barrack, near a wood-burning stove. With winter weather to arrive soon, they wanted to be certain that their beds were reasonably close to the source of heat. Using the bed sheets they brought with them, Katusha and Nikolashya made two small straw mattresses for their bunk beds, and one straw mattress for Konstantin. Meanwhile, Luba and Alexei made a large straw mattress for themselves and placed it on the bare plank floor next to their children.

"This whole thing is crazy," grumbled Alexei. *"A cruel plan put together by cruel and stupid criminals. I made a terrible mistake by not shooting a couple of them in Horodok."*

"To verno (that is true), *"* responded Luba tearfully as she settled into their straw bed, *"these damn Bolsheviks have crushed our hopes and dreams. One day they will get their asses kicked. I will be the first in line to do that kicking."*

Still, this was not the time for recriminations. *After all,* thought Alexei, *even the act of feeling sorry for oneself can sap a person's strength and resolve.* As catastrophic as was the deportation and the exclusion from the environment of their ancestors, Alexei was no stranger to adversity. He knew the challenges before him—first, he had to keep his own spirits up and second, he was now responsible for the survival of each member of his family, much as had been the role of his father before him. Things could have been much worse. What if he had been separated from his family and sent to a different camp or left in the wilderness without food or clothing? Maybe even put to death?

The next morning, Alexei and Konstantin were up at sunrise. Looking around at their surroundings in the midst of a boreal forest generally known as the Russian taiga, each realized that escape from the logging camp would be an impossible dream. At the perimeter of the clearing were empty sentry boxes and only one armed guard accompanied by a guard dog stationed at the entrance to the camp.

The extreme winter temperatures which would surely arrive in November, followed by average daily winter temperatures of -30 degrees Celsius, would soon challenge the family's resolve. Better to think about the summers which, although short, were generally warm and humid. Even though in dire straits and the hour being early morning, the atmosphere seemed surprisingly relaxed when an NKVD official, approaching the barrack, declared, *"You kulak thieves are very lucky. Your destination is a logging camp. Other prisoners are not so lucky."*

"Not so lucky? What is their fate?" asked Alexei.

"Who knows? They are probably somewhere beyond the Arctic Circle. It's cold up there, damn cold. They don't last long up there. Your destination is this special settlement camp and not a corrective labour camp where your chance of survival would be small."

Somewhat relieved to receive some encouraging news, Alexei got sufficient courage to ask the NKVD official, *"A special settlement? What is that?"*

"Da, you were sentenced without a court hearing, weren't you."

"You say that this is a logging camp? But, where are the roads to get the logs and lumber to market?" enquired Alexei.

"Roads? Why, you miserable stupid kulak, we have the two best road systems in Siberia. You saw our railway system, the very best in

the world. Soon you will see our river system, which is Mother Russia's greatest road for transporting logs to our saw mills."

Back inside the barrack, the NKVD official who had spoken to Alexei just moments earlier entered the barrack. Sporting a neatly trimmed beard and moustache, bushy eyebrows, and dressed in a Red Army uniform, he gave the appearance of being an offspring of a Mongolian tribe who invaded this part of Siberia so many years earlier. Short, stocky, and quick of movement, the official's order was blunt, loud, and to the point, *"Get up, you no good scum of the earth. I am Commandant Systovsky. By seven o'clock you will make for yourselves a small breakfast of porridge. You may then rest for the balance of the day. Do not leave the perimeter of this work camp. We have guard dogs and ammunition. Work starts tomorrow."*

He would not be the only official to visit Barrack One. Systovsky's earlier appearance was in contrast to the scraggly-looking Brigadir, the next visitor to the barrack who addressed the new arrivals, *"My name is Brigadir Lashkov. Here is a pot of buckwheat for this barrack. Decide who will prepare your breakfast. Divide the porridge equally. Use the utensils you brought with you. Each person will get one slice of bread for the day."*

In listening to Lashkov, Alexei must have concluded that it was unusual for NKVD officials to introduce themselves. Perhaps the introduction came from Lashkov's realization that the deportees would be seeing much more of them in the coming days and that the appearance of the development of a positive working relationship, at least in the beginning, would do no harm. The introduction, however, did little to dispel the impression that Lashkov treated the newcomers with a good measure of disdain, as if to say that their working relationship, as well as their time on earth, would be a short one.

During that one-day rest period, the slave labourers left behind in the work camp and who had not been transferred to another work camp, must have felt that they had hit the jackpot. Along with the newly-arrived deportees, they were also given a day off. This gave the inmates of the four barracks an opportunity to mingle and meet the NKVD staff who would direct their lives in the coming days, perhaps for years to come. During that day of rest, the new arrivals learned about the organization of the logging camp. Commandant Systovsky and Brigadir Lashkov worked as a team; Systovsky responsible for the general operation of the camp, while Lashkov took care of issuing logging equipment each morning, work assignments, and the performance of each team.

Camp security was an important function in the logging camp. In this camp, the Commandant had eight Red Army militia soldiers at his disposal. In turn, the militia had four trained guard dogs: two German Shepherds and two Black Russian Terriers. Dressed in their Bolshevik uniforms, the militia brutes, with dark, weathered faces, and sunken eyes, looked more like fierce Mongolian warriors and not your regular Russian soldiers. In addition to the militia men, the Commandant was assisted, when necessary, by several labourers who had earlier adopted the principles of the Bolshevik Party. Their assistance was particularly helpful in cases when disciplinary actions became necessary.

Once the prisoners were washed and shaved, the second step in the process of turning men and women into anonymous zeks was the job of determining which deportees would require camp clothing. In some camps the wearing of standard camp uniforms was mandatory, while in other camps the labourers could wear their own clothes, if such were available to them. In Camp 27, the labourers were permitted to wear their own clothing. The decision seems, in practice, to have been left up to the whim of each camp.

In the end, it did not always matter. By the time the deportees reached the camp, many prisoners' own clothes were in rags, if they had not already been stolen. Those who arrived without their own clothing were issued camp clothing. As well, each received a pair of long underwear, a black tunic, quilted pants, one long quilted outer jacket, a felt hat with ear flaps, rubber-soled boots, and one pair of fleece-lined mittens. No effort was made to ensure that sizes matched the prisoners' weight and size. It was not unusual to find prisoners trading items of clothing in an effort to come up with the right size.

Staying warm in a Gulag barrack.
Source: Gulag History Museum, Moscow.

A prisoner in a Siberian labour camp.
Source: Gulag History Museum, Moscow.

The Kozlov family was full of questions about the local geography and the existence of any other work camps in the region. However, neither the Commandant nor the Brigadir seemed in a mood to discuss any matters pertaining to the various functions of the camp or the local geography. From others in the camp, the new arrivals learned that the Omsk region was situated on the confluence of the Irtysh and Om Rivers and that the oblast was located in Western Siberia. The highest point in the oblast, which covered an area of 140,000 square kilometers, was no more than 300 meters above sea level.

The oblast of Omsk was bordered by the oblasts of Tyumen to the west, Tomsk and Novosibirsk to the east, and the Republic of Kazakhstan to the south. To the north was the *taiga,* the sub-arctic lands consisting of coniferous and evergreen forests. To the south and southwest was a stretch of forest *steppes* and fertile black soil. The Irtysh River, navigable throughout the year, unless confronted with an unusually cold winter, made it crucial to the logging industry.

Founded in 1716, Omsk, 2,555 kilometers east of Moscow (three time zones), was already a bustling industrial town and was quickly becoming an important administrative and transportation center. Served by the Trans-Siberian Railway and located in a region rich in natural resources, the deportees would soon discover that its location was preferable to many other destinations in Russia's Eastern Empire.

During that fateful year of 1930, over 1.5 million deportees and prisoners would be exiled to this region of Siberia. The following year, an additional 200,000 prisoners would be forced to work as labourers in the Gulag. They would produce a third of the country's gold, much of its coal and timber, and a great deal of almost everything else. However, this kind of information was never made available to the camps' occupants—each slave labourer was kept in the dark, forbidden to read or write until such a time as permitted to do so by the Camp Commandant. Any kind of discussion, other than that having to do with daily tasks, was frowned upon.

It was a period when Stalin's Soviet Secret Police began to build several hundred camp complexes, each comprising thousands of *lagpunkts* (individual labour camps). In turn, each lagpunkt contained from a few hundred to many thousands of prisoners. These prisoners would soon work in almost every industry imaginable—logging, mining, construction, factory work, farming, designing airplanes and artillery—and live, in effect, in a country within a country, almost a separate civilization. They would ultimately be the ones who would be instrumental in building the Soviet Empire.

Living and working conditions in the camps varied significantly across time and place depending on the impact of national and international events. Country-wide famines, food shortages, waves of terror, and the sudden influx or release of large numbers of prisoners had a direct impact upon working conditions. To one degree or another, the large majority of prisoners faced meager food rations, inadequate clothing, overcrowding, poorly insulated housing, poor hygiene, and grossly inadequate health care.

With a dearth of food supplies in the camp, the first order of business in the barrack was the pooling of food resources that had not already been confiscated by the guards. Unlike their experiences on the train en route to Omsk, there was no opportunity to sequester or hide food from others in Camp 27. To do so would bring the wrath of all of the inmates upon the perpetrators' shoulders.

At the end of that first day's rest, the inmates in the barrack were served a light meal of cabbage soup and boiled potatoes. As was the case on the night of their arrival, at nightfall everyone in Barrack One was ordered to bed. However, sleep came slowly to Alexei. Cuddled next to him in their bed of straw, Luba also had difficulty falling asleep, each with their own private thoughts, yet surely of a like mind. Although there might have been plenty of tears at the outset of the journey, all of that was now over. Reality was finally setting in and sleep came slowly, albeit fitfully.

At daybreak, everyone in the barrack was roused by a guard who ordered the women to make a large pot of porridge for everyone. To everyone's surprise, Brigadir Lashkov brought in a small container of milk which was shared by the deportees. After a rationed breakfast, he addressed the logging teams, *"At the end of the day, you must complete your assigned tasks which are established for us by our superiors. If you fail to meet your quota, the food rations to your barrack will be reduced. Your barrack foreman will supervise your work. You will be reminded if your pace of work is too slow. Now, get to work, you dumb lazy bastards."*

Following the standing order for the day from Lashkov, the logging foreman for Barrack One addressed the group, *"This barrack is organized into work units as prepared by administration. I will read the names on each team."* As the names were read out, Alexei was relieved to learn that Konstantin was assigned to his five-man team. *"I will assign the equipment and take this barrack's logging teams to the work site. The women and children will remain behind and take care of camp duties. Their duties will include the provision of firewood for all barracks and gathering lichens and reindeer moss to supplement the camp's food supply."*

With that brief instruction, the four logging teams from Barrack One were assigned their logging equipment and provided with a small ration of food and water for a mid-day break. Leading the four teams to their work site was an armed Red Army soldier. At the rear of the logging teams was another heavily-armed Red Army soldier accompanied by a fierce-looking guard dog. During the march, Alexei's team stuck together and made small talk.

As they left the work camp, Alexei noted that not one of the four sentry posts was occupied. In fact, few if any logging camps in the region were fortified. The perimeter of most of the logging camps in the Omsk region was marked only with posts. Yet, this absence of any obvious fortifications did not make escape any easier. The new arrivals to the camp would soon learn that escape was deterred by the harsh elements as well as tracking dogs that were assigned to each camp. In some cases, a prisoner might be assisted by a native tribe in his attempt to escape, while in other cases the same tribe would return the escapee to the NKVD for a cash reward. Successful escapes were rare.

The four logging teams from Barrack One arrived at their timber destination within an hour at which point the foreman explained, *"Your job is to fell fir trees, limb them, and cut them to length. This timber area is assigned to your barrack. We have several other timber locations for Camp 27 logging teams. Once I see the quality of your work, you evil bastards, I will name a leader for each of the four teams."*

The instructions were clear and there was very little need for talk. Each logger wanted to get acquainted with his fellow workers, learn how to fell trees so that they dropped in the right direction, how to limb each, and how to cut each tree to desired lengths. Each knew the penalty of a sub-standard performance. As the day progressed, the foreman carefully watched the performance of each of the four teams. At mid-day, the foreman called a break.

"Kozlov, you may be a thieving kulak, but you do know something about logging. You will be the leader of your logging team. Make certain that you meet your daily quota. If you don't, you will be replaced."

Each logging team received a work assignment for every working day. Included in the assignment was the minimum number of trees to be felled, trimmed, and cut to desired lengths. With the use of grappling hooks, the logs were manually stockpiled to a height of two meters. Later, the logs would be transported to the nearby Irtysh River or to the railway siding. Ultimately, the destination for the logs would be a saw mill which would transform the logs into lumber for a variety of domestic and commercial uses.

As the leader of his logging team, Alexei set out to develop a sense of teamwork. After all, he was fully aware that food rations made available to the barrack would be tied directly to the team's work performance. As a consequence, the loggers were left to their own devices. Camp administration saw little need to reinforce this guideline. Meanwhile, a rumour circulated that a cafeteria for the camp would soon be in operation.

Barrack One would serve as a center of activity for the women of the lumber camp in the preparation of basic meals. As well, they would also be charged with the responsibility of sewing and mending work clothes, making yarn at those times when wool was made available, and knitting mittens and sweaters. Since the barrack provided a limited amount of space for all of this activity, it was not unusual for fierce fights to break out. Luba and her two daughters were not used to this type of behaviour and took immediate steps, as best they could, to protect their own territory in a barrack that was now their home.

The initial shock of being dressed as zeks was only the first stage in a long initiation. Immediately afterward, the prisoners underwent one of the most critical procedures in their lives as inmates—the selection and segregation into categories of workers. This selection process would affect everything that happened to each labourer, from the type of barrack he lived in to the type of work assigned. This, in turn, would determine whether a labourer lived or died.

This selection was meant to reflect a deportee's social origin, length of sentence, and state of health. Prisoners were put into three categories: those with sentences under five years, working class prisoners with sentences of over five years, and those sentenced for counter-revolutionary crimes for an indeterminate length of time. Most of the newcomers fit the category of working class prisoners with sentences of less than five years of hard labour. This is why their destination was a logging camp, reflecting the requirement for minimal security.

In the oblast of Omsk, winter can come very early or it can come late. Days become short, cold, and rainy overnight. In advance of the first snowfall in early November, the Kozlov family experienced something they had never suspected could happen to them in Siberia, a sandstorm. But then, neither did the family know much about the geography of the region.

Geographically, Omsk is close to Kazakhstan, a Russian Republic that to a large degree is sand-covered. As a result, whenever a strong wind blew in from the southerly direction, it was not unusual to experience a sandstorm. New residents soon discovered that during the fall and spring seasons, a sandstorm signaled a severe change in the weather. With the coming of the first major snowfall, a new set of challenges befell the camp. Up until this point, the residents were able to supplement their meager rations with mushrooms and berries. With the coming of snows, this was no longer possible. More and more, the inmates had to turn to the use of the soft and edible mosses from the taiga in the daily staple of cabbage or potato soup.

During those first weeks of labour, Alexei discovered, to his horror, that the three teams from his barrack rarely filled their work quota. He wondered if this inability to fill a basic quota came about by design or because the teams were short of talent and strength. The kulaks were no strangers to work; however, they appeared to be strangers to hard work. On one particular day, the four units were not supervised by either of the foremen. As a result, the mid-day break extended to a two-hour nap. The loggers would not return to work even when Alexei insisted that they do so. This resulted in a meeting with the four team leaders on the following day. On his desk, the Commandant had a copy of the Soviet penal code from which he quoted, *"A penalty is available for those who elect to sabotage the working order of the mighty communist society."*

He made it clear that the management of the logging camp was not immune from punishment, something they would wish to avoid at all costs. He ended his orders by saying, *"Each team leader is responsible for himself and his team members. The results of your work presented to me by Brigadir Lashkov are pitiful."* Fixing his stern gaze at Alexei, his question was direct and clear, *"What do you have to say, Kozlov?"*

When Alexei rose with the intent of speaking, the Commandant told him to sit down, that he didn't want any bullshit, just more hard work. Having heard that exiles disappeared for lesser fault, Alexei took the reprimand very seriously. He promised the Commandant that he would do better. In turn, each of the other team leaders made a similar promise. These promises were important in light of what happened the very next day, an event that sent shock waves through the barracks.

On a clear and cold winter's day, several rifle shots were heard. Rumour had it that two prisoners attempted an escape from a nearby work group and were promptly shot by a guard. In way of explanation to his superior, the guard said that coercive and motivational elements applied to these two labourers failed to increase their performance. Their work quota was never met. It seemed that the only explanation provided by the guard was that their faces pointed away from the work camp. This was sufficient proof that escape was on their minds.

Other problems began to develop in the barrack. A couple of the women began to vomit and retch continuously during the night. They said that with the windows being closed at all times, the suffocating odours in the barrack made them sick. This caused one of the women to open a window even during the coldest of nights, leading to more complaints.

Another woman complained about being raped in the middle of the night by one of the labourers in the barrack. When asked why she did not scream out, her retort was, *"I was afraid to scream, to wake the others in the barrack."* This led to the realization that in the darkness of night you could hear screams from this woman or that woman, followed by oaths and noise of scuffling only to realize that the source was not from a bad dream or a nightmare but from being sexually attacked. Such behaviour led to the creation of a vigilante group of males to protect the women in the barrack from unwanted advances. However, even this did not fully stop all the aggressive behaviour, sexual or otherwise.

One Sunday, the inmates of the barracks gathered in Barrack Three, the largest of the four barracks. It was a day off for everyone and they were about to be addressed by a special visitor from Moscow. Before the visitor addressed the group, a member of the Bolshevik Party played a couple of Russian melodies on a mandolin. *"People,"* said the Bolshevik visitor, *"I want you to realize one thing—you are here to work. Perhaps you will be here forever. You will live here and many of you will die here. Do not harbour any illusion that it is only temporary and don't expect a miracle. I want you to settle down and arrange your lives accordingly. If you work hard, we will try to better the living conditions and make your life more pleasant. "*

To those gathered to hear the hard truth, the words of the Bolshevik agitator were of limited comfort. Rumour had it that all new deportees received this kind of welcome only to find out that movement from one camp to another or from one economic initiative to another was not unusual. It occurred to Alexei that his family could be broken up and individual members transferred to other camps. However, one part of the speech rang true; it was common knowledge that thousands of deportees ended up somewhere in this vast area known as Siberia. Unfortunately, countless numbers ended up in Far East Russia where most perished without a trace. Survivors and their offspring often ended up in permanent exile.

Since this logging camp was not a secure detention camp under armed guard, fathers who had a family in camp were allowed to wander around in the surrounding forest. Administration felt that the head of a family would be unlikely to try to escape from a labour camp. One day, while wandering around in the timber reserve to the south and across the Trans-Siberian Railway, Alexei discovered an agricultural kolkhoz. He knew better than to tell anyone about his discovery.

In time, Alexei found out that this particular kolkhoz had been created just two years earlier and that it operated in a manner at odds with kolkhozes in Ukraine. While the traditional kolkhoz paid its workers a share of the collective farm's product and profit according to the number of workdays, a *sovkhoz* employed salaried workers. However, in Omsk, no such distinction was necessary; all of the kolkhozniks were forced labourers.

The importance of a kolkhoz within about 20 kilometers of the logging operation cannot be underestimated. As time went on, it was not unusual to find individuals in one group or another breaking the rules by developing a system of barter. Neither was it unusual to have one individual exchange a piece of clothing for an egg or two, some milk, or some vegetables. However, to get caught meant severe punishment and even expulsion to another work camp.

The forest turned out to be the source of nourishment in unexpected ways. During the summer months, there would be no shortage of wild berries which could be turned into preserves and, for the more enterprising, homemade wine. In the fall of the year, all one had to do was to bend over and fill a basket with a variety of mushrooms.

Initially, Camp 27 was not filled to capacity; however, this would soon change as new deportees continued to arrive. Meanwhile, the six women and the four teen aged girls in Barrack One developed a routine for carrying out the domestic tasks of cooking, cleaning, and general duties. The 15 teen aged boys began their orientation to the world of work by carrying out a variety of assigned tasks, one of which was the preparation of logs for a new barrack. This left 69 males, all assigned to logging and lumbering duties. Following two months of routine assignments, a considerable amount of stability was attained.

Eventually, the Commandant allowed the prisoners to write a letter to family in Ukraine. However, there was no guarantee that the letters ever found their destination. And, even if they did, one could be assured that its contents would be read by NKVD officials. As a result, it was not unusual to develop some sort of a code in order to communicate one's thoughts while at the same time deceiving the officials. In the end, few, if any letters ever reached their destination. Curiously, during that first winter no one in the labour camp received a letter from home.

Before long, a number of small group associations developed for the purpose of socializing. On the one hand, those with families tended to congregate as a unit, while the single males and females formed another group. Despite the close surveillance by camp management and militia, it soon became clear that it would be impossible to control the actions of every individual. Three enterprising males discovered a family in the agricultural kolkhoz who operated a small but secret apiary. The family sold honey to those who could pay a small price for it, while at the same time keeping their mouths shut. When Alexei heard about the operation, and even though he loved honey, the alarm bells went off. He knew full well that should these three individuals be discovered, they would be severely disciplined, if not eliminated.

With the frequent arrival of new prisoners, it was not unusual to find that the composition of a particular work group also changed. However, these changes were carefully controlled by the foremen. At all times, the foremen wanted to approve each and every replacement. In this way, the opportunities for escape would be minimized. As a method of ensuring that each assigned team member arrived for the day's logging operation, the foremen devised a clever scheme. At the end of each work day, each labourer would hide his work tools. If a prisoner arrived at the logging site the next morning and was not able to locate his tools, this was sufficient proof that an illegal replacement had taken place. This meant that an escape from the logging camp was contemplated or had already taken place.

In one such case, two prisoners arrived at the work site and were unable to locate their tools. To Brigadir Lashkov, it was obvious that an exchange without authorization had taken place. The two prisoners were immediately marched back to the barracks and transferred to the newly-established Vorkuta labour camp in far northeast Siberia. As for the two prisoners who arranged the exchange, a week later the Brigadir reported, *"Two prisoners escaped last week. I can report that those two rats were reported to the NKVD by a native tribesman and have since been eliminated."* If nothing else, the event had a subduing effect on anyone attempting escape.

Camp 27 was witness to two severe punishment procedures carried out by administration in order to place a damper upon escape and improve the work habits of labourers. In one case, a particularly aggressive foul-mouthed labourer was great in the use of profanity but less so as an effective labourer. The Brigadir wanted more production and less profanity out of him. As a result, he was singled out for some extreme torture. His arms and legs were tied behind his back and he was suspended upside down from the ceiling of a punishment cell for several hours.

In another case, a zek was forced to drink water until he nearly drowned. An NKVD guard then forced him to lie on his back, tied his hands and feet securely to the sides of the punishment cell, placed a plank on his stomach, and jumped up and down on the plank. As other labourers watched, the force of his weight on the zek's stomach caused the water to squirt long distances from his mouth and nose. Witnessing such punishment, the work ethic of all labourers improved. However, even with the increase in performance, prisoners continued to be shuttled from labour camp to labour camp.

With dwindling food supplies during the winter months, the prisoners relied more and more upon the various lichens which grew on rocks, trees, timber stumps, and the top of tundra in the forest. Reindeer moss not only provided food for the reindeer in the region but also for the labourers. Infrequently, the prisoners had a few grams of wild game or fish. However, such occasions were rare, more often replaced by the regular fare of cabbage soup mixed with edible leaves, roots, and reindeer moss processed in a special way. First, the cook would leach out the acids from the reindeer moss that could cause severe intestinal irritation. He would then make a powder which would be added to the soup to thicken it. Many were convinced that the lichens held special healing powers, especially if one were coming down with a high fever. Still, each week brought news of a prisoner dying from illness.

Perhaps one event, more than any other, changed the dynamics of Camp 27. Sixteen-year old Katusha and 17-year-old Anna Timskaya were assigned by Brigadir Lashkov to the logging operation. Lashkov was heard to say that the camp lacked the necessary manpower to skid the logs to a collection point for transport to the Irtysh River. The work was not easy and the two girls were unable to skid the larger logs to the collection point. On an early winter's morning, Brigadir Lashkov observed that Timskaya was not pulling her weight exclaiming, *"Why, you lazy little no good bitch. You are not pulling your weight."*

"Not pulling my weight," retorted Timskaya, *"if you are so strong and smart, why don't you skid a few logs yourself? Is this a job for a little girl?"*

Lashkov did not say a word. His ruddy face rising in colour, he slowly and deliberately extracted his pistol from his holster and shot Timskaya right between the eyes. Katusha was horrified with the suddenness of what occurred. For a moment, she thought that the Brigadir would also shoot her. Her father, working nearby with his team, heard the shot and rushed to Katusha's side. Soon, the two were joined by Konstantin. No one said a word. Finally, Brigadir Lashkov retorted, *"I'll report the incident to the Commandant. This camp does not need any lazy mouthy bitches."*

That evening, word about the senseless killing spread like wild fire. In particular, the parents of Anna could not hide their grief. The very next day, word filtered down to the labourers in Camp 27 that Brigadir Lashkov would soon be re-assigned to another work camp. Meanwhile, Katusha told her parents that their assignment came about because Anna rejected the sexual advances of Brigadir Lashkov, who fancied himself as a lover with an insatiable appetite for sex. This information infuriated Anna's parents who vowed that Lashkov would pay the ultimate price for taking Anna's life.

The logging operations continued unabated. However, in contrast to the first months of hard labour in the primitive logging operation, things began to change as production quotas decreased with the coming of winter. Labourers had more time to think and to talk about their circumstances. Some said that the Soviet leaders dreamed of doing away with guards, barbed wire, and labour camps in favour of more humane settlements where prisoners would till the soil, log the forest, and become productive citizens in a self-reliant frontier. There was even the rumour that Camp 27 would be one where some of these new ideas would find a home.

If this were the case, there was very little evidence to indicate that changes would take hold in the foreseeable future. Indeed, the opposite seemed to be happening. Suddenly, it was confirmed that three of the labourers in Barrack One were transferred to another work camp. Rumour had it that Camp 27 had been receiving special treatment and that changes were now in the offing. But then, how was one to know? Inter-camp visitations were forbidden, as was any communication with other camps.

Deportees continued to arrive in Camp 27, even during the winter months. Unfortunately, many had frozen to death en route as a result of the extreme temperatures and their frozen bodies had been dumped along the railway. With the coming of snow, severe temperatures, and a decrease in rations, the foremen found that the process of felling the thick trees for the socialist cause was quickly losing its importance. Labourers frequently turned on each other, on the camp staff, and on the two nurses who would visit the camp from time to time.

Siberia can be cold, very cold.

There was no shortage of reports about killings, theft, marauding, rapes, and dying. Others were injured as a result of conflict. Several either feigned injury or injured themselves in an effort to escape the drudgery of hard work, the crippling cold, and the loneliness of camp life. For those slave labourers who continued to reject the redeeming qualities of hard work, the NKVD had a number of behaviour modification techniques, including solitary confinement, starvation, beatings that left no marks, intimidation, humiliation, and sleep deprivation. Prisoners were dying from exhaustion, starvation, and hard labour. It seemed as though it was the criminal in their midst who had the best chance of survival by avoiding, to the degree possible, physical labour. Stalin was quickly turning human beings into animals.

"What was Stalin thinking?" asked Luba. *"Why would he send hungry, unshod prisoners without proper supplies to this Godforsaken land? To build his stupid brave new world?"*

"Shush, Luba. Don't allow these thoughts into your head. Our best chance to survive is to keep quiet. We must do what the Brigadir tells us to do. That is our only hope."

Chapter 8

LABOUR WITHOUT END

Bone chilling cold that numbs the extremities

A lexei may have been well versed in mixed-farming operations, but he never imagined that he would find himself inside a Soviet labour camp felling fir trees which were up to two meters in circumference. Even more difficult to accept was the camp's policy of tying production to food rations. The total of a logger's work measured at day's end would determine if he ate or starved. In essence, Alexei and Konstantin were now responsible not only for their own survival but that of the other members of the family as well.

The rations allocated to labourers in the Gulag were generally measured in grams. Depending upon circumstances, these allocations ranged from as little as 100 grams to as much as 800 grams per day for nutrients classified as dry goods, moist food, or liquid food. About 200 grams of soup would be equivalent to one cup of soup, while 400 grams of dry bread would be equivalent to two slices of bread.

As a farmer, Alexei had developed an easy-going and unhurried manner. Working as a lumberjack made the task of felling trees all the more challenging. Each worker was given 400 grams of half-dried bread to tide them over the ten-hour work day. When the workers arrived back at camp after a hard day's work, they soon realized that the meals being served were woefully inadequate. How could they be satisfying? The most common fare was watered-down cabbage soup laced with a potato or two. At other times it was chicken soup that looked like the cook prepared the concoction by running a chicken through a pot of boiling water and then adding a small amount of mashed potatoes or dried mushrooms to the mixture to give it some body.

Yet, all was not lost. Working with a small group of kulaks, Alexei soon discovered the fundamentals of survival. Obviously, it would be counter-productive to have one member of the group outperform all of the other members. This would only result in the establishment of increasingly higher performance standards. The decision to put a plan into place was precipitated, in part, from a remark made by a member of his team, *"Believe me, Kozlov, those guards have everything. They make kasha every day and eat it with butter. Their cabbage soup is made with meat and there is so much bread they can't eat it all. And, what easy work they have!"*

"You have seen all of this?"

"Da, I have. And, how do they come by all of these privileges? Simply by kissing the asses of their superiors and embracing soviet bullshit. They are ready to battle the evil enemies of the state and are encouraged to treat labourers brutally to prevent their escape."

Just thinking about the injustices rampant in a labour camp caused Alexei to pause and consider how the guards would accompany the labourers to the work site commanding them, *"A step to the left or a step to the right is considered an attempt to escape. We will shoot without warning."* This was sufficient proof of sadistic guard behaviour toward the labourers. When one labourer was recently shot by a guard, it was covered up by the simple words, *"Attempted escape."* Propaganda hammered home the supposed perversions and dangers of these anti-Soviet, virtually sub-human prisoners. It was always the intent of Gulag authorities to keep guards from getting to know prisoners on a personal level. The NKVD wanted the labourers to be treated in the same way at all times—at arm's length and badly.

Without even having to discuss the matter, Alexei's logging team developed a plan to attain and then maintain a standard of performance acceptable to Commandant Systovsky. To do otherwise would have put at risk the weaker members of the crew as well as members of other logging crews who would have to meet the performance standards established by Alexei's crew. Although Alexei's logging team did develop an effective work-to-rule plan, the NKVD officials seemed none the wiser for it. Weakened by some of the worst food in the civilized world and in winter temperatures that frequently went as low as fifty degrees below zero, it was a miracle that any member of the work group survived.

A religious family with Christian beliefs, the Kozlovs were saddened with the idea of not being able to observe their first Christmas in Siberia. It was no secret that the Communist officials who ran Camp 27 hated Christians and especially the very thought of any labourer wanting to celebrate Christmas. This upset Luba, who characterized it this way, *"The Communists not only hate Christians and Jews, they hate each other. They hate everything and everybody. When they quarrel, the Communist with the upper rank will try to get rid of the other by having him transferred to another work camp."*

"Shush, Luba. The best we can do," responded Alexei, *"is to celebrate Christmas in silence. We can even say a silent prayer when we go to bed."*

Even though the Commandant did not allow anyone to acknowledge or celebrate the birth of Christ, he seemed to understand the necessity of maintaining a positive attitude within the work force. After all, this particular lumber camp was for kulaks and not hard-core criminals who were destined for hard labour camps where the life of a prisoner was doubly dangerous. In those camps, the fear of gang violence and rape was very real. Serious conflicts between criminal and political prisoners were common as were conflicts among inmates from different ethno-linguistic groups.

Unlike the previous month when each team came under the surveillance of two foremen, it now became a common practice to be under the control of only one foreman. In time, the work group gained the confidence of the NKVD and the foremen gave the prisoners more and more freedom, to the extent that on some days they would complete a day's work without any supervision.

During January in Siberia, everything vanishes beneath a deep blanket of whiteness. Rivers, fields, trees, and forest roads disappear, and the landscape becomes a white sea of mounds and hollows. On days when the sky is gray, it is hard to see where earth merges with the sky. On this particular cold winter's day, the sky was a rich blue, the sunlight, refracting the light, blinding as if millions of diamonds were scattered on the snow. Unfortunately, the magic of the day was about to unleash a storm. Not one person came forward with an answer to the Commandant's question, *"Where the hell is Lashkov?"* This was the evening that Systovsky was to meet with Brigadir Lashkov to plan the logging activities for the ensuing month. Lashkov, however, had not returned from his duties of the previous day.

It would not be until the next morning that Alexei, accompanied by the Commandant, would find Lashkov. The news was not good. There, under a huge fir tree lay the frozen body of the Brigadir. Curiously, the fallen log was on the perimeter of three contiguous logging operations and no one seemed to know what happened. All enquiries were met with stoic silence. Rumour among those in Camp 27 had it that this was retribution for the death of Anna Timskaya. Commandant Systovsky filed a report with NKVD headquarters with assurances that he would fully investigate the incident.

In the end, Systovsky had no alternative but to punish all those who were part of the work crew on that fateful day. Food rations were decreased and Camp 27 would not return to normal operations for the next two weeks. Meanwhile, Katusha was convinced that justice for her friend had now been served. Re-assigned to camp duty, she felt relieved that the tragedy of Anna's death was now behind her. In reflecting upon the incident, Alexei remained skeptical about the Commandant's assurances that he would fully investigate the tragic death of the Brigadir.

As the cold winter weather continued unabated, it was not uncommon for a prisoner to get severely frostbitten. At times, it was difficult to determine whether a member of the group deliberately exposed his fingers or toes to the extreme cold to invite frostbite just to get a few days away from the lumber camp. Other prisoners justified their transport to the hospital in Omsk by inducing an infection. This could be accomplished by pulling thread through the plaque between their teeth and then running the thread through a few inches of flesh with a needle. To discourage these kinds of practices, the NKVD officials immediately placed such perpetrators into solitary confinement in an unheated cubicle, a penalty that many did not survive. On other occasions, many of the labourers who tried to escape from the work camp were shot and their frozen bodies left at the entrance to the camp as a reminder to others who might be contemplating escape.

Once a sufficient number of logs had been cut to length and stockpiled, an NKVD official ordered the logging foreman to begin the process of manually skidding the logs to the Om River, a tributary of the Irtysh River which drains into the Ob River before emptying into the Arctic Ocean. These two river systems provided Siberia with an ideal system for floating logs to saw mills downstream. In addition, some of the logs would soon be loaded onto sleighs for transport to the nearest railway siding before being freighted to a saw mill in Omsk. Since over one-quarter of the land mass in the region was covered by pine, cedar, spruce, fir, birch, and aspen, the logging crews had in inexhaustible supply of logs.

Siberian logging camp operations.
Source: Gulag History Museum, Moscow.

Although the logging camp did have a structure to house horses, it did not have its own draught horses or hay to feed them. The Commandant was aware that Alexei had draught horses on his farm in Horodok and that he knew how to work them. Consequently, Alexei was selected to join two newly-assigned camp foremen to pick up horses, sleighs, and other skidding equipment from a kolkhoz in the region. During the twenty-kilometer walk to the kolkhoz through heavy snow, Alexei feigned surprise when a foreman informed him that the agricultural kolkhoz existed near the logging operation. To admit that he already knew of its existence would bring the wrath of hell upon his shoulders. After all, the loggers were always under the impression that all labour camps and kolkhozes operated in isolation, far removed from each other.

When Alexei asked the foreman about the location of the kolkhoz, the foreman's guarded response was, *"The kolkhoz is somewhere in this region. Only a select few have knowledge of this. You are ordered to keep it so. If you don't, you will join Comrade Lashkov."*

The next morning Alexei and the two foremen returned to the logging camp with two sleds, six draught horses, and a sufficient supply of hay for a couple of weeks. Systovsky must have recognized Alexei's work ethic and leadership because he ordered him to operate a two-man sleigh to haul logs from the timber logging site to the nearby railway siding. With the deep snow cover and snow drifts along the wagon trail to the railway siding, Alexei and Konstantin set out to prepare an acceptable snow-road by shoveling a narrow passage through those locations that had excessive snowdrifts. Once this task had been completed, two additional sleighs were commandeered from the kolkhoz for the transport of logs.

Alexei was elated with his new responsibility. This gave him time to think about his present circumstance and what the future might hold for him and his family. In some ways, this new assignment helped to alleviate his feeling of hopelessness, desperation, and fatigue from the exhausting work schedule. It was also during the log-hauling operation that Alexei would discover that the region contained a considerable amount of agricultural land, some of it already under cultivation by collective farms.

Not all activity in the work camp was related to the production of logs and lumber. In February of 1931, the Commandant called a meeting of all workers in Camp 27. *"Today,"* was his opening remark, *"I shall be providing each member of the work camp with a standard Soviet passport which will serve as your identification card. You will be required to carry it with you at all times and produce it when asked to do so by any Soviet authority."*

The labourers accepted the new guidelines without being given an opportunity to raise any questions as to the necessity for a Soviet passport. Alexei, just for a moment, considered asking Systovsky about the adequacy of their Ukrainian passports but decided against it. To do otherwise might result in unforeseen circumstances. *"These internal passports,"* explained Commandant Systovsky, *"will replace your current passports. Some passports will be valid for five years, others for a shorter period of time. The NKVD office will decide which of you will be provided with 6-month identity cards."*

To Alexei, the provision of internal passports meant only one thing: some of the prisoners would be coming into contact with officials outside the camp, which would require them to present an internal passport. Later, it became apparent that the prisoners receiving the 6-month identity cards were the ones earmarked for relocation to another work camp. Throughout the process, no explanation was provided, all of which led to considerable speculation.

Unlike other camps where some of the workers would soon come from Poland, Latvia, Lithuania, and Belarus, nearly all of the workers in the Omsk lumber camp came from Ukraine. Throughout the process, it became the goal of the NKVD to establish and maintain complete control over all those who came to Siberia. However, despite the stringent controls and oppressive attitude of the guards, the atmosphere at times seemed somewhat relaxed.

After the passports were issued, the workers all returned to their regular duties not knowing what the immediate future held for each prisoner. Unfortunately, rumours began to circulate that internal passports produced for slave labourers who had been shot by the NKVD were being resurrected and used once again by unscrupulous Soviet officials who were intent upon providing a new identity for a prisoner in exchange for money or some other favour.

Meanwhile, a working relationship of sorts began to develop between Alexei and the Commandant. In reflecting upon the situation, Alexei was never quite able to put a finger on why or how the seemingly mutual understanding developed. Perhaps it started with the Commandant's sincerity in describing the benefits of the communist way of life at every opportunity and Alexei's apparent willingness to listen. *"You know, Kozlov,"* Systovsky would often muse, *"the very meaning of Bolshevism is majority. It comes from the word 'bolshinstvo.' Bolshevism captures the very essence of the principle of democratic centralism, military leadership, and support of the worker."*

"You have truly embraced Bolshevism, Commandant?"

"That is what Vladimir Lenin told us before the October Revolution in Saint Petersburg. It was the concept of these soviets that became the model for the Bolshevik Revolution in 1917. Do you understand me?"

Alexei did not discourage the Commandant from talking about his time in Saint Petersburg. As a young Bolshevik revolutionary, Systovsky supported Lenin's desire to organize the party in a strongly centralized hierarchy that sought to overthrow the Russian Tsar and achieve power. According to the Commandant, the Bolsheviks were not completely of one mind but rather based their beliefs on the notion of democratic centralism characterized by a rigid adherence to the leadership of the central committee. Systovsky recounted how the party refused to co-operate with liberal or radical parties which were often labeled as bourgeois (middle class). *"Most important,"* the Commandant would emphasize, *"our Party took an important position—solidarity among all of the workers of the world. Kozlov, you will soon belong to this world class of workers."*

Although Alexei may have been aware that Bolshevism had quickly become the official ideology of Soviet Russia, what he did not know was that all opposition was about to be suppressed and opposition leaders executed.

As each day of labour stretched into the next, the Kozlovs realized that the NKVD never did confirm the length of their banishment to Siberia. True, there was a common understanding that the standard length of a kulak's sentence was five years. However, all that the family knew was that they were sent to a relatively remote district that possessed rich forests awaiting logging operations and agricultural land of questionable quality. In the midst of these potential economic riches, rumours began to circulate that within their own camp, many continued to die from starvation. Others drank themselves to death from bad liquor made locally. To add to the stress, the population was composed of fewer than 15 percent women. This imbalance provided little opportunity for socializing with the opposite sex, leisure activity, or entertainment.

Following on the heels of prison reform, which started in Europe and quickly spread to Siberia, the Bolshevik leaders began to shed some of their previous harshness. Regimes grew lighter and policing more lax. In contrast to what was to come after the outbreak of World War II, the present circumstance of the slave labourers seemed hardly an onerous punishment for the relatively small group of men and women who ended up in Omsk. In the work camps, the inmates received a certain amount of favourable treatment as productive workers rather than as criminal prisoners. As time went on, those labourers who survived their first year in exile were allowed to have limited access to books, paper, and writing implements. However, all reading materials required prior approval of the NKVD. Paper, pens, and pencils were in short supply.

The numbing cold of the winter days made it all the worse when each day brought only seven hours of daylight. Even the world's largest terrestrial biome, the taiga, brought little relief to Alexei and Konstantin as they hauled the logs from the logging camp to the railway siding, a distance of twenty kilometers. That winter, copious amounts of snow came with bitterly cold winds which blew in from Northeast Siberia. This made the task of hauling logs more difficult than might be the case in warmer weather. Still, both Alexei and Konstantin felt lucky to escape the difficult work of felling trees from morning light to sunset.

During those times when Commandant Systovsky wanted to talk, he liked to refer to Siberia as one large prison. *"You know, Kozlov,"* observed the Commandant, *"Siberia is now my home. Escape from here is impossible. Many of those assholes trying to escape our camp are caught by the killing temperatures or the bounty-hunting natives who turn those dogs in to our NKVD officials. To escape, you would have to walk unimaginably long distances through deep snows and forests, and deal with wild animals."*

"You have experienced this, Commandant?"

*"To verna (*that is true)*, I know all of this. We see survivors who are caught, returned to camp, and then lose their frozen limbs. In other cases, a criminal is returned to camp and our justice system removes one or both of his legs. In that condition, he can no longer escape. Others die on the operating table, often performed by a person claiming to be a medical doctor."*

"You say that operations are performed without the use of an anesthetic? Damn, that is cruel. Very cruel," shivered Kozlov.

"Punishment under our leader takes place away from other people and is rarely humane. Who would witness such things? Dead men don't talk, do they? Before Stalin came along, the criminals died from being tortured in Moscow. Now they die from starvation, hard and exhausting work, cold winters, and disease."

What struck Alexei is how little he knew about Siberia. Few survived their sentence of punishment and the horrors experienced by survivors rarely found their way back to civilization. There were even stories about how the original prisoners to Siberia had to walk to the place of their exile from their homes in European Russia. Often the journey took years—the distances walked sometimes measured thousands of kilometers. Many prisoners walked from one transit prison camp to another without any long-range plans. They were able to do this because the supervision of exiles was extremely negligent. Convicts had to beg their way because there was almost no food provided for them. It was rare that doctors would accompany the exile parties and there were very few prison hospitals. The lack of record keeping was such that officials often didn't know where the exiles had come from, what crime they had committed, and what their destination should have been. Perhaps this was the reason that Stalin was so keen on the development of better controls through the issuance of internal passports.

"I should know about this," explained Commandant Systovsky, *"I was one of those who had to march."*

"You survived all of that? Perhaps, Commandant, this logging operation is a blessing."

"When I was exiled after the Revolution as a member of the White Army, we were divided into hard labour convicts, penal colonists, those deported by the Bolsheviks, and the volunteer followers—the women and the children."

"You were banished? For what crime?"

"That is none of your business. I can tell you that the convicts were banished for life and deprived of all civil rights, branded, or tattooed with a hot iron and later with deep tattoos."

"Were you punished, Commandant?"

"Da, I spent three years in a Siberian mine. I never want to go back there. My re-education is now complete. You should work hard to complete yours."

According to Commandant Systovsky, many of those exiled had lived outside the prisons in barracks or in little cabins that weren't very different from dog kennels. The more serious convicts lived in the prison, often in iron shackles that they would have to wear for years. Most convicts worked in the mines where they would not see daylight for months. Their whole life consisted of two things; work and sleep. The daily ration consisted of some brown bread, a morsel of boiled meat, and some tea—with rare appearances of cabbage soup. Almost nothing was done to protect prisoners' health and those with infectious diseases were not separated from others. Some hospitals didn't even have beds; people had to lie on the cold, filthy floor receiving no medical help due to a frequent lack of doctors, nurses, and medicines.

"After my release, I elected to stay in Siberia as a free worker," proudly announced the Commandant. *"Many others who survived their*

terms of hard labour also elected to stay in this great country. Some even wrote back home and brought their families to Siberia."

"Things are changing today?"

"Da, of course. Most of those who arrive in Camp 27 are kulaks or political prisoners who have been accused of treason, espionage, sabotage, and anti-Soviet propaganda. Few, if any, are guilty, perhaps much like you, Kozlov."

An increasing number of political prisoners found their way to Siberia, even during the cold winter months. To many of them, it occurred that the purpose of arresting innocent people was to destroy not only the opposition but the idea of rebellion itself. Those arrested included people neutral to the regime as well as dedicated communists who helped to expose enemies of the Soviet people, truly believing that they were doing the right thing until they themselves were arrested. Belatedly, they realized that a large proportion of the fellow prisoners were not guilty of any crime.

Late each night as Alexei and Konstantin returned to Camp 27, they were once again confronted by the extremely harsh conditions. In the deep of winter, the daily rations were once again reduced drastically as compared to the rations received at the outset of the winter. Many labourers in the camp were abused by fellow labourers and guards. Reports of workers freezing to death continued to come in while others continued to die from starvation. NKVD guards did not view them as human beings and didn't think of them as workers but rather as prisoners. It is little wonder that Commandant Systovsky looked forward to the spring of the year and a replenishment of the work force.

Still, no two labour camps in Siberia were alike. There were differences in the organization of daily life and work, different sorts of guards and punishments, and different kinds of propaganda. Over time, the Gulag went through cycles of relative cruelty to that of relative humanity. Siberia contained a wide variety of camps from the lethal gold mines of the Kolyma region to the luxurious secret institutes outside Moscow where prisoner scientists designed weapons for the Red Army.

At times, certain prisoners improved their lot by working in relatively comfortable jobs. Within each camp there was a prisoner hierarchy. Some prisoners were able to climb this hierarchy at the expense of others or with the help of others. At other times, the Gulag was overburdened with women, children, and old people. Suddenly, and without explanation, many were suddenly released by Stalin in mass amnesties. It sometimes happened that whole categories of enemies suddenly benefited from a change in status. The opposite was also true; in the Soviet Union the perpetrators could become victims themselves. Gulag guards, administrators, even senior officers of the secret police could be arrested and find themselves sentenced to detention or work camps. Not every poisonous weed remained poisonous. However, every single group of Soviet prisoners lived with the constant expectation of death.

The primary purpose of the Gulag was economic and, as a result, far from humane. Within the system, prisoners were treated as cattle. Guards shuttled them around at will, loading and unloading them into cattle cars, weighing and measuring them, feeding them if it seemed that they might be useful, starving them if they were not. They were exploited and treated as a commodity and, unless productive, their lives were worthless to their masters. Within the Gulag, prisoners died, not as a result of the captors' efficiency but due to gross inefficiency and neglect. Prisoners were locked in punishment cells until they died of cold and starvation, left untreated in unheated hospitals, or simply shot at will for attempted escape. The Soviet camp system, as a whole, was not deliberately organized to mass produce corpses—even if at times it did.

Reading the accounts of those who survived, one is struck more by the difference between the victims' experiences than by the differences between the camps. In the Siberian wasteland, you could die in a logging accident or you could die in a cattle train. One's survival, simply put, was tantamount to playing Russian roulette.

Even at this early stage of the development of the Gulag, there was extreme secrecy. This promoted a wide proliferation of padded statistics and false reports. More and more, it appeared as though work was being done only for the sake of appearance, deliberately falsified with inflated indicators in official reports. After all, the supervisors, managers, and Soviet hierarchy responsible for the work camps had to show Stalin that his Five-Year Plan was producing good results. As a consequence, many of the positive economic indicators of the camp economy were overstated. They were not achieved through normal organization of production but through predatory exploitation. In the end, not only did this save the lives of numerous slave labourers, but their bosses as well. It would be during the winter of 1931 that the Politburo suddenly considered some changes to the manner in which it utilized the labour of its slaves.

Survival in Siberia was much like playing a game of chance. A prisoner rarely knew the rationale for any decision made by those in command. The Kozlovs would soon discover just how unpredictable was their own situation.

Chapter 9

RELOCATED

Why can't I serve my sentence in this logging camp?

After months of subzero temperatures, Siberia gradually began to warm up but not before several of the labourers in the logging camp succumbed to the extreme temperatures. The sounds of happy frogs singing and spring rains were definite signs that spring had finally come to Camp 27. The thick ice on the Om River was slowly melting and very soon the logs, which earlier had been skidded to the stream, would find their way to the Irtysh River before floating downstream to a saw mill. As well, the snow that had blanketed the ground throughout the region began to melt, loosening its wintry grip upon the region's rivers.

The coming of spring was especially good news for Alexei. Prior to his family's banishment to Siberia, it was the time of year that a well-rested farmer's thoughts turned to the seeding of crops and the planting of the family garden. The Kozlov family was about to observe its eighth month in Siberia, still not knowing the length of their sentence. At the same time, the logging camp was full of rumours about impending changes. The question on everyone's lips was what would these changes bring? Would they simply bring a change of location or a change of occupation from a logging camp to one of the most feared mines in Kolyma, Norilsk, or Vorkuta? Most loggers were of the mind that change in the Gulag was not always for the better.

As the winter began to relinquish its grip on the logging camp, another realization came to the fore. Despite the imbalance between the number of males and females, love and sex were common occurrences in the camp. This had much to do with the structure of Camp 27 which had difficulty separating men from women and the unwillingness or inability of the Communist Regime to punish every disciplinary infraction committed by camp personnel. This often encouraged arbitrary and abusive behaviour towards labourers as well as an ambiguous attitude towards sexual activity in the camp.

This matter came to a head when Katusha asked her mother, *"Do you know a logger named Igor from the next barrack?"*

"Tak, tak, child, I know of him. What about him?"

"Well, mother, Igor frightens me. Yesterday he grabbed me from behind and squeezed my breasts. It was difficult to fight him off me."

"He did that to you? Why, that sniveling little mudak (bastard). And what did you say to him?"

"I told him to leave my breasts alone, that I was not interested in him or in sex."

"You fought him off you?"

"When he pinned me to the ground, I gave him a vicious kick, right in his groin. He was barely able to move for the longest time. He left holding his private parts like a little pasek (dog), yelping all the while."

"Dobry (good). Alexei will talk to that animal. He had better stay away from you or I'll have Alexei castrate him like he did the piglets on the farm in Horodok—without the use of an antiseptic. That would be a lesson he would never forget."

Commandant Systovsky was aware of the NKVD's concern about sexual misconduct, not only in the logging camp but also throughout the

Gulag system. Camp 27 was not immune from this problem. Although the number of women in the camp of child-bearing age was relatively small, the pregnancy rate amongst that group was inordinately high. This led to the difficulty of harnessing pregnant women and nursing mothers in the economic activity of the camp. The NKVD was also concerned about the costs associated with the upkeep of children born in the camp itself. However, any attempt to control or contain such behaviour proved futile.

Alexei had to admit that the logging camp had made some progress on several fronts. Luba organized a women's sewing and knitting club, and Katusha, assisted by her younger sister Nikolashya, organized a kindergarten class of sorts for the younger children. Permission for the creation of the kindergarten class came directly from Commandant Systovsky, who said that it was a part of Stalin's new plan to improve the conditions in Siberia's labour camps. However, Alexei was not convinced that the approval of the kindergarten was a part of Stalin's new plan. Instead, it was probably the Commandant's recognition that new incentives would need to be provided for the labourers and their families if production quotas imposed by the NKVD were to be met. In the end, the Commandant did not have to rationalize his decision. In turn, NKVD officials responsible for the operation of the logging camp did not lodge any objection to these initiatives.

New arrivals from other camps continued to arrive in Camp 27. They confirmed that the working conditions in Camp 27 were in stark contrast to those of other labour camps where prisoners frequently lived in a camp zone surrounded by a high fence or barbed wire, overlooked by armed guards in watch towers. For them, life was brutally violent. Their stinky barracks were overcrowded and poorly heated. Prisoners competed for access to all of life's basic necessities and violence among the prisoners was commonplace. If a labourer survived hunger, disease, and his fellow prisoners, he might succumb to the arbitrary violence at the hands of camp guards. All the while, prisoners were watched by informers—fellow prisoners looking for any misstep to report to Gulag authorities in the hopes of getting a personal reward for ratting. As one thoughtful Camp 27 logger described it, *"The Gulag was conceived to transform human matter into a docile, exhausted, ill-smelling mass of individuals. Prisoners live only for themselves and think of nothing else but how to appease the constant torture of hunger. Their only concern is evading kicks, staying warm in a cold climate, and surviving ill treatment."*

Ever worried about the survival of his family, Alexei was aware of the rumours swirling about having to do with transfers of labourers to another camp. Fearing that the news would be bad, no one had the courage to approach the Commandant to seek clarification about these rumours. On May 1, Alexei was called aside by Commandant Systovsky with a simple command, *"I want to see you in my quarters."*

When Alexei entered the Commandant's quarters, he was not surprised to see a stranger waiting for him. He had heard a rumour that an important NKVD official had arrived the previous day. Dressed in his military uniform, the visitor to Camp 27 introduced himself as Polkovnik (Colonel) Podgorny. *"Kozlov,"* was his opening remark, *"I have here, in writing, for you the decision of the NKVD Special Board."*

"A decision of the NKVD? Is it good news?"

"That is none of your affair. My work is to carry out all orders of my superiors."

"What is that decision?"

"Your sentence is two years of hard labour followed by three years of re-education. You have now served one year of your hard labour sentence. During the next period of time, you must become a good soviet worker and shed your capitalistic tendencies."

"I do not have capitalistic tendencies."

"Don't argue with me! You have not completely embraced the ideals of Bolshevism. However, your work and that of your family has been acceptable to the Commandant of Camp 27. That is why you will soon be assigned to another camp for more re-education."

"Re-assigned? Further education? Why the transfer? I like it here."

"That, Kozlov, is the decision of the NKVD and cannot be appealed. Perhaps the NKVD has concluded that your work is more valuable elsewhere. You will get your specific orders within one week."

"What about my family, Colonel?"

"This transfer order includes all members of your family."

Alexei knew better than to ask any more questions. He also knew that the five-year sentence handed down by the Special NKVD Board was not unusual. Other kulaks had received similar sentences—with the proviso that the attitudes of this class of deportees had to show marked improvement in order to keep the sentence to the minimum of five years. In other cases, kulaks received a minimum sentence of three years of hard labour, followed by two additional years of re-education. Either way, the time of detention was five years, similar in length to Stalin's first Five-Year Plan. However, repatriation to one's country of origin would not always occur automatically at the end of the sentence. In many cases, a deportee would have to serve additional time in exile so that the process of re-education might continue to a successful conclusion.

When he quietly broke the news of his sentence to his family, each seemed, more than anything else, relieved. After all, the sentence could have been harsher. *"Maybe, there is a God after all,"* remarked Luba. *"Perhaps the Bolsheviks have some common sense. Let us all pray that our next deportation will not be farther east."*

147

Always fearful that a careless remark would lead to trouble, Alexei cautioned Luba, *"I agree, these Bolsheviks are stupid animals. But, we must keep these thoughts to ourselves."*

"You have worked with Systovsky. Why don't you ask him for a transfer to a work camp that requires less manual labour?"

"I will approach the Commandant once that Polkovnik bastard leaves our camp. Maybe I can get Systovsky's approval for a re-assignment to an environment more suitable to us than this stinking logging camp."

If Alexei wanted a quick decision as to his re-location, he would be disappointed. The Commandant seemed in no hurry to tell him the news. But, that seemed not to matter. With the coming of spring weather, along with the muddy conditions, the lumbering operation was reduced to a skeleton logging force and he could do little else but await the decision. In the meantime, the news filtered down that new deportees were scheduled to arrive from Ukraine in the coming weeks to replace those who did not survive the winter months and those about to be reassigned to other camps.

Damn these Bolsheviks, thought Alexei, *this could turn out to be bad news for our family. What if Systovsky decides to break up the family and send our children to some other work camp? Maybe even send Luba to one labour camp and me to another camp?*

Although labourers in Camp 27 continued to die from starvation, the news from other regions of the Soviet Union was even worse. One such report came directly from an NKVD guard who said that Ukraine was in the midst of a famine. This, according to the guard, would have a chilling impact upon the adequacy of supplies delivered to the camp. Still, the biggest concern and discussion in the camp centered round the destination of those zeks about to be transferred. No one seemed to know what ministry the orders came from, regional or national. Even more uncertain, a deportee never really knew whether a transfer was of a temporary or permanent nature. A camp prisoner simply phrased it this way, *"These orders come from above, either signed by Stalin or as good as."*

In mid-May, the Kozlov family finally got their marching orders. Seemingly out of the blue, Alexei was approached by Commandant Systovsky with a simple order, *"Pack your belongings and that of your family. You will be escorted to the train station by an NKVD official. Once you arrive at the railway siding, you will be told of your destination."*

"But," objected Alexei, *"I like it here. So does my family. We have been in this logging camp for less than one full year."*

"That, Kozlov, is no concern of mine. The NKVD must have given you credit for one full year for your time in the logging camp. You have two hours to pack your belongings and those of your family. We will have a wagon waiting for you."

"You will have a wagon? But, we walked here from the railway."

"Sometimes, even a slave is treated like a person. Who knows?"

A thousand thoughts crowded into Alexei's head. *Where are they taking us now? Is it deeper into Siberia or is it back to civilization? Will the journey be made by horse and wagon or will we board a train at the same railway siding that brought us here last fall?*

His thoughts were suddenly interrupted when several of the zeks selected to remain behind in the lumber camp came over to say goodbye. Once the family was loaded onto the wagon, Alexei noted that there were no NKVD guards, only one armed NKVD wagon driver. The trip took about five hours to arrive at the same railway siding that first brought the family to Camp 27. However, the NKVD driver did not stop at the siding. After crossing the railway, he continued his journey in a southerly direction. The Kozlovs suddenly realized that unless there was another railway siding that would take them to some other location in Siberia, their destination was either another lumber camp nearby or an agricultural kolkhoz. Either way, they were cautiously optimistic.

By mid-afternoon, the Kozlov family arrived at what appeared to be a modest kolkhoz. A rather large yard featured two large barracks, several small log houses, and an assortment of farm buildings adjacent to a small brook. In the horizon, within one kilometer of the kolkhoz, one was able to see a small village. Each one of the log houses in the village appeared to have a small garden. Several of the homes had one or two other buildings on the property, perhaps for the use of farm animals. The kolkhozniks were aware that May would bring an influx of new kulaks and prisoners. As the Kozlov family entered the kolkhoz, several kolkhozniks appeared in the farm yard to welcome the Kozlov family.

Beyond the brook stretched what appeared to be a considerable amount of cultivated land for grain fields, pasture, and kolkhoz gardens. Interestingly, it appeared as though a new barrack and warehouse were under construction. Beyond the barracks and far into the distance, new land was being cleared. There was only one conclusion that Alexei could reach, this kolkhoz was about to expand its operations.

Noting the curious gazes, the NKVD wagon driver who doubled as a guard, declared, *"You are now in Zarya (Sunrise) Kolkhoz. We have to feed you scum of the earth. Maybe that is why our leader wants to cultivate more land and develop a new food processing industry."*

Of course, the NKVD guard would not have known that Alexei and Konstantin had visited an agricultural kolkhoz in the same region during the winter months to commandeer draught horses for Camp 27's logging operation. Although it was not this particular kolkhoz, it was now apparent that collective farming was taking hold in the region, not far from the evergreen forests and the lumbering industry. This explained why newcomers to Camp 27 said that the food rations were superior to what they had experienced earlier. From these comments, Alexei concluded that some of the agricultural products from the local kolkhozes were being diverted to the logging camps in the region.

Upon the arrival of the Kozlov family at the agricultural kolkhoz, the camp manager, Commandant Matsunova, instructed the NKVD driver to take them to one of the log houses recently vacated by a family transferred to some other location. Looking around, Alexei was uncertain what the future held; however, one thing was clear—the new accommodation seemed to be superior to the barrack they had just left behind. Still, Alexei did not want to express his joy at the sudden turn of events. That evening, out of earshot of others, he asked Luba, *"Who should we thank for this re-assignment? Would it be Systovsky? Did the Anna Timskaya incident have anything to do with this transfer?"*

"Maybe," responded a perplexed Luba, *"this transfer had something to do with the accidental death of Lashkov."*

If Alexei expected an official response from an NKVD official, he would have been greatly disappointed. Few had the courage to ask a superior about any decision of the NKVD. For those who were foolish enough to risk such a question, their tenure in the Gulag could quickly come to a sudden end from the barrel of a revolver. Alexei could only reach one conclusion—the Kozlov family would never know for certain who gave the order for a transfer to a kolkhoz. Suffice it to conclude that all directives came from Stalin or his henchmen and were quickly swallowed up in the vastness of a cold and formidable land.

The very next day the Commandant addressed the new arrivals from the lumber camp and from European Russia by saying, *"All of you will be joining a work brigade and the work of Zarya Kolkhoz will continue without interruption. You are here for two purposes: work and re-education. Through obedient work and meeting our quotas, you will soon become worthy soviet workers and citizens. Otherwise, your existence is without worth. Do you understand that?"*

Immediately following the brief and somewhat harsh words of welcome, everyone was assigned a task according to their age and strength. At first, the Kozlov teenagers were assigned to load and unload things, provide each barrack with firewood, and bring water from wells in wheelbarrows to those who were working in the mixed farming operation and in the fields. Once settled in, Konstantin was assigned as a cow herder, while Alexei joined a farm brigade. Luba, Katusha, and Nikolashya were assigned to gardening and domestic duties. Their first domestic task was to clean up the log house. The walls were damp and there was only one small coal-oil lamp inside.

Siberian log cabin, similar to that built by the Kozlovs in Zarya Kolkhoz.

A Siberian Village, much like the one near Zarya Kolkhoz.

The Kozlovs were mistaken in thinking that they would be able to make their new quarters livable in a short period of time. To their surprise, the log house was infested with bedbugs which were soon intent upon eating the family alive. Worse yet, just as soon as the house was heated, the bedbugs would multiply. Instead of burning wood, the Kozlovs turned to burning coal and filling the house with smoke and fumes. But, the bedbugs seemed to have minds of their own. When the smoke was severe and the coal-oil lamp was lit, they would go into hiding. The moment that the lamp was turned off, those bloodsuckers started crawling all over each member of the family once again. Most nights, the family had to keep the lamp burning all night just to keep the bedbugs at bay. It took several weeks of mopping, whitewashing, boiling all the clothing in hot water, and sleeping on a bare floor before the bedbugs were finally exterminated and the log house made livable. Meanwhile, it took quite a toll on the sleeping habits of the whole family.

To add to the family's problems, the new Commandant was like a wild animal. He had a broad and ruddy face, bushy eyebrows, and eyes that pierced like thorns. Every day he would walk from one end of the kolkhoz to the other and from one end of the adjoining residential village to the other, peeping in the doors to see what the enemies of the people were talking about and to find out if they were getting together in the evenings. He seemed to be suspicious of everybody and everything. This made the kulaks extremely nervous, especially so since he always carried a sidearm and took great joy in waving it in the air from time to time.

True, you could question his character; however, he seemed to know how to operate a cooperative. He set out by structuring each work brigade with an eye for effectiveness and efficiency. Each brigade had a worker from each of the three broad categories of *bednyaks* (the poor peasants), the *seredniaks* (peasants of moderate wealth), and the *kulaks*. Notably missing, however, was the worker that came from the category of *batraks* (the landless agriculture workers for hire). The Kozlovs would soon learn that most batraks ended up in mining operations.

Still, this categorization was lost in the eyes of Commandant Matsunova. After all, he had a quota to meet—a quota that had little regard for labels but rather an emphasis upon production and meeting kolkhoz quotas as set by the NKVD. Although Commandant Matsunova was an unpredictable tyrant who ruled with an iron hand, his style of management might have been necessary. After all, the kulaks deported from Ukraine were joined by the native Siberians who had resided in the region for many years. Neither group was particularly happy about having to work on a Siberian kolkhoz. All those working on the kolkhoz were aware that they were selected by the NKVD for such a re-location with the belief that they would unlikely attempt escape. As a result, the kolkhozniks had a certain amount of freedom of movement.

Unlike their time in the logging camp, Katusha and Nikolashya, although beyond elementary school age, now had an opportunity to attend a village school, two kilometers from their log house. Among other aims, the kolkhoz manager wanted everyone to abandon their Ukrainian heritage and become fluent in the Russian language. The school seemed to have little regard for structured content in the elementary grades, concentrating on the basics of reading, writing, and arithmetic—offered only in the Russian language. To no one's surprise, most every lesson of the day made reference to or was a testimonial to the greatness of the Bolshevik leader, Josef Stalin.

The parents of the children attending the elementary school questioned the very purpose of education when there was little opportunity of advancement. As Alexei put it, *"Why should our children study if they won't be accepted into technical secondary schools? They won't even be able to peep through the doors of these institutes."*

The kolkhoz Commandant would never agree to let the children of the enemies of the people attend a school outside the collective farm. It was impossible to change his mind. All requests were categorically refused with one phrase, *"It is prohibited."* Even in elementary grades, many of the children of the prisoners weren't able to continue their studies because the teachers would automatically give them bad marks and put their names on the list of weak pupils. Despite these difficulties, all the children in the village and the kolkhoz would soon become fluent in the Russian language. At home, the Kozlov family continued to communicate in Ukrainian.

With the new work assignment, Konstantin became convinced that there was no such thing as truth in the world. To him, there was his family and the world outside, which consisted of two kinds of people, those who oppressed and those who were oppressed. *"Mother,"* was his question, *"do you believe that the world created villains such as Matsunova just so that they could oppress humble people?"*

"I don't know who created villains. All I know is that Stalin surrounded himself with plenty of heartless villains. But, whatever you do, keep those thoughts to yourself. We don't need more punishment."

What Konstantin did not know was that the villains' troubles were no less than were theirs. After all, the villains were, in all likelihood, overwhelmed with fear because they had children and relatives of their own. Most of all, they were well aware that if they did not embrace the ideals of communism, they too would soon become the oppressed.

Katusha, now sixteen, dreamed about attending gymnasia (secondary school) back in Ukraine, dating, and falling in love. Nikolashya wanted to see her school friends and her pet kitten Musha. But, this was not to be. The village had no secondary school, and even if there were one, it is doubtful that the Commandant would allow her to attend the school. However, after an appeal to the Commandant, Katusha and Nikolashya were permitted to attend the elementary school in the nearby village during the winter months for three days each week. The only proviso was that they assist the elementary grade teacher with the instruction of kindergarten children.

The two Kozlov girls soon discovered that meanness was everywhere, and a good measure of it came to visit upon their family. Since the school was intended for the children of those who had lived in the village for a number of years, everyone understood that the children of the kolkhoz labourers were in attendance only because the NKVD allowed them to attend. As a consequence, the children of the foreigners were humiliated everywhere they went and, like their parents, they were not able to rid themselves of the cruel burden of their fate. Why? What had they done? What was their crime? They could not find the answer to these bewildering questions.

Communist slogans began to appear everywhere, slogans such as, *Work for the Glory of Your Country, Stalin is With Us,* and *Work is Glory.* What glory was there when one could wander no farther than three to four kilometers from the village? Still, as time went on, things began to change ever so slightly.

With the added freedoms and decreased surveillance, the Kozlovs realized that not all of the kolkhozniks were deportees from Ukraine or Russia. The physical appearance of many of the villagers would indicate that they came from Kazakhstan or the Caucasus, a region of a mountain range in southwest Russia. In other cases, the appearance of the children would indicate that they had a Mongolian or Turkic heritage (Mongolia borders Kazakhstan to the east while the Turkic peoples comprise a collection of ethnic groups living in Western Asia).

Several of the buildings which served the kolkhoz looked relatively new. Perhaps this reflected Stalin's recent policy of confiscating privately-owned agricultural lands and facilities from farmers before consolidating them into a kolkhoz. Unlike the career criminals and political agitators who ended up as slave-labourers in penal colonies, mines, railroad construction, and lumber camps, the NKVD screened out the hardcore criminal element in favour of deportees, such as the kulaks, who would be unlikely to create problems. Those who ended up at Zarya Kolkhoz were specifically selected by the NKVD as labour colonists, given the new label of special settlers, deprived of their civil rights, and put to work in an especially harsh environment to exploit the agricultural resources of Siberia.

During this same time frame, the Communist leaders struggled with a variety of terms that they might apply to the deportees who ended up in settlements within the Soviet Union. The NKVD wanted to simply call them *labour colonists*, while Stalin's statisticians preferred to categorize them as *special settlers, exile settlers, and administrative exile settlements*. Most were victims of ethnic cleansing, accused of being subversives, and deported to Siberia in order to prevent a perceived threat.

According to Stalin's plan, 75 percent of the 500,000 people deported in 1930-1931 as labour colonists were to work on farms and in the forests. Within two years, they were supposed to have freed the state from any expense for their support and then begun producing merchandise that would allow the state to recover the expenses incurred in the operations of deportation and settlement of the contingents. Another 500,000 were scheduled to work in the sectors of fishing, crafts, and mining. In all of this, the real challenge for Stalin was the matter of procuring sufficient food supplies to ensure survival of the deportees for a period of time to make them useful to the state before they perished.

To ensure success of the deportation-colonization, the Bolsheviks intended to bring into production a million hectares of virgin land and create hundreds of labour villages at the rate of one village for every 500 families. Within every village would be 100 living units of 65 square meters, each sheltering 20 people. Each labourer would be allotted an area of 27 square feet of living space. During the first year, baths, an infirmary, a hygienic station for removing lice and other parasites, stables, and a garage for machinery were to be constructed. During the second year, a school, a cafeteria, a reading room, and a store were planned. Any other facilities that might be required in the third year of operation were left up to Stalin's planning committee. Perhaps the biggest obstacle to meeting this challenge was the projected requirement of about 250,000 tractors to mechanize the farming operation in Siberia.

In order to accomplish this grandiose plan, the NKVD estimated that they would need millions of board feet of lumber, tons and tons of iron and sheet metal, tons of nails and, in addition to other materials, tons of glass. To administer these villages, the NKVD planned to develop Chekist Commanders who would be assisted by militiamen, technicians, agronomists, physicians, and health officers who would have broad powers. This initiative required that all reports would be submitted to a main managerial office especially created to run the labour villages. Even at the outset, the NKVD admitted that transportation of the human contingents and equipment would be the biggest problem—especially farther east beyond where the rail lines or waterways ended. To help accomplish this initiative, the planners requisitioned hundreds of trucks, thousands of horses, and hundreds of tractors for deployment in Siberia alone.

Stalin's foolhardy plan would soon lead to dire circumstances. The Party leadership stripped Ukraine of many of the most progressive farmers, the kulaks, and then raised the grain targets for obligatory deliveries imposed on the kolkhozes as well as on individual peasants. This decision was taken despite the fact that a poor harvest was predicted for 1932 and that many reports from Ukraine, the North Caucasus, the Volga region, Western Siberia, and Kazakhstan reported problems with food supplies. All signs pointed toward a coming famine. By mid-October of 1932, only 20 percent of the procurement campaign was realized.

The peasants in Ukraine, often with the complicity of the kolkhoz's management, used all kinds of stratagems to avoid delivering part of the harvest to the state. Thefts of the collective harvest were subject to a draconian law of ten years of forced labour in camps or the death penalty. This, however, seemed at most to be a minor irritant and by no means the complete deterrent as intended. Wheat was buried in pits, hidden underground, ground up using homemade hand mills, or stolen during transportation and weighing. What, in particular, upset Party planners was that many kolkhoz managers sided with the people they were supposed to be managing. Some even showed overt opposition to the state's procurement plans.

With Stalin's realization of the many instances of ineffective agricultural practices throughout Ukraine, it is little wonder that a number of kulaks, the Kozlov family among them, were re-assigned from logging operations to kolkhozes. Earlier in Ukraine, the assaults on the kolkhozes and peasants led the Central Committee in Moscow to conclude that the objectives of Stalin's first Five-Year Plan, which started in 1928, were fulfilled earlier than expected. Despite a particularly alarming situation in the agricultural sector and considerable resistance from the Ukrainian Communist Party, Soviet officials celebrated the triumph of socialism. In fact, the Soviet propagandists went so far as to say that the first Five-Year Plan was accomplished in four years and three months.

But, Stalin now saw a new threat. Although the kulaks had been defeated, the enemies of socialism no longer acted overtly. Learning from their past mistakes and wanting to escape prosecution, they masked their intent and became veritable mutants, carrying on a particularly vicious war of sabotage that could take place in a kolkhoz itself, while others would leave the kolkhozes in large numbers and spread false rumours to discredit collectivized farming. Still others would infiltrate factories or major construction sites in order to carry out acts of sabotage. According to Stalin, the criminality and social deviance would constitute the chief threat to the construction of socialism.

Suddenly, the exodus of peasants from Ukrainian villages and kolkhozes was reaching alarming numbers. This led Stalin to order an end to this mass exodus on the pretext of going to look for bread. Special patrols were set up in railway stations and on highways to intercept all runaways leaving Ukraine and, *"All those refusing to return home should be arrested and deported to labour villages or, in the case of criminals, to labour camps."* Of course, for those who were intercepted and sent home, it meant certain death in villages that were already suffering from famine and had been left entirely to their own fate without the slightest aid in securing food.

Confronted by a growing chaos caused by the influx of millions of peasants fleeing collectivization in 1932, the authorities decided to implement the ambitious program of ridding the major cities of these undesirable elements. In order to maintain control of its peoples in the Soviet Union, the Communist Party initiated a program of *passportization* of the urban population in 1933. With the new passports, the program of identifying individuals was now to be far broader and more systematic.

Its first objective was to control migratory movements and to limit the immense rural exodus triggered by the forced collectivization of the countryside. The new passports identified those not working, kulaks, country residents, those stripped of their civil rights, those sentenced to exile, and all criminals. To implement the program, the NKVD recruited and trained thousands of additional police officers. Passport offices were set up in government agencies and local police stations.

This explains, in part, why so many in Moscow and Leningrad (Saint Petersburg) who found themselves without the means or the credentials to qualify for a passport were promptly shipped to Siberia, further swelling the ranks of detention centers and camps. Individuals arrested without a passport were subject to a particularly summary administrative procedure. Within 48 hours, the sector inspector sent a list of the persons arrested to a special police committee, whose sole task was to deal in an extrajudicial manner with matters connected with passportization. Penalties consisted of immediate expulsion and deportation to a special village where they would be under house arrest while others were sent to a work camp for a maximum of three years. Most were sent to the largest transit camp in Tomsk, before being deployed to other camps farther east.

As a result of these events, the Kozlov family was relocated to the Zarya Kolkhoz. Agricultural specialists first chose those people who were in the best physical condition, while obviously weak and sick individuals remained behind. Those who were seriously ill were placed in quarantine at the stations or hospitalized, but no one knew what happened to them after that. The deportees were widely dispersed into small district towns, villages, farms, and remote farm outposts. To ensure continued orderly deployment, the NKVD set up a number of special police detachments responsible for maintaining the special regime under which the deportees lived.

Interior of a typical labour camp barrack. Source: Gulag History Museum, Moscow.

Women in a women's barrack. Source: Gulag History Museum, Moscow.

The segregation of young children in a labour camp barrack. Source: Gulag History Museum, Moscow.

With the arrival of so many deportees, Zarya Kolkhoz was hard pressed to feed them all. As a result, hunger and famine conditions were constant. It was not unusual to see entire families wandering about pale and with swollen bellies, even going so far as to search for animal carcasses, or wild onions and various grasses to sustain themselves. Many of the grasses were not digestible and frequently led to diarrhea and dehydration. The children were particularly vulnerable. Many of them came down with colds and influenza-type diseases leading to a high rate of mortality. Konstantin went so far as to drink milk directly from a cow's udder, always in mortal fear of being discovered.

As Alexei reflected upon the situation in Zarya Kolkhoz, it began to look as though Stalin's collectivization program was turning out to be a ghastly failure. The full impact of his policies were about to unfold in Siberia and in Ukraine.

Chapter 10

TRAGEDY STRIKES

Siberia's harsh winter climate claims a loved one

Just about the time that the Kozlovs were being transferred from the logging camp to Zarya Kolkhoz, Stalin had great plans for the creation of collective farms and tractor stations to increase production. While addressing the new class of soviet worker, he declared, *"He who does not work, neither shall he eat,"* adding as an afterthought, *"let them perish!"* Far from recognizing the right of the whole population to food, Stalin specified two groups, the class enemies and the idlers who deserved either repression or starvation, and declared that those stealing from the kolkhoz in order to eat should be killed. In particular, his anger was aimed at those who profited from the work of others saying, *"A man with two coins is an enemy of society and should be sent off to a labour camp."*

Unfortunately, Stalin soon discovered that the collectivization process was not going as well as planned. This was especially true in mainland Russia, Ukraine, and Belarus. Peasants often reacted angrily to the forced seizure of land and herds, slaughtering much of their livestock rather than turning them over to the state. Famine plagued the countryside and the entire agricultural sector was in severe economic decline. As a result, some incentives were given to appease the peasantry in order to improve and ease the collectivization process.

The goal of the incentives was that the peasants would join the new collective farms with less resistance. However, in protest the peasants had already slaughtered much of their livestock. The losses of livestock hurt the Soviet economy. As a further concession, the government decided to allow each household to farm upwards to 2.5 acres of land and to raise a limited amount of livestock, including cows, sheep, and pigs. Unfortunately, Stalin soon realized that these measures were far too little and too late to stave off a full-blown hunger crisis in Ukraine.

Soviet poster urging women to join the collective farm movement.

Soviet poster urging men to join the collective farm movement.

Harvesting on a kolkhoz.

Stalin moves to mechanizing kolkhozes by introducing tractors.

The problems of agricultural quota and supply extended all the way to the Zarya Kolkhoz. Unlike the kolkhozes in Russia where the enterprise was a form of agricultural production cooperative of peasants that voluntarily united, presumably for the purpose of joint agricultural production based on collective labour, there was nothing cooperative about the agricultural enterprise in Zarya. Zarya Kolkhoz was not managed according to the principles of socialist self-management, democracy, and openness with active participation of the members in decisions concerning all aspects of internal life. Emerging after Stalin's collectivization campaign, the kolkhoz did not have many characteristics of a true cooperative. After all, this was Siberia and those working the fields were not exactly there of their own free will. Any participation in the fruits of their labour was completely out of question.

The Omsk region, even as early as 1931, was home to hundreds of Russian kulaks who had developed their small farms in this new land into successful farming operations. Earlier, Communist Party activists had been sent into the countryside to agitate for the collective farms. Most of the peasants were afraid, but determined not to give up a centuries-old way of life and to make a leap of faith into the unknown. When these small farms were first collectivized, very few kolkhozes had tractors or modern implements. They were badly run by people who knew little about agriculture and who made crude mistakes. This discredited the whole process of collectivization. Peasants who had spoken out against collectivization were beaten, bullied, tortured, threatened, and harassed until they agreed to join a collective farm. NKVD authorities recognized that the Zarya Kolkhoz needed an influx of kulaks from Ukraine in order to increase the amount of cultivated land and to improve productivity.

Undoubtedly, this was one of the reasons why the Kozlov family was selected for relocation from a logging camp to this particular kolkhoz. However, no one knew for certain. Records, if maintained, were not available to outsiders for examination and, at the local level, the matter was never addressed. What emerged, particularly in Siberia, was a process of rubber-stamping the plans, targets, and decisions of the district and oblast authorities. The oblast would nominate preferred managerial candidates and implement the detailed work programs. This resulted in the creation of cooperatives as an offshoot of the state sector which, in essence, became *sovkhozy* (the state-owned farm), rather than a *kolkhozy* (the workers' farm cooperative).

The most basic measure of the internal organization of the kolkhoz was to divide the workforce into a number of working groups, generally known as brigades. Unlike mainland kolkhozes which encompassed from 200 to 400 families, the Zarya Kolkhoz was measured not so much by the number of families, but by the number of exiles, deportees, and prisoners within the compound. At the time of its creation in 1928, Zarya Kolkhoz had 75 workers. Headed by a brigade leader, each work force consisted of 15 to 20 workers, or three to four families charged with the responsibility of putting into place a successful agricultural enterprise.

Initially, the kolkhoz utilized basic farm implements powered by draught horses for a whole range of agricultural operations. Under normal circumstances, as envisioned by Communist leaders, the kolkhozniks would have been paid a share of the farm's product and profit according to the number of workdays they contributed. But, Zarya Kolkhoz was a sovkhoz where the Communist managers were paid a small salary and the kolkhozniks a meager ration of vegetables and grains. Even at that, the kolkhozniks would not have been allocated anything had it not been for the purpose of preventing their stealing the same items from the kolkhoz in the first place. In a small number of cases, kolkhoznik families were permitted to plant their own small gardens.

Members of the kolkhoz were required to work a minimum number of days each year in agriculture as well as on other nearby government projects. In cases where a kolkhoznik did not fulfill the required minimum of days, penalties could result in the confiscation of their private plot or a trial in front of a People's Court. This could result in three to eight months of hard labour in the kolkhoz, a year in a corrective labour camp, or deportation to another labour camp deep within Siberia. Above all else, the kulaks wanted to avoid deportation to any such secure detention camp where few, if any, survived.

Although Communist policy dictated that some of a kolkhoz's profits would be distributed among the workers even in Siberia, this turned out not to be the case in the Zarya Kolkhoz. Payment was made in the form of a small food ration, insufficient for survival in many cases. Residents were required to live on what they grew in their own garden, supplemented by meat and eggs from their chickens and domesticated geese, and milk from their goats. Although promised, there were no tractors at the time of the arrival of the Kozlov family. As a result, the peasants ploughed kolkhoz fields with horses which were kept, for security purposes, in a special stable near the kolkhoz offices.

Zarya Kolkhoz, although young by any standard, had two dormitories which accommodated about a dozen families along with several dozen labourers. However, not all kolkhozniks lived in dormitories; a few were assigned accommodation in small log houses or rented rooms in the nearby village. For the Kozlov family, life on the kolkhoz mirrored, to some degree, the life they had experienced in the logging camp with one important difference—in addition to the farming operation, the kolkhoz did have a small meat factory which was able to provide limited employment opportunities for members of the Kozlov family. Much of the products from the meat factory were earmarked for nearby logging camps and for sale in markets in Omsk and Tomsk.

In a strange way, the Kozlov family was lucky. Numerous other kulak families exiled from Ukraine after 1930 ended up in special settlements farther inland which, in essence, were primitive and isolated camps. Most of these camps consisted of a few barracks built by exiles in which several hundred people slept on wooden planks, while others lived in earthen dug-outs, or were housed in abandoned churches, buildings, cattle sheds, and barns. The barracks, which were meant to house 250 people with small window openings here and there, actually housed three or four times their capacity. To add to the problems, the latrines in these special settlements consisted of a fenced-off area, making it impossible for residents to find privacy. In most cases, the inhabitants prepared their food outside on camp fires, while the source of water came from a nearby river.

Technically, Zarya Kolkhoz was not a form of imprisonment even though a full report had to be filed with the local police each month. The kolkhoz was made up of Russians, Ukrainians, Volga Germans, and Siberians. Housed in one of the barracks, the authorities even went so far as to provide one single classroom for the children of kolkhoz.

As if to symbolize their renunciation of the peasant culture into which they had been born, Katusha and Nikolashya were forced to cut their braids which were traditionally worn by peasant girls until they were married. On opening day of school, the Commandant of the settlement gave a speech in which he told the children that they should be grateful to Soviet power which was, " . . . *so good and kind that it allows even you, the children of the kulaks, to study and become good Soviet citizens.*" The Communists believed that a *perekovka* (reforging) of human beings who did not fit the mould of the Soviet personality was an important ideological feature of the Gulag system.

The early winter of 1932 started out cold and things did not improve during the balance of the winter months or during the spring of 1933. The winds seemed always to blow in from all directions, particularly from the northern reaches of Siberia. If this were not bad enough, the winds would shift to the southeast and blow in from Kazakhstan. Suddenly and without warning the snows, mixed with sand from the faraway desert, descended upon the Zarya Kolkhoz. This caused the roof of one of the barracks to collapse under the weight of the heavy snows, resulting in several fatalities. Those who survived had to seek shelter in a barn. The men of the kolkhoz were of no help; most, including Alexei and Konstantin, were on loan to Camp 27 for the winter's logging operation. According to Commandant Matsunova, the influx of new prisoners into the logging camp to replace those who died or were transferred made it necessary that several experienced loggers be brought in to train and supervise the newcomers.

As a result of the heavy snowfall, the school-aged children, assisted by male labourers who were not assigned to the logging camp operations, were all mobilized to repair the damaged roofs and to clear the snow off the roofs not damaged. These tasks were undertaken in extreme temperatures. Luba, Katusha, and Nikolashya were not immune from participation. They, too, had to join the construction crew. Their task was to skid aspen logs from the nearby forest into the yard of kolkhoz where they would be hewn and then used to shore up the collapsed barrack.

With the interruption in the deliveries of food supplies during the severe winter, the kolkhozniks lived off the few remaining supplies stored in the root cellar. Supplemented by food stuff brought to the kolkhoz by the new arrivals, there was barely sufficient food for survival. Weakened by hunger and fatigue, several people were struck down with typhus and had to be isolated in one of the smaller barracks. In the absence of any medicine, the sick were left to fend for themselves. Similar in many ways to cholera or tuberculosis, the viral form of typhus was more prone to strike a poverty-stricken kolkhoz where rodents may have come into contact with the labourers. At first, several kolkhozniks came down with a headache, then a high fever, followed by nausea, vomiting, and diarrhea. Many typhus victims perished that winter. Unfortunately, their bodies could not be laid to rest in the frozen ground. This task was not accomplished until the spring thaw.

Sadly, when Alexei and Konstantin returned to the kolkhoz in March, they discovered that one of the victims of the winter's typhus season was

Luba. She was fine when they left the kolkhoz the previous fall. After hearing the shocking news, the first question that Alexei asked Katusha was, *"Good Lord, when did mother pass away? What happened?"*

"Mother passed away on December 25," replied a tearful Katusha.

"How did she die? Where is the body?"

"Mother's frozen body is in storage in the small wooden morgue in the village. Commandant Matsunova told us that all those who perished during the winter months would not be buried until April, when the ground thaws."

"Were you and Nikolashya with mother when she died?"

"Tak, on her last night Nikolashya and I spent the whole night praying with her and for her. We assured her that we would be here for each other, no matter what. On mother's last breath, a tear flowed down her cheek. She found peace with the Lord at last, and that thought is what helped us get through the experience of losing our beloved mother."

"Did you ask that stupid, senseless Matsunova if you could send word to us?"

"Tak, I did father, but he said it was no use."

If nothing else, the death of Luba, who was the matriarch of the family, brought the remaining members of the family even closer together. Still, the images of the past winter would not go away. The kolkhoz labourers were not given any food, perhaps a part of a deliberate policy to reduce the population of the kolkhoz. To survive, many turned to eating tree bark. They even went so far as to uncover a pile of rotten potato plant roots in the snow from the previous fall's potato harvest, mashing the roots, and then baking them into edible cakes. It was heartbreaking to watch their stomachs swell up. Those who did not die from typhus, died from dysentery, an inflammatory disorder of the intestines.

Slowly, ever so slowly, the snows of a severe winter gave way to the sounds of spring and the Kozlovs turned to other duties on the kolkhoz. Being descendants of ancestors who worked hard on their land in Ukraine for centuries made it easy to once again work the land. Commandant Matsunova named Tarasov Komarowski as the brigadir in charge of all planting operations. Meanwhile, Alexei and Konstantin were ordered to join Komarowski's brigade, while Katusha and Nikolashya were placed on a brigade responsible for planting a large garden. With so many deaths, new brigades were organized to take charge of the cattle, horses, hogs, poultry, and other farm animals. As new deportees continued to arrive, the work force in the kolkhoz gradually increased from 200 to more than 500 workers.

When the last vestiges of winter began to dissipate, Commandant Matsunova discovered that the population of Zarya Kolkhoz had been decimated. The frozen bodies of those who perished during the cold winter months were simply taken out of storage and buried in a graveyard near the kolkhoz without the benefit of any kind of a religious ceremony. Luba's grave was marked with a simple wooden cross.

Organizing the brigades into effective work units required planning, coordination, and communication. Yet, communicating about any matter was frowned upon, especially if it had to do with Stalin or communism. Despite the damper placed on communication, there was no shortage of rumours about new arrivals or about those exiles that had to walk for two days to reach the kolkhoz only to find that the accommodations were abominable. Without the help of others, even more exiles would have perished. Many were held in cellars for a week, sleeping as best they could on their meager baggage or on the bare floor. Others were housed in a workshop, where everybody slept on the cement floor. Despite the deprivations on the kolkhoz, most tried to keep their dignity. They refused to be like slaves to the authorities. With a daily ration of only 200 grams of bread, the death rate in the kolkhoz continued to take its toll.

Still, in comparison to the lumber camp, things developed in a different way in Zarya Kolkhoz. As a result of the decline in available food for labourers, Katusha and Nikolashya were given permission, under the control and guidance of an NKVD guard, to pick mushrooms in the nearby pine forest. Before setting out for the mushroom pick, the Brigadir warned them, *"When you pick wild mushrooms, you must stay within five kilometers of the kolkhoz. You will be under the guidance and control of an NKVD guard. Do not do anything stupid."*

"How will we know which mushrooms are edible," enquired Katusha.

"Don't worry, the NKVD guard knows his mushrooms. He will tell you which mushrooms are safe to eat and which are poisonous. If you eat the wrong mushrooms, nothing much will happen to you."

"Nothing much? What does that mean?"

"The worst that can happen to you is that you will die. In the end, you will all die anyway. This will just hasten the process."

Before a group of seven teenaged children, with sacks over their backs, set out for the mushroom pick, the NKVD guard provided them with some basic information, *"Mushrooms have a long history as a food in Siberia. Our kolkhoz needs more food to survive. Your task is to help us survive."*

"How many species of mushrooms will we pick?" questioned Nikolashya.

"Siberia has hundreds of species of fungi. We will pick only three types of mushrooms in this forest. The red pine mushroom which has a milk cap (Lactarius deliciosus), the brown bun mushroom which has a large brown cap (Boletus edulis), and the red-headed one."

"The red-headed one? That's an interesting name. What does it look like?"

"It is a mushroom with a woolly milk-cap. We like to call it the bearded milk-cap (Lactarius torminosus), a favourite of mine. Once the mushrooms are picked, you will bring them back to the kolkhoz, dry some of them, and preserve some in brine."

In order to survive, risks were taken. In time, several enterprising youngsters were able to gather mushrooms, not only for the kolkhoz but also for their own little initiative. They went so far as to set aside and sell for a few kopeks small quantities of mushrooms to residents in the nearby village. Later that summer, older children in the kolkhoz would sneak into the large gardens at night to steal potatoes from the fields. Some of the parents even got involved in this questionable activity in order to provide for their families.

Alexei struck a deal with the workers of a nearby slaughter-house, helping them build their wooden houses in exchange for cattle blood, which, unlike meat and bones, would not be missed by the authorities. He became sufficiently enterprising to make blood sausage during the summer and fall months without being detected. Alexei was of the view that Commandant Matsunova was aware of some of this activity but elected to turn a blind eye. Perhaps the relaxation of the attitude on the part of the Commandant had much to do with the decrease in the daily bread ration during the summer months from 200 to only 50 grams per day. The negative result of this decrease was predictable when the kolkhoz had to deal with an ever increasing number of deaths from malnutrition.

Luba Kozlov's final resting place in Siberia.

The Kozlovs, despite the loss of Luba, were able to remain together as a family. For many, the experience of deportation was synonymous with fragmentation of the family. Often, the children were sent to various children's homes and never heard from again. In other cases, it was not uncommon for deportees, especially if they were young and unattached, to take their chances living on the run in Siberia, hoping somehow to find their way back to their homeland. By the end of the summer of 1933, escapes from special settlements had become a mass phenomenon with tens of thousands of kulak runaways. Of the 500,000 who attempted to escape, only about 92,000 were ever caught. What happened to those who were not caught is left to one's conjecture.

During the summer of 1933, the remaining four members of the Kozlov family devoted all of their time to the farming and gardening operations, while at the same time grieving the loss of Luba. It appeared that Commandant Matsunova had taken pity on the family, going so far as to assign Alexei the task of assisting Brigadir Komarowski with the operation of the kolkhoz. In the final analysis, it became obvious that during the time of food shortages, the kulak deportees fared better than did the other exiles.

With the seemingly never-ending arrival of new exiles, the barracks were once again filled to capacity. Despite all of the frenetic activity, each person in the kolkhoz harboured some sort of a dream, in some instances for his family while in other cases for himself. For fear of reprimand, these dreams were seldom shared with others. Perhaps it was from this sort of impetus that Alexei turned to Komarowski with an important question, *"Brigadir, would it be possible for me to build a new log house for my family near the kolkhoz? I could then give up the present log house to new arrivals?"*

Brigadir Komarowski seemed not to hear the question. Perhaps he was fearful of being involved in any discussion or activity that would be contrary to the stated policy of the Communist Party. To Alexei's surprise and just about the time that three new tractors were being brought to the kolkhoz in advance of the harvest season, Commandant Matsunova called him aside asking, *"Kozlov, I hear that you want to build a log house for your family, is that true?"*

Checking to make certain that no one was within earshot, Alexei nodded in agreement, *"That is true, Commandant. With all of the crowding in the barracks, a log house for our family would help everyone. We can build this log house ourselves."*

"We'll see. Remember, this is a labour camp, not a holiday camp."

The discussion on the topic of building a log house was very short. Conversations with management were always short. Even the conversations with other exiles were guarded or non-existent. No one wanted to be deported to another settlement or to a logging camp for speaking against the policies of Stalin or criticizing kolkhoz management. Most preferred life in the kolkhoz to that of a logging camp or a mining camp in Eastern Siberia.

As the crops were being taken in, rumours once again began to circulate about shortages of food in Russia, Ukraine, and Belarus. These struck a chord with the kulak deportees because they must have been thinking about the coming winter and how best each might survive if agricultural, gardening, and meat supplies were to be totally confiscated by the Communists. It seemed as though everyone living on the kolkhoz wanted to commandeer, even at great risk, sufficient grains for the coming months.

Other rumours of tragedy began to circulate. A teen-aged girl became pregnant during the summer and died as a result of an attempt to abort the fetus. In several other cases, exiles were found to be missing during a roll call. Most were rounded up, but several were never heard from again. No one knew what happened to them. Those who were rounded up were immediately sent to special settlements. Some said that their destination was the Stalinsk metal works to toil as penal labourers where they lived in dugouts made of branches and pine needles along the river bank against the outside of the factory wall. Here, the prisoners even made their own rudimentary furniture and carved their own cups, spoons, and other utensils.

Having developed a reasonable working relationship with Brigadir Komarowski, Alexei decided to once again pursue the question of the length of his family's exile to Siberia. *"Brigadir,"* was his direct question, *"I do know that the sentence of my family is five years, two years hard labour followed by three years of re-education. However, is it possible, through hard work, to shorten our sentence to two years of hard labour and two years of exile?"*

True to form, Brigadir Komarowski did not have an immediate response. However, as the last of the vegetables were taken in and without discussing the matter at length, the Brigadir did share with Alexei that it was his understanding that the Kozlov expulsion was for the standard period of five years for kulaks consisting of two years of hard labour and three years of exile. *"It is most unusual,"* concluded Komarowski, *"for the NKVD to shorten a sentence."*

Recognizing that the family was approaching its third year of hard labour, the response from Brigadir Komarowski was most disappointing. Since the family's sentence was never confirmed initially, Alexei assumed that it might well be for a period of less than five years. Still, Alexei was optimistic that the authorities might reconsider the length of the sentence. At the same time, Alexei had to admit that it could have been much worse. During the Kozlov's first year in Siberia, a number of co-workers were selected for re-assignment to labour camps that housed hardcore criminals, dissidents, anti-Bolsheviks, and under-achievers. The survival rate in these labour camps was less than 50 percent during their first year.

As the last vestiges of the harvest crops were harvested in the Zarya Kolkhoz, Brigadir Komarowski approached Alexei, addressing him directly with an order, *"Kozlov, I am making a trip into Omsk next week. New markets, you know. You will accompany me on that trip."*

Alexei felt his heart skip a beat. Somehow, he felt that the trip to Omsk would change his life forever, perhaps that of his children as well. He tried hard not to show any emotion.

PART 3

ESCAPE

Chapter 11

DREAMING THE IMPOSSIBLE

Just who is this mysterious man from Kazakhstan?

As Alexei thought about his upcoming trip to Omsk, he reflected upon the Soviet culture that was developing in the kolkhoz. By the fall of 1933, the modest school had a collection of over three dozen worn books which formed the basis for instruction. Gospozha Antonina Mikhailyvna Golovna, a proud member of Komsomol, the youth wing of the Communist Party, taught the basics of reading, writing, and arithmetic without the benefit of being certified. A daughter of a family deported from Saint Petersburg with only three years of formal education, she was often heard to say, *"Everyone should learn to read and write."*

The idea of literacy in the Russian language was fully embraced by Josef Stalin, and Golovna was sufficiently dedicated to the Party to urge the younger children to attend school and to join the Young Pioneer organization. Nikolashya, the only Kozlov sibling eligible to join the Young Pioneers, limited to children between the ages of 10 and 15, did not need much coaxing. The Organization's motto was *always prepared* and its activities included crafts, sports, and the eradication of illiteracy. Although one of the aims of the Young Pioneer organization was to provide young people with an opportunity to participate in a summer vacation or a winter holiday, such activity was not permitted for the children of deportees in Siberia.

Even the primitive living conditions in the crowded barracks and the small space set aside in one of the barracks to serve as a classroom did not dampen the children's willingness to learn. The crowding in the barracks was quickly becoming the norm and grudgingly acceptable to its occupants. The luxuries enjoyed in the past were all gone. In those same barracks, it was common to see women sleep with blankets in place of quilts. The men, sequestered in their own barrack, simply slept in their tunics to keep warm. Needless to say, all of this made the barracks smell bad, like a barn.

Although Alexei approved of Golovna's initiative, he disliked the idea of the Communist Pioneer movement taking root in the kolkhoz, especially since it soon became an unwritten policy for youngsters to snitch on their parents, neighbours, and relatives. Children entered the Pioneer Club in elementary school and continued until adolescence at which time they typically joined Komsomol. There were no separate organizations for boys and girls. Thousands of camps built exclusively for Young Pioneers would soon appear throughout the Soviet Union.

Knowing that a careless word might get him into real trouble, Alexei never spoke against Stalin to his children. Like other fathers, he was afraid to drop any kind of unguarded word because his daughter might inadvertently mention it in school, where the teacher would report it to the authorities who would ask the child, *"Where did you hear that?"* and the child might answer, *"Father says so and father is always right."* And, before you know it, father would be punished. Making matters worse, Pioneers who failed to inform on their families might be treated with suspicion and regarded as lacking in vigilance. In rare cases, such children might themselves be denounced and stigmatized.

To illustrate this, a kulak by the name of Ivan arrived that summer and befriended Alexei by telling him that he fell into an anti-Soviet position with his experience in Austria as a prisoner of war during World War I. He described how he returned to Ukraine with a love of Austrian order, convinced that the bourgeois small-holdings which he had seen in

Austria were the key to agricultural wealth. Ivan saw the mistakes of the first period of collectivization as chaos, not a temporary complication. Unfortunately, it was his own daughter who reported him to the NKVD. *"That is how,"* Ivan confided in Alexei, *"I ended up in this pigsty of a kolkhoz in Siberia."*

In another case, it was actually a kulak's son that turned his father in to the NKVD authorities. Dmitri's son already knew that his father had been identified as being anti-Soviet. Not wishing to harm his own prospects for a career within the Communist Party by being expelled from the Pioneer movement or the Komsomol and then barred from colleges and professions, he elected to report his father to the NKVD.

Grigory, another recent deportee from Belarus, told Alexei that his nephew turned him in to the NKVD by saying, *"I renounce my uncle, an ex-priest. For many years, he deceived the people by telling them that God exists. For this reason, I severed my relations with my uncle."*

"You accepted this false accusation without telling the NKVD the truth?"

"I accepted the false accusation," explained Grigory, a member of the Russian Orthodox Clergy, *"with the belief that my nephew would be spared deportation to Siberia."*

Many of these renunciations were encouraged by the parents themselves who recognized the need for their children to break from them if they were to advance in Soviet society. Many children accepted and expressed the view that, *"My real father is the Komsomol, who taught me the important things in life; my real mother is Our Motherland, the Union of Soviet Socialist Republics, and the people of the Soviet Union are my family now."*

In major centers throughout Russia, films, books, and songs began to feature the exploits of ordinary heroes from the proletariat—engineers, model workers, aviators, ballerinas, and sportsmen—those who were all bringing glory to the Soviet Union. Soon, some of this propaganda would reach Zarya Kolkhoz. This was a method of encouraging young people to believe that they could emulate their achievements, provided they worked hard and proved themselves as worthy Soviet citizens.

What is strange about all of this is that it *did* happen, especially to the children of kulaks where the children grew up with the stigma of their origins and where they wanted to be regarded as equal members of society. Some renounced their kulak relatives while others claimed that all of their relatives were dead. Such acts of denial were often necessary for survival. It became a case of the children prospering while their parents disappeared into Siberia. When families were deported, they did not always stay in one camp for a very long time. Those who survived were often shuttled to other work camps. Many decided to live on the run, picking up odd jobs in factories and mines, wherever they could find a loophole in the passport system, splitting up and hopefully reuniting once again.

With the introduction of the passport system, the police were instructed to step up their campaign to exclude from the towns the socially impure: kulaks, priests, merchants, criminals, parasites, and prostitutes. This drove millions to conceal their origins so that they might become socially acceptable. In many cases, false papers could be easily obtained through bribery or purchased from forgers where clean biographies could be developed. Many people simply threw away their old papers and applied for new ones from a different soviet, going so far as to change their family name. To add to systemic problems, Soviet officials and police were themselves notoriously inefficient and corrupt.

As Alexei waited for the day that he would join Brigadir Komarowski for the trip to Omsk, he realized that his family had not celebrated Christmas the previous year. Any such celebration was forbidden by Stalin in 1929. However, deportees were told that although the practice of placing a Christmas tree in the home would not be reinstated, they would soon be allowed to use a fir tree as an indication of Father Frost during New Year's celebrations, at which time gifts could be exchanged.

Although Stalin occasionally did show some signs of kindness in his policies, all of this changed when, in 1932, his wife, Nadezhda Allilueva, committed suicide. This made Stalin distrustful of everybody in his entourage and would eventually trigger another round of purges. Those suspected of being duplicitous by concealing their real aspirations and deceiving the Party under the cover of a false oath of loyalty were suddenly drummed out of the Party, many never to be seen again. Once Stalin weeded out the dissenters, he urged his new team to close ranks behind his leadership.

To consolidate his relationship with Brigadir Komarowski, Alexei tried hard to demonstrate an attitude of a march towards communism. The idea that this was a life or death struggle against capitalist elements came with the territory. Even in remote Siberia where any news of the latest developments on the world stage was hard to come by, many put aside their doubts about communism. Stalin urged them to join the struggle against a perceived new enemy, Hitler and his Nazi Party.

Most new arrivals exhibited a lack of commitment to the ideals of communism. *"This,"* explained the Brigadir, *"is the reason why they are here in the first place."* At the same time, he recognized Alexei's efforts to embrace the fundamentals of communism. For the first time, Komarowski referred to him as comrade, a word of comradeship generally reserved for those imbued with the spirit of communism. *Perhaps,* reasoned Alexei, *if I can show the Brigadir that I have made progress in re-forging and re-educating myself into the image of a good communist, the NKVD authorities will release me and my family from bondage earlier.*

The eventful day for the trip to Omsk finally arrived. Alexei, however, was not prepared for what he was about to experience. Komarowski, always guarded about what he said, made small talk during the five-hour horseback ride to Omsk, but nothing about the purpose of the trip. The Brigadir explained that the Omskaya Oblast was about to be created. The oblast would border Kazakhstan and boast an area of 140,000 square kilometers. Even as the oblast was being created, it already possessed six small cities and seventeen urban villages.

Upon visiting the first of several markets in Omsk, Alexei took every opportunity to listen to the conversations of those trying to barter for items of clothing, footwear, vegetables, and meat. However, not all the talk was about the activities in the marketplace and how best to prepare for the winter. For the very first time, Alexei listened to talk about food shortages in Ukraine and the number of people who perished as a result. On a relatively cold fall day, it was a shock for Alexei to note that many of those attending the market were so shabbily dressed. It was most obvious that those living in Omsk had fallen on hard times.

Looking around the market, Alexei observed a woman from a village who had her eye on a cotton nightshift. In exchange, she was prepared to barter a fine crop of potatoes and carrots. In other cases, deportees talked about receiving parcels from their families back home. But, not everyone in attendance was bent upon bartering personal items for foodstuff. In the crowded market, there was plenty of evidence that both locals and deportees had fallen on hard times, as was apparent from the number of individuals begging for a piece of bread. In cases where a beggar became too aggressive, it was not uncommon to suddenly see the appearance of a police officer, an NKVD official, or a member of the OGPU urging them to keep moving.

After spending the night in the town's central park, Alexei and Brigadir Komarowski made their way through the original wooden Tobolsk Gate to the main market of Omsk which was located in the confluence of the Irtysh and Om rivers. Many years earlier, Tobolsk Gate stood as witness to the beginning of *Tsar's Road* and the point of entry into Siberia. To Russians, it is the cultural and spiritual center of the city. In the midst of a region that had developed a Siberian Tatar culture in an outpost of Russian colonization, there was also evidence that many at the market were kulak deportees from Ukraine.

Even though loose talk or idle conversations about Stalin's policies were forbidden, there was plenty of guarded talk about Stalin's crimes in Ukraine. It seemed as though Stalin had declared war on his own people when in 1932 he sent Commissars and OGPU secret police to crush the resistance of Ukrainian farmers to forced collectivization. Ukraine was sealed off and all food supplies and livestock were confiscated. OGPU death squads executed anti-party elements. Furious that an insufficient number of Ukrainians were being shot, Stalin promptly set a quota of 10,000 executions a week. During the bitter winter of 1932-1933, twenty-five thousand Ukrainians were being shot or died of starvation each day. Cannibalism became common. Eventually, seven million Ukrainians would perish, three million of them children. Those who spoke out about the genocide were branded as fascist agents. Stalin also ordered the arrest and execution of many of the Soviet Union's ablest statisticians because they were either too precise or misunderstood the degree to which the regime wanted to support collectivization by distorting grain production and population figures.

Later in the day, Brigadir Komarowski ordered Alexei to look after the horses while he paid a visit to the director of the market. As Alexei reflected upon the order, he concluded that the Brigadir was about to negotiate prices for the supply of vegetable, grains, poultry, and meat being supplied to the market. He was thankful to be able to spend some time on his own without having to guard his every word and movement.

Deep in thought, he was suddenly startled by a question posed to him, *"Ukrainian deportee, I presume?"*

"Why do you ask?"

Looking around to make certain that no one was within earshot, the stranger quietly responded, *"Just a simple question. You look like a Ukrainian kulak. And, nyet, I am not an OGPU agent or a policeman."*

Not being certain about the tall, thin stranger with a handlebar moustache, all Alexei would offer him is that, *"Tak, I am a deportee from Ukraine."*

At this point the stranger introduced himself as Oleg Parsimov, saying that he spent five years in a labour camp in Kazakhstan. *"After five years,"* continued Parsimov, *"I was transferred to Omsk. In Omsk, I accepted work with the Trans-Siberian Railway. The OGPU extended my exile for an additional three years of re-education."*

"You were not re-educated during your five years of exile?"

"Who knows? The party wants to re-educate me in the ideals of communism. But, tell me, what the hell does that mean?"

"Is all your work in Omsk?"

"My work takes me to Kazakhstan from time to time. Who knows? Maybe the authorities will transfer me back to Kazakhstan."

If Alexei did not know where the conversation would take them, he did not have to worry. In a few brief moments, always being aware that Brigadir Komarowski might return unexpectedly, he learned that Parsimov was a Ukrainian deportee with an understanding of the political atmosphere in the region. While digesting what Parsimov told him, Alexei was startled to hear the manner in which the next question was phrased, *"Your family is with you, are they not?"* It was not so much the question, but rather the inflection in his voice that left the impression that he already knew the answer. Even though this raised a lot of questions, Alexei decided not to let his curiosity get the best of him.

"To Pravda (that is true)," explained Alexei, *"I was arrested for being a kulak. Without warning, we were deported to Siberia."*

"How is your family doing?"

"We're doing fine except for my wife."

"Your wife? What happened to her?"

"She died," explained Alexei.

Even though in Siberia one rarely knew who his friends were, Alexei accepted at face value what Parsimov was telling him. Deep in thought, Alexei was surprised with Parsimov's offer, *"I think I can help you. When you are next in Omsk, why not look me up? The local railway station master will tell you where I live."*

"You want to help me? Why? How?"

"There are troubled times ahead, especially for deportees."

This was not the first time that Alexei heard that stiffer measures may be in the horizon for deportees. *"What is it that you are suggesting, Parsimov?"*

"You should be thinking about surviving the difficult times which are sure to come."

Alexei was suddenly full of questions, *"What difficult times do you see? Shouldn't I be happy with my present work? Are you offering me an escape plan?"*

"Da, I have heard that our leader will be executing many political dissidents. I want to help you. But, there is a small cost for this help which has many rewards."

"A small cost?"

"I do not think that you can put a price on freedom, especially when it is only 50 rubles. Think about it. If you want more information, come back and see me at the railway station."

Just as suddenly as Parsimov first appeared, as though in a dream, he disappeared into the market crowd. Alexei thought about his every word. For some unknown reason, he could not help but compare Parsimov's moustache with that made famous by Ukraine's poet laureate, Taras Shevchenko. The very thought left him with a smile. Trying to make sense of it all, Alexei's smile turned into a frown. *Should I trust a complete stranger,* thought Alexei, *or should I turn the matter over to the NKVD? Should I tell Komarowski about Parsimov?*

Alexei and Brigadir Komarowski spent one more day in Omsk before returning to the kolkhoz. Alexei learned that those who fell ill were often taken to a hospital in Omsk. However, the last thing a kolkhoznik wanted was to fall ill. As far as the NKVD was concerned, the patient was already half way into the grave simply because he could not work. Occasionally, the really sick people were allowed to rest in the hospital. Deportees applying for hospitalization were examined by doctors, predominantly female, who let them expose everything for them to see. The medical check was quite simple. All a doctor needed to know was how much flesh was left on the patient's buttock. This was accomplished by pinching the buttock and the results came back in three categories: *one, two,* or *okay.* Those placed in the category of *okay* were admitted to the hospital for recovery.

Yet, despite all of these sufferings, the NKVD guards rarely, if ever, abused the kolkhozniks or prisoners arbitrarily. They were under a strict Red Army rule that prohibited private sanctions in the organization. If they broke the rule, they had to be ready to find themselves on the opposite side of the barbed wire in detention centers or to contend with some other form of discipline.

Zarya Kolkhoz was populated with deportees, local residents, and peasants from nearby villages who had earlier established small farming operations but were now forced to join a kolkhoz. As a result, the deportees found themselves working in the fields side by side with local farmers. The local farmers took pity on the kolkhozniks, often offering them food, even though their lot seemed no better than that of the deportees. These acts of kindness gave the Kozlov family the impression that the local Russians were an open-hearted and generous people.

In assessing all of the information gleaned while in Omsk, Alexei concluded that there were, perhaps, a few signs of an improving economy. It seemed as though the authorities would once again pay prisoners a small monthly stipend for their labour. Now living in a small log house that the Kozlovs built near the kolkhoz, Alexei realized, if the gossip was true, that he would be able to buy food with the money earned. Even vodka, which had been strictly prohibited, would soon come into circulation. The NKVD was intent upon improving the morale of its slave labourers, going so far as granting them the privilege of taking a bath once a month. Many would soon take advantage of the availability of hot water to deal with their life-time enemies: lice and bedbugs. By 1934, the political situation, nationally and on Zarya Kolkhoz, attained a modicum of stability. Transfers out of the collective farm were minimal and those who died from labour or disease were quickly replaced by an influx of new arrivals.

Unlike the previous year, many of the prisoners arriving in 1935 were women. And, with the direct threat of starvation somewhat alleviated, the female prisoners switched their preoccupation with bread and potatoes to that of assessing their own femininities. Some of them even moonlighted to make money off their physical charms. As to the question of getting pregnant, they would simply shrug their shoulders saying, *"Nyet, our children will be Stalin's children and they will be well taken care of. Hopefully, they will grow into fully-recognized Russian citizens. Besides, if war breaks out, Russia will need all the manpower she can muster."*

The very nature and structure of the labour camps in Siberia did little to discourage women from being preyed upon from all quarters. During their transport to the camps, they were often raped on the transport ships or in the railroad cars by NKVD guards. Upon arrival at their destination they would be paraded naked in front of the camp officials, who would select those they fancied, promising easier work in exchange for sexual favours. Officials preferred German, Latvian, or Estonian women who most likely would never see home again, over native Russian women who might one day return home. Women not selected by the camp officials became prizes for male and sometimes lesbian criminals. Besides the everyday tortures of starvation, work exhaustion, exposure to the cold of the far north, and physical abuse, the more intractable prisoners of either sex were frequently subjected to isolation, impalement, genital mutilation, and in extreme cases, a bullet in the back of the head.

By 1935, Alexei noted that his family had been in Siberia for nearly five years. For some reason, however, the NKVD authorities would not tell Alexei when his family would be repatriated to Ukraine. Even more troublesome was the rumour that the sentences of all kulaks would be increased. Critical food shortages, malnutrition, and hard work caused a sudden spike in the death rate of forced labourers. As a result, Stalin decided to replace those who died by simply increasing the length of the sentences imposed upon all kulaks.

In the midst of this uncertainty, Alexei saw a potential for other problems that might visit his family. Katusha, now 20 years of age, was being courted by a young Bolshevik revolutionary. Meanwhile, 21 year-old Konstantin gave all the appearances of embracing the ideals of communism. Even Nikolashya, now a mature 17 year-old, displayed flashes of artistic talent in small theatrical performances put on by the kolkhozniks to portray the life and times in Siberia. Could it be that Stalin's re-education plan was taking root?

Like most other detention camps and kolkhozes in Siberia, each member had, in his or her own way, two lives: one that on the surface portrayed an adherence to the principles of communism while on the other hand harbouring a secret desire to leave it all behind. Although it is true that the Kozlov family now worked in a kolkhoz, it was also true that Omsk was now facing an increased demand for manpower, not only in the kolkhozes of the Omsk Oblast, but also in the logging camps. In addition, there was an increasing amount of activity in industry—in furniture-making, woodworking, engineering, and oil refining. This made it much easier, first for Alexei, and now his son Konstantin, to dream of spending their remaining days in exile in a vocation other than logging or collective farming. All of this new activity led to the development and maintenance of reading rooms, cultural clubs, libraries, and art clubs—sometimes within the confines of a kolkhoz, but most certainly in cities and towns.

In light of these cultural developments, the Kozlov siblings looked forward to the day that they might also be able to take a trip into Omsk to visit the Prosvita Ukrainian cultural center. However, during those troubled times, everyone was well aware that the NKVD kept a close eye on any activity that might give it the appearance of being anti-soviet. This fear of possible dire circumstances did not stop Konstantin from asking permission of Brigadir Komarowski to make just such a trip to Omsk.

—•❋•—

As the year of 1935 came to a close, Brigadir Komarowski did approve the request which would allow Konstantin to travel to Omsk. In retrospect, the Brigadir should have withheld his approval. In the end, the NKVD made certain that Komarowski paid the ultimate price for his decision. Worse yet, this seemingly innocent decision would unleash a sequence of startling events for the Kozlov family.

Chapter 12

ESCAPE FROM THE GULAG

My name is Mikhail Baranov

O ver-burdened with the problems of survival during a time of famine in Ukraine and Russia, the kulaks in Zarya Kolkhoz must have felt like snow-covered trees after a major snowfall. While taking in the crops and the gardens, there is little doubt that they wanted to talk to one another about their problems but were afraid to do so. As soon as one kulak gave in to the temptation to talk, he would undoubtedly be overheard by someone else and just like that he would suddenly disappear, never to be heard from again. Each knew that they could get into trouble as a result of a single conversation, so most entered into a conspiracy of silence with their friends. As one kulak described it, *"Talking could be dangerous at the best of Soviet times, but during these times, a few careless words were all it took for somebody to vanish forever. Informers are everywhere. Today a man talks freely only with his wife—at night, with the blankets pulled over their heads. Even then, there is no guarantee."*

Since his family now lived in a small log cabin at the perimeter of the kolkhoz, Alexei felt a bit more comfortable talking to his children about the risks they faced if they elected to talk about Stalin's grandiose plans. Knowing that Konstantin had recently gained permission from Brigadir Komarowski to visit the main market in Omsk, he had some advice for him, *"Watch your tongue or you will get into trouble. When you are in Omsk, see if you can get away from the NKVD long enough to talk to Oleg Parsimov."*

"Parsimov? The railroader who you met in Omsk? What do you know about him?"

"I do not know much about Parsimov except that he is a railroader and that he took an interest in me. He seems to know what is happening in Siberia."

"He took an interest in you, father? Is he a spy? Should I trust him?"

"I'll be damned if I know. He sounded like a person who wanted to help a fellow kulak. I have some reservation about asking you to meet him. You can find out where he lives by making an inquiry at the main railway station. Do not tell anyone about him. Find out what he has in mind."

"You say that he is tall and has a handlebar moustache?"

"Tak, he is tall and slim, like a poplar tree. Be suspicious of him. He could be an agent of the NKVD. How did he know that my family was with me in this kolkhoz? I do not have any answers."

Recognizing that every second person was likely to be an informer, Konstantin, with strict instructions from Brigadir Komarowski, set out in the company of an NKVD guard for the main market in Omsk. The two were asked to confirm the delivery dates for the products negotiated earlier for Zarya's agricultural and meat products. The fact that he was allowed to make the trip in the company of only one guard was, perhaps, a reflection of the confidence that the Brigadir had in him. On the other hand, the NKVD was aware that Konstantin's father and two sisters remained behind in the kolkhoz. They would provide some assurance that Konstantin would return to the kolkhoz.

During the horseback ride to Omsk, Konstantin thought about his tacit agreement with his father not to talk about political events. He knew that anyone could be arrested by a member of the NKVD and forced to incriminate his friends by reporting such conversations as evidence of their counter-revolutionary activities. In the political climate as it developed by 1936, to initiate political discussions with anyone except one's closest friends or members of the family was to invite suspicion of being an informer or provocateur.

Konstantin thought about the camp system where the inmates were put to work in every aspect of hard labour—building railroads, roads, canals; forestry, mining, construction, and agriculture. He thought about the women, although housed in separate barracks, who often shared the same work with men. Most troubling was the basic daily food ration, now set at 400 grams of bread, which accounted for little more than half of the prisoner's required daily calories. Of course, daily rations did vary, depending on whether the prisoner was a shock worker, an invalid, or a Stakhanovite. The most productive workers received a food bonus of fish, potatoes, porridge, or vegetables to supplement their ration of bread.

Konstantin felt fortunate that his father had obtained permission to build a log home. At six o'clock each morning, the Kozlovs had to join the workers living in the barracks, in time for breakfast at six-thirty, roll call at seven, followed by work until sundown. After a skimpy dinner, their duties consisted of chopping firewood, shoveling snow during the winter months, gardening, road repair, and other duties as assigned by the Brigadir. During Siberia's summer months, the days were long and the nights short. At eleven in the evening, it was lights out—but not before the coal-oil lamps were re-filled in readiness for the new day. The more he thought about his lot on the kolkhoz and his little brother Pyotr back in Ukraine, the angrier he grew.

While at the market in Omsk, Konstantin told the NKVD guard that he wanted to relieve himself in an outdoor toilet provided for the general population. Instead, he hurriedly made his way to the main train station, trying to imagine what Oleg Parsimov would look like. At the railway station, a freight train chugged its way through the town, festooned with Party propaganda banners stating, *Spirit of Creative Construction* and

Labour In The USSR Is A Matter Of Valour And Glory. Another freight train, traveling in the opposite direction, had slogans of its own: *Camp Workers, Let us complete the ground preparation at a level of 150 percent,* and *Better Provisions for Shock Workers!*

When Konstantin enquired about the banners, he was told that a shock-work system, complete with worker competitions, was being instituted by Stalin. Konstantin recalled that even Zarya Kolkhoz published a brief newsletter that urged labourers to work hard for the glory of the Party. The newsletter strove to cultivate worker enthusiasm and a spirit of creative construction in society. Whatever his thoughts, Konstantin was disappointed to learn that Parsimov was out of town until the next day undertaking some railway repairs east of the city. Returning to the main market, the NKVD guard was waiting for him with a question, *"Where have you been, Kozlov? That was a very long crap."*

"Upset stomach. It must be the food I ate."

Rather than return to Zarya Kolkhoz that day, Konstantin suggested that they stay overnight in order to complete their business enquiries the next day. That evening, when they joined the market crowds, Konstantin reflected upon the cross-section of buyers and sellers. There was no shortage of Christians, Muslims, kulaks, political dissidents, and criminals. Evident also were the homeless and the hooligans who had been, once too often, tardy at work.

The following day, Konstantin once again told the NKVD official that he was still experiencing stomach problems and that he needed some time to himself. Quickly, he scurried back to the railway station to meet Oleg Parsimov. Looking Parsimov over from head to foot, it struck him that he did look like a darker image of a moustached Taras Shevchenko, Ukraine's Poet Laureate.

"Tak, my name is Oleg Parsimov. Should I know you?"

"My name is Kozlov. My father's name is Alexei Kozlov. He asked that I meet you in person, that you might have some news for me."

"You say your name is Konstantin Kozlov? Da, you do look like your father. Come with me. I shall talk to you as we walk along the platform of the railway station."

Looking at Parsimov in his regular Soviet-style work clothes, slender build, moustache, and the unmistakable odor of the railway, Konstantin thought about the brief description his father had shared with him.

"Gospodin Parsimov, my father told me that you are well informed and knowledgeable."

"I am from the same region of Ukraine as your family. When I first saw your father, he reminded me of my best friend back home."

"You're a kulak, then, aren't you?"

"To verna, in a way of speaking. I am a railway foreman. I build and maintain railways. I was deported to Omsk because of my comments about Bolshevism."

"Do you like it here, Parsimov?"

"It could be worse. What I wanted to tell your father, I will share with you. I see many new arrivals in Omsk. I heard that Stalin is about to unleash a new campaign. What kind of campaign, I do not know. Maybe it is about those who have spoken out about government policies. They are called the counter-revolutionaries. Maybe even those stupid Whites are the culprits. Perhaps it is the Whites who will face the music."

"The Whites? Who are these Whites?"

Oleg seemed surprised to learn that Konstantin was not aware of the Whites. *"You don't know? You don't know that the Whites were the Russian forces which fought the Bolsheviks after the October Revolution?"*

Now in a defensive posture, Konstantin decided to explain it this way, *"Da, of course. I know that the White and Red Army fought the Russian Civil War from 1917 to 1921."*

"Actually, that civil war continued into 1923 in Eastern Russia," Oleg shot back, pounding his chest as he did so.

"You said that the Whites will face the music? If there are troubled times ahead, is there something that I should be doing?"

"These are difficult times for all of us. Give some thought to what I have said. Think about yourself and your family. When you have a plan, come back to see me."

"You want me to develop a plan? Can you tell me something about the plan you would expect from me?"

"Think with care about what I have said. Where do you want to be in the coming days? Where would you like to be next year?"

"My father told me that your help will cost 50 rubles. Is that true?"

"Da, there is this small cost for a new identity, a new passport, and a new assignment. Without these documents, the plan cannot work."

"The service you provide seems important."

"Very important. Aside from your father, never ever say anything about our meeting."

Returning to the marketplace, Konstantin was once again admonished by the NKVD official for his tardiness in returning from the outdoor toilet. On the horseback ride back to the kolkhoz, Konstantin could not get Parsimov's words out of his mind. Two things appeared clear: Parsimov seemed to have an inkling of the terror that Stalin would soon unleash, and it looked as though he wanted to extend a helping hand to a fellow deportee from Ukraine. What was less clear was Parsimov's motivation. Was it solely money or was there another motive?

When Konstantin arrived at the log cabin which served as the family's place of residence, he found it empty. As well, all the family's possessions were gone. Not only that, but there were signs that new occupants were in the process of moving in. Upon making an enquiry in the main barrack, he was told that Commandant Matsunova, accompanied by four Red Army officers, arrested Brigadir Komarowski the previous day. No explanation was given.

"What about my father and sisters? Where are they?"

"Your father has been re-located to a kolkhoz in Rodina and your sisters to Iskra."

"Where are these kolkhozes?"

"They are both in this oblast."

Konstantin did not have to be told that he had landed in the midst of a hornet's nest. How did all of this suddenly come about? Why was Brigadir Komarowski arrested? Was it because he was getting too friendly with some of the deportees? That evening, Konstantin was assigned a bunk in one of the barracks all the while wondering what the new day would bring. To whom would he now make the report about the local market in Omsk?

At seven in the morning, just before the traditional serving of porridge, Commandant Matsunova addressed the kolkhozniks. After the customary remarks about the advantages of the soviet way of life and the progress made during Stalin's first Five-Year Plan, he got right to the point, *"We are now well into Comrade Stalin's second Five-Year Plan. Our leader wants to accelerate the plan. We must make some changes. Brigadir Komarowski has been replaced by Brigadir Bilinkov. A number of the kolkhozniks have been relocated. Under the leadership of the new Brigadir, this kolkhoz will continue to meet its objectives."*

Following breakfast and roll call, Brigadir Bilinkov addressed the kolkhozniks. Once again deep in thought, Konstantin seemed not to hear what the Brigadir was saying until he heard his name being called. Looking up, it was none other than Brigadir Bilinkov, *"Kozlov, come with me. I want to talk to you."*

Brigadir Bilinkov led him to the log cabin previously occupied by his family. Suddenly, it occurred to Konstantin that it was the new Brigadir who had taken over their place of residence. When they arrived at the log cabin, the Brigadir explained, *"This log cabin has been assigned to me by the Commandant. The destination of Komarowski is none of my business. It is none of your business either."*

"My father and sisters have been re-located?"

"Da, your father has been transferred to another kolkhoz. His expertise will be required there. The same goes for your two sisters. Their help is needed in yet another kolkhoz. You will be taking the place of your father, assisting me with my duties."

Looking at Brigadir Bilinkov, Konstantin didn't know what to say, what questions to ask. In the end, he had none. Just to know that his father and his two sisters may still be alive was blessing enough. It was now time to plan for the future. Although the days dragged on and there was no shortage of challenges during the winter of 1936, what was most important was to make contact, if at all possible, with his two sisters and his father. One thing seemed clear; Brigadir Bilinkov was far more dictatorial than was his predecessor.

With more new arrivals, the three barracks once again became over-crowded. Those not gainfully employed in the various tasks in the kolkhoz were immediately transferred to logging camp operations and, in a small number of cases, to mining operations in the Far East.

As the first signs of spring began to appear in 1936, Konstantin decided to risk asking Brigadir Bilinkov for permission to travel to visit his sisters and his father. To his surprise, the Brigadir granted permission, saying that he expected him and an NKVD guard back in three days. The horseback ride to Iskra, twenty kilometers from Zarya Kolkhoz, took the better part of one day. There was no shortage of tears as he embraced Katusha and Nikolashya.

He didn't know what to say when Katusha announced that she had fallen in love with a Red Army officer and had consented to marry him that coming summer. Nikolashya, as well, seemed buoyant and bubbly. *Was she in love as well? What was happening to his family right before his eyes? Were they not aware that their time of banishment to Siberia was about to end? That they might be repatriated at any time?*

On his return to Zarya Kolkhoz, Konstantin detoured to meet with his father in the Rodina Kolkhoz. Interestingly, all three kolkhozes, Zarya, Iskra, and Rodina were separated by virtually the same distance. Konstantin's father was aware that Katusha and Nikolashya had been re-located to a kolkhoz in Iskar. Not wishing to raise any suspicions,

Konstantin quietly asked his father, *"Are you aware that Stalin is planning a Reign of Terror?"*

"Tak, that is what I have heard. Best not to say much about politics, otherwise we might meet with the same fate as did Komarowski."

"Do you know what happened to him?"

"Nyet, but I can guess. Either way, he is no longer with us. This is why we must continue to work hard, keep our thoughts to ourselves, and never speak against Stalin."

"Father, I have met with Parsimov."

"You have? What did he say? Anything important?"

"He said that there are troubled times ahead, that dissenters will be terrorized and heads will roll. I have been thinking about a lot of things. I am worried. Worried for all of us."

"My son, I know what you are thinking. Your chance of survival is very slim. Very few survive the ordeal. Work hard. Who knows, we may soon be repatriated. Our five-year sentence has already been fulfilled. This is our period of exile. Our time of re-education."

"Father, do you know what happened to Komarowski? Is it possible that you and I have been tainted by his friendship? Are we destined for the same fate? All of this worries me."

"Do you feel that we might be earmarked for elimination?"

"Tak, I had a bad dream last night. I believe that this is the calm before the storm. Otherwise, why was our family split up?"

Arriving back at Zarya Kolkhoz, Konstantin could think of little else but a plan to leave Siberia behind. Word had filtered back to Zarya Kolkhoz about a prisoner suddenly leaving the kolkhoz headed for Kazakhstan with the hope of reaching Turkey before finding his way back to Ukraine. Several other zeks had disappeared into the western reaches of Siberia with the hopes of reaching Ukraine on foot. Once those individuals left, they were never heard from again. Still, it encouraged Konstantin to think about these possibilities. Not wishing to leave his future to chance or to the Bolsheviks, he was now ready to take matters into his own hands.

During April of 1936, at a time when the farming implements were being readied for seeding, the opportunity to travel to Omsk arose once again. Checking to make sure that he had his internal passport with him, he set out for Omsk with two NKVD officials. Permission to undertake the trip was granted by the Commandant with a clear order to arrange for the delivery of meat products during the summer months.

Once at the Omsk market, Konstantin used devious means to extricate himself from the two NKVD officials long enough to meet Parsimov at the railway station. Konstantin wanted to share his vision for the future. Only this time, unlike his first meeting with Parsimov, he was ready to share the contents of his plan.

"Good to see you again, Comrade. How is your father?"

"Fine. My father is fine. He has been transferred to another kolkhoz. He is doing more re-education. Also, my sisters have been transferred."

"Did you get to see them?"

"Tak, in fact, I did."

"Well, you and your family are very fortunate. When the NKVD authorities break up a conclave of kolkhozniks, they like to send each to different work camps. It does appear as though the officials thought that your family members have served their time of hard labour and want to use them to continue to develop Stalin's agricultural program. It looks as though they have been spared."

"That, however, has not made it any easier for me."

"What of your plan, Kozlov? Do you have one? What do you want to do with your life?"

"I am ready to do whatever is necessary to be repatriated, to find my way back home."

Konstantin could see that to spend more time with Parsimov could put both of them at risk. As a result, he expressed his thanks saying, *"I have some tasks to complete for the Brigadir at the local market before returning to the kolkhoz."* But, as Konstantin was about to leave, Parsimov gave his arm a gentle tug.

"You know, Kozlov, I too have family in the Ternopil Oblast. It would do my heart good to make contact with them. In my coveralls, I have all the instructions for you. Here is the code. It has the names of railway contacts in Tyumen, Sverdlovsk, Kirov, Kazan, and Moscow. Each contact will be able to help you. When you reach Moscow, you will be on your own."

"You mean, Parsimov, that these names are included on this piece of paper?"

"Da, but it is not that simple. Each letter of the name of the person you are to meet is increased by one increment up to the count of six. Then, the count begins at one once again. You will have to study these. Get the names right and memorize them. No ordinary person will be

able to decipher my notes. Be careful with this information. Do not ever mention my name to anyone!"

"Where will I begin my journey?"

"Why, you will begin your journey right here. I will determine how you will be able to hitch a train ride to Tyumen. There, you will meet a contact. Once you have memorized the coded information I have given you, destroy it."

"What about the 50 rubles?"

"Have them with you when you are ready to leave."

On the horseback ride back to Zarya, Konstantin could hardly contain his excitement. The first and most important task was to work hard and gain the confidence of Brigadir Bilinkov. Only then would he be ready to put into place his plan, a plan that offered the ultimate reward, even though it might put his father and sisters at risk. In all of this, one question kept coming back, should he or should he not tell his father and sisters about his plan? Or, did his father already suspect that he was planning a trip of no return. His biggest challenge would now be to put together the 50 rubles required for the services of Parsimov.

Back at the kolkhoz, Konstantin decided to put his plan on hold. With the arrival of new farming equipment, including four new tractors, Bilinkov informed him that in addition to the traditional grains, the kolkhoz would begin to specialize in sugar beets, construct a processing plant and a refinery, and turn out coarse slightly damp brown sugar. The Brigadir even intimated that the kolkhozniks would receive a portion of their payment at the end of the month in the form of a couple kilograms of sugar, a treasure on the black market.

The fields set aside for the planting of sugar beets, which stretched for hundreds of hectares, were now being ploughed by four new tractors, each pulling multiple ploughs. True to rumour, the age of mechanization had arrived.

Later that summer, the same tractors were used to pull multiple ploughs to uproot the beets. Equipped with buckets and advancing in a line, Konstantin supervised the workers who collected and dumped the beets into conical piles. A tractor with a trailer would later take these to the new processing plant.

Unfortunately, the beets often with only the leaves showing sometimes lay on top and sometimes under the shallow layer of earth. The constant bending down to tend to the beets soon became a torture to the young and old. Brigadir Bilinkov, an unsmiling man, would frequently visit on horseback. On his first visit, he sent the pickers back over the ground saying that too many beets had been overlooked. From the second visit forward, it was Konstantin's job to pace the work of the kolkhozniks. Everything had to be done to a *norma*, the fulfillment of a plan conceived somewhere higher up for tough grown-ups used to hard labour, specifying a certain number of standard-sized piles per day. At the end of each day, a record of each worker's performance was maintained by Konstantin.

Each mid-day break was a welcome relief, although rather short. Work resumed even though the workers were still hungry. As time went on, Konstantin discovered that some of the workers became quite resourceful, going so far as to create a small pile of earth and then quickly covering it with beets. This practice continued unabated until Brigadir Bilinkov discovered the subterfuge. Not only did the kolkhozniks get into trouble, but so did Konstantin. That evening, Brigadir Bilinkov called a meeting of the beet pickers. He had a stern message for them, *"If you don't manage the norma, it only costs you your sugar and maybe your freedom. If you continue this sabotage, I will bring in the NKVD. Then, instead of a month here, you could be doing much harder work in the snow in the north for a few years. Don't let me catch you at it again."*

This was warning enough to all the workers to increase their performance. Like most workers, however, the kolkhozniks could not wait until they got a day off during the weekend. Many would gather behind the small school building in the evening, light a little fire, and sit around telling jokes, singing songs, and smoking *Makhorka* cigarettes rolled in *Izvyestya* or *Pravda* newspaper. On other weekends, some of the girls in the nearby village would invite several of the kolkhozniks to a *vyecherinka*, an evening gathering where everyone would join in song and dance. The boys and girls would sit side by side on a long wooden bench, cracking sunflower seeds. A balalaika, guitar, or an old accordion would be brought along to provide music. After a while, the village boys and girls would start dancing, mostly not in couples but one by one, doing a solo round with their arms on their hips or crossed on their chests. Some of the boys could perform a variety of *kozachok* steps, but before returning to the bench, stop in front of the dancer of the opposite sex. That person would then take the floor to dance. Some celebrants danced better, some worse.

On one such occasion, Konstantin discovered that there were two reigning champions, a young man named Serhiy and a young girl named Marusya. There was no formal competition for the title—it was bestowed by popular acclaim and could, in due time, be lost to a better dancer, if one arose.

Later that evening, a young man from the village showed up with a kolkhoz horse harnessed to a long empty hay cart. The merrymakers got permission to go into the nearby woods and to continue the party after they built a campfire. Someone showed up with a bottle of home-made vodka, which was passed around. Each person took a small swig so that there would be enough for everyone. Others sang what they called *chastushki*, or little pieces from popular patriotic songs. During the evening, new lines for the *chastushki* were continually composed. As the evening wore on, the songs got more and more ribald, many revelers using phrases that would rarely be heard in formal settings.

Unfortunately, the beet norma took quite a beating on the next day of work. Brigadir Bilinkov suddenly declared an end to all parties until the norma could be attained and maintained once again. The kolkhozniks realized the urgency of Brigadir Bilinkov's directive, working each day from dawn to dusk. The Brigadir wanted to make sure that the beet crop could be harvested in time to meet the kolkhoz's commitment to the market in Omsk.

Time passed quickly and the snows came early. With the new arrivals in the Zarya Kolkhoz, the living quarters were again becoming increasingly crowded. On the final day of November a messenger arrived at a gallop on horseback from the regional center with a telegram for Brigadir Bilinkov. The news was not good for a number of the kolkhozniks. No one seemed to know how the selections were made; however, within the next week fully 50 percent of the labourers in the barrack were suddenly re-assigned to other camps. Stalin was about to unleash his campaign of terror. Each passing day brought some relief when, at the end of the day, Konstantin discovered that he was not on Brigadir Bilinkov's list.

When the spring of 1937 finally arrived, everyone in Zarya Kolkhoz was aware of Stalin's Reign of Terror. Those who were re-assigned to another camp were not heard from again. No one knew what happened to them. With this fear constantly gnawing at his very heart, Konstantin was speechless when Brigadir Bilinkov ordered him with the words, *"Kozlov, I want to have a word with you."*

"Right now?"

"Da, right now."

Konstantin was virtually certain what would come next, a journey deeper into the frozen taiga of Siberia. Looking at Konstantin and pointing to the east, Bilinkov had a message, *"I have some news for you."*

"News? What kind of news?"

"In my possession I have the official document from Commandant Matsunova. You are being transferred to a work camp east of here. In Omsk, you will take a train to Novosibirsk where you will be met at the railway station by NKVD officials for your new assignment."

"Re-assignment? What about my father and sisters?"

"I know nothing about them. They are under the supervision of other kolkhozes."

That was all there was to it. The talk was short. There seemed little need to discuss the new assignment. After all, not everyone had the opportunity to be re-assigned during the initial stages of Stalin's Reign of Terror. Many were simply annihilated, even if they were innocent of any crime. Others simply vanished as if into thin air.

Arriving in Omsk under NKVD guard, Konstantin noted that six other kolkhozniks were also being transferred eastward. At the train station, there was a beehive of activity as dozens awaited the arrival of the Trans-Siberian train. During his wait on the crowded platform, Konstantin heard someone near him say, *"Don't even look around. Take this packet of clothing."*

"Is that you, Parsimov?" whispered Konstantin.

"Da, da, quickly, in this cubicle put on this cover-all and jacket over your present clothes and act like a railway worker. Do not get on the train going east."

"Where will I hide? The NKVD will soon be taking a roll call."

"You don't have to hide. Just wait here on the crowded platform. There is a train going west. I'll get you on it as a railway worker."

"What about the 50 rubles? I have them. Do you want them now?"

"Da, leave the rubles with me. You will have to destroy your current identification while you are on the train bound for Tyumen. Don't get caught with your old passport."

With all of the activity on the railway platform, Konstantin had no difficulty in changing into the railway workers' coveralls and jacket. An NKVD official shouted out the names of those about to board the train for the eastward journey. With his heart pounding, Konstantin heard his name being called. He could not believe his ears when someone yelled, *"Present."* But it was not his voice. Someone else confirmed his presence. *Had someone else assumed his name?*

In short order the train was loaded and with a couple of loud whistles set out on its eastward journey. At that moment, a smaller crowd started to gather for the train which would take them from another railway platform to Tyumen. As those about to board the train milled about, Konstantin, now wearing a railway work jacket, heard Parsimov give him the final instructions, *"Your internal passport and documentation are in your jacket pocket. Do you remember the code that I gave you earlier? Have you memorized the names of your contacts by applying the secret mathematical code I gave you?"*

"Da, I have memorized each name in each city."

"Dobro. Your name is Mikhail Baranov. Remember, you are now Mikhail Baranov. You have been brought up as an orphan in an orphanage in Novosibirsk. You do not know your father or your mother. If asked, just say that you know nothing more than that. You are on assignment with the Trans-Siberian Railway."

"I am a railroad worker?"

"Da, that is true. Your railroad assignment is in your packet. The name of your first repatriation contact is only in your head. When you arrive in Tyumen, you will report to the Brigadir of the railway for your work assignment."

"How will I be able to answer questions raised by the NKVD?"

"That is your challenge. You are now on your own."

In the gathering darkness, Konstantin could barely make out the face of Parsimov. Somehow, he looked different than he had remembered him. Had he changed his appearance for some reason? About three dozen passengers boarded a railway car that reflected the barest of amenities, a bench along each side of the car with double-decker bunks at each end. Also boarding were several Red Army soldiers and what appeared to be four NKVD officials. As the train pulled out of the Omsk railway station, an official checked the credentials of each passenger. When it came Konstantin's turn, he quickly answered, *"My name is Mikhail Baranov. My destination is Tyumen."*

"Are you a railway construction specialist?"

"Da, I am. I will be working in Tyumen."

"Do you have your papers with you?"

"Da, I have my passport and my re-assignment document. I was told by the Commandant that my working papers will be waiting for me at the railway station in Tyumen."

Mikhail reached into his jacket pocket for his passport and his re-assignment document. However, even before he was able to present his credentials, the NKVD official motioned him to return the documents to his pocket. Konstantin was surprised that neither his identification nor his re-assignment documents were fully examined. This suddenly raised many questions. Who had assisted Oleg Parsimov? Why? How did Parsimov come up with the name of Mikhail Baranov?

There was no shortage of frantic activity at the Omsk railway station. Stalin's new campaign was suddenly taking hold. One thing was clear, the name Konstantin Kozlov was now retired. This would be the first day in the life of Mikhail Baranov.

Chapter 13

TREK OF TERROR

A systematic liquidation of elites and socially marginal people

If Mikhail Baranov were to select a time in history to undertake an escape from the Gulag, he could not have selected a more dangerous time. The human cost associated with the so-called Stalin Revolution was appalling. It all started in earnest with the initial emphasis on collectivization, retreated to a relative calm from repression in 1934 and moved quickly to Stalin's *Reign of Terror* in 1937. At least 90 percent of all executions carried out by police organizations in this period occurred during the two deadly years of the Great Purges in 1937-1938. The politicized risk factors were social in origin and encompassed ethnicity, religion, criminal background checks, any association with anti-Stalin factions, and resulted in police tracking and surveillance. Thousands of Soviet citizens became suspect when they were denounced by a neighbour or by a member of one's own family.

In 1933, nearly 46,000 people escaped from camps of which only about 50 percent were captured. The local population was often terrorized by the escapees. This led to ongoing requests on the part of camp bosses for additional guards. Not being able to meet this request, the NKVD instituted tighter controls. In extreme cases, it was not unusual for guards to shoot a prisoner and then get a reward for thwarting an escape.

As the purges unfolded in the summer of 1937, the NKVD received the green light to include Party officials, administrators, managers, professionals, military officers, intelligentsia, and ordinary citizens. It began with the pre-emptive roundups called *mass operations* and proceeded to the enemies which were hidden from discovery. Throughout, Stalin constantly pressed for an upward revision of his original quotas even as organizational zealousness ran completely amok and was quickly replaced with mass executions in place of incarceration as the people-removing method of choice. In 1938, the NKVD sent out a communiqué which stated that, *"Despite a series of orders on conducting a decisive war against prisoners' escapes from camps, serious improvements in this matter have yet to be made."*

On a Trans-Siberian train en route to Tyumen, staying away from other passengers and not entering into any conversation was challenge enough for Mikhail Baranov. Even more difficult was the matter of never leaving the impression that he was eavesdropping on another person. Still, Mikhail found it difficult not to listen to what others were saying about themselves and their work. At one point, a fellow railroader turned to him saying, *"I have not seen you before. Have you worked on the railway east of Omsk?"*

"Neither have I seen you," answered Mikhail, making no effort to get into any discussion. Adding, as an afterthought, *"My place of work is up to my superiors."* Knowing that silence may well be the best policy, no attempt was made by anyone to engage in conversation unless the other party was willing to do so. Not knowing the identity of the questioner made Mikhail all the more suspicious about his surroundings and fellow passengers. Despite these misgivings, none of the workers portrayed the characteristics of socially dangerous elements: terrorists, criminals, or petty thieves. From this, Mikhail concluded that they, too, were railway workers being assigned to a workforce in Tyumen.

At one point, one of the workers commented that, *"All the ethnic Chinese arrested in the Omsk region were shot for political crimes."* Another worker joined in by saying that these criminals, *"Are known to be associated with money lending and opium-smuggling,"* adding as an afterthought, *"Several of these scum had ongoing contacts with relatives living abroad and were shot for espionage."* At no time did Mikhail enter into these conversations.

Mikhail was happy that he had deciphered and memorized the name of his first contact in Tyumen. After all, there seemed to be plenty of suspicion to go around and even having the secret code on his person might have led to dire circumstances had he been discovered. Just to make sure that he had no incriminating evidence, he meticulously went through each pocket of his coveralls and his jacket to make sure that these contained only his new internal passport and re-assignment papers. Having satisfied himself that he had no incriminating evidence, he awaited the first signs of the morning sun.

Mikhail recalled how he was able to apply to each of the five scrambled code words the formula given him by Parsimov. In this way he was able to come up with the five contacts on his escape route to Moscow. The first letter of the first code word *jyvlnt* was *j*. To the letter *j* Mikhail added one increment to come up with the letter *k*. He continued applying the formula to each successive letter of the code word until he determined that the first contact in Tyumen would be a *Brigadir* by the name of *Kashin*.

Using the same secret formula, Mikhail determined that his second contact would be *Brigadir Beketov* in *Sverdlovsk*. However, *Perm*, his third stop, was changed by Parsimov to the city of *Kirov* and a meeting with *Brigadir Rubashkin*. His fourth stop would be in *Kazan* and a rendezvous with a brigadir by the name of *Novikov*. If all went well, his final contact would be *Brigadir Popov* in *Moscow*. Once in Moscow, he would set a course for more familiar territory, the final destination being

Horodok. Each contact was indelibly committed to memory. There was no room for mistakes.

Before reaching Tyumen, Mikhail made one more critical decision. Not wanting to risk being caught with his original passport which he still carried in his inner-trousers, he spent a considerable amount of time tearing this document into tiny pieces, mixing the mixture with tobacco, and then smoking it. As can be expected, the smell emanating from the rolled cigarette was most foul. When a fellow passenger asked, *"Must you smoke that stinking shit?"*

The reply from Mikhail was instantaneous. *"You have to be a real man to smoke this stuff. Can I roll you one?"* For a moment, it appeared as though a fight would break out. One thing was clear, by the time Mikhail finished his third cigarette, the last vestiges of his old passport vanished along with the acrid smoke. This turned out to be a most fortunate decision. When the train arrived in Tyumen, Mikhail was startled to see that the train station was virtually under siege by the Red Army. *"What's going on here?"* Mikhail asked no one in particular.

An answer came back promptly from one of the passengers, *"Just as I predicted last night. The credentials of each passenger will be checked by the military police and the NKVD. Anyone without a work permit and the proper identification will be put to sleep, forever."*

Waiting for his turn to be interrogated, Mikhail broke out in a cold sweat. Although the wait was short, it seemed as though the whole process was put into place with an exclamation mark upon Stalin's Reign of Terror. It did not take the police long to ferret out those who did not possess the necessary credentials. When it came Mikhail's turn, he did not wait for the questions to come. He knew what they would be. His remarks were curt and to the point, *"My name is Mikhail Baranov. Special duty, Trans-Siberian Railway System."*

An NKVD official peered closely at Mikhail, briefly examined his credentials, and then waved him aside. Mikhail was glad that neither the officials nor the police saw his knees shaking. After all, it was one thing to have questionable credentials, it was quite another to say that you worked for the Trans-Siberian Railway system. Now that his credentials were cleared, the next task was to keep a sufficiently low profile so as not to raise the suspicions of those he met in the transportation car. With the hustle and bustle in and around the main railway station in Tyumen, it occurred to Mikhail that this would not be his destination. Approaching an NKVD official, he asked, *"Excuse me, is this where railway workers get off the train?"*

"You are a real dumb bastard," declared the official, *"your credentials say that you are a railway worker and you don't know the station to which you should go? Go to platform 4 and take that oblast train for a short distance to the railway workers' station."*

At the railway construction and maintenance station, the Commandant checked Mikhail's credentials and confirmed, *"Da, I do know Vladimir Kashin. What is your business with him?"*

"I am to report to him."

"Report to him? Why?"

"I can only submit my credentials to Bigadir Kashin."

"Wait here. Brigadir Kashin will be here shortly."

Mikhail did not have to wait long. *"Brigadir Kashin, my name is Baranov. Mikhail Baranov. I have my re-assignment papers for your examination."*

Brigadir Kashin thoroughly examined Mikhail's passport and re-assignment document, and nodded affirmatively. *"So, Baranov, you want to work with my crew? Dobro. I am in charge of a railway work team. You will be staying in the workers' barrack near here. I will take you there. Tomorrow you will join my work crew."*

Mikhail was not surprised at the brevity of their conversation or with his assignment to the work gang. He knew that it would not be possible to continue his journey to Sverdlovsk without first working in Tyumen long enough to gain the confidence of Kashin and obtaining his re-assignment papers. *"This is Tyumen Yard for Railway workers,"* Kashin informed Mikhail as he escorted him to the accommodation barracks, *"and the other station is the Voynovka Railway Station used for the transport of freight."*

Mikhail's welcome in the barrack, which featured double-deck sleeping bunks for 32 workers, was less than cordial when one of the workers looked him over saying, *"A fat cat, eh? Give our Brigadir a couple of months and he will have you looking trim like the rest of us."*

"A fat cat, you say? Well, this cat knows how to work."

After this brief exchange, the tensions eased somewhat as others joined in the conversation. *"This section of the railway in Tyumen,"* remarked a worker, *"was completed in 1885. It is an important link to other centers and communities in the oblast."*

"These other centers," Mikhail asked, *"are they agricultural or lumbering centers?"*

"Da, agricultural and logging centers. Further inland we have mining. This railway serves the historic city of Tobolsk to the northeast and Sverdlovsk to the west."

At first, Mikhail believed that his work with Brigadir Kashin would be relatively short before getting his credentials to proceed to the second leg of his journey. However, with Stalin's Reign of Terror showing no signs of abating, Mikhail thought it best to continue to work hard in

Tyumen and say little. With the whispered reports of arrests and killings by Stalin's henchmen, the best that he could do was to play a waiting game. Meanwhile, no one questioned his knowledge of railroading. What he lacked in expertise, he made up with his work ethic.

Days turned into weeks and it was difficult to get an accurate read as to what was happening in other regions of Siberia. Mail from the western regions of the Soviet Union stopped, as it were, in its tracks. Suddenly, even the NKVD officials were not receiving any mail or parcels from home.

Tyumen, located on the Tura River, turned out to be a beautiful town. Founded in the 16th century, Tyumen was first a Russian outpost in Siberia and had always been an important settlement. The town was now in the midst of developing into a small military settlement. In particular, mining engineers recognized that the region was rich in oil stretching from the Kazakh border to the Arctic Ocean. *Little wonder,* thought Mikahil, *that I was dispatched to serve on this important transportation hub.*

No one can argue with the importance of Tyumen in the history of Russia. As early as the middle of the 18th century, the trade center had a population approaching 10,000. In 1862, the first steamboat in Siberia was built in Tyumen, the first telegraph came in the same year, and water mains were laid in 1864. However, the real spurt in development did not come until the Trans-Siberian Railway came as the easternmost railhead. This made Tyumen the principal trade and industrial center of West Siberia. During the Russian Civil War, which lasted from October, 1917 to October, 1922, Tyumen was at first controlled by Admiral Alexander Kolchak and his Siberian White Army in support of the Tsarist Monarchy. However, on the 5th of January, 1918, Tyumen was taken by the Red Army and solidly in communist control during Stalin's Reign of Terror.

When Mikhail landed in Tyumen in 1937, the city was already a major industrial center. This would also be the year that steamboats and cargo ships would ply their trade in furniture, fur, and leather clothing—all of which were locally produced. For these reasons, the Stalin Regime wanted to maintain the transportation corridor by employing the very best that the deportation system had to offer.

With the coming of the first frosts, Mikhail felt sufficiently comfortable to approach Brigadir Kashin, *"Brigadir, when would it be a good time for me to take my skills to another railway center, perhaps to the city of Sverdlovsk?"*

"To another center? To Sverdlovsk? Are you aware of the dangers?"

"Da, da. I am aware of the elimination of a number of prisoners, criminals, petty crooks, and the laggards. But, I think that I have much to offer."

"Be ready on Sunday morning, Baranov. I will prepare the work papers for you. Be sure that you have 50 rubles for me for the transfer papers."

Mikhail was surprised to discover that the Brigadir wanted exactly the same number of rubles as did Parsimov. This, in itself, raised several questions. However, even to pay Kashin this amount depleted his meager savings. Having paid the Brigadir, it occurred to Mikhail that the amount of time he would spend in each railway work station en route to Moscow would depend upon the wage he was paid. In turn, most of what he earned would be used to compensate his contacts along the way for the service that they would provide. From this, it was obvious that all of the risks resided with the person taking the decision to move on.

By eight o'clock on Sunday morning, Mikhail found himself in the company of a brigade of railway workers, all destined for Sverdlovsk. Arriving one day later in Sverdlovsk, Mikhail learned that the city had plenty of history and was quickly becoming the location of the largest heavy machinery factory in Europe. At the railway workers' station located three kilometers north of the center of the city, Mikhail was informed that Sverdlovsk was a hub to a number of other centers in the Urals. Mikhail's contact, Brigadir Beketov, a large and robust bear of a man, immediately assigned him to a special railway work crew.

"The work crew you will be joining, Baranov, is responsible for the repair and maintenance of our major railway bridges. Keep a lookout for saboteurs. The order from our leader is that we must ferret out all criminals. Keep in mind," continued Brigadir Beketov, making a sign as if to decapitate a victim, *"no one is immune. Once those saboteur bastards are identified by the Red Army officers, they disappear as though into a bottomless pit."*

"The Red Army makes these bastards disappear? How is that?"

"No one really knows how or cares. Not only that," added Brigadir Beketov, *"but no one around here is brave enough to even ask such a question. Who knows but that the questioner may well be next on that shit list."*

As a result of this admonition, Mikhail once again adopted a stoic code of silence. However, this code of silence was broken when a member of the railway crew made a dastardly discovery near the town of Revda. When he wandered some distance from the railway to relieve himself, he stumbled upon a shallow burial grave for the victims of one of Stalin's killing fields. This led to a considerable amount of discussion within the work crew as how best to handle the discovery. In the end, the Brigadir declared, *"I don't want anyone mentioning one word about this discovery to anyone. Never! If you do, you too could be marked for elimination!"*

November, 1937, brought an unusually heavy dump of snow. Coincidentally, this seemed to mark the end of Stalin's initial campaign to rid the Siberian landscape of those who might present a problem to the Soviet Government. Having survived the most dangerous moments in the campaign, Mikhail decided that the time was right to seek an assignment in Kirov, the next stop on his trek back to Ukraine. Learning that the unusually high snowdrifts near the Ural Mountains provided the railway crew with additional work, he approached Brigadir Beketov with a question, *"How are the rail lines in and around Kirov?"*

"Good, very good," replied the Brigadir. *"Why do you ask?"*

"Well, I just want to be of help. I want to help to make sure that the Trans-Siberian Railway continues to operate efficiently."

Not much more was said between the two until the end of November when word came to Mikhail from a crew member, *"Comrade Baranov, the Brigadir wants to see you."*

"See me? Why? Did he say why?"

"Nyet, not one word."

With that, Mikhail set out to see Brigadir Beketov in his special railway car set aside for railway management. When he knocked on the Brigadir's door, he was taken aback when an angry response came, *"Stop pounding on the door, you idiot. Enter."*

"My name is Baranov. You wanted to see me?"

"Baranov, we have problems with the railway bridge over the River Vyatka. Kirov is 320 kilometers north of Kazan. I want you to join a bridge crew which leaves here on Monday."

"Kirov? You say, Brigadir, that it is north of Kazan? What kind of a town is Kirov?"

"Kirov is an important city situated on a river plateau. It is an engineering, chemical, woodworking, and leather industry center. The railway system also serves a waterway system."

"This train that will take me to Kirov, is it a work train or a freight train?"

"A regular work train. The train will stop in Perm. In Perm, the Red Army will be clearing the region of spies, counter-revolutionaries, and the criminal element."

"Should I be concerned about this train stop?"

"Of course, you should be concerned. Your credentials must be in order. This is why you are paying me 50 rubles to make sure you don't end up in Vorkuta."

Right on schedule on Monday, Mikhail boarded a special car set aside for the railway work crew. Since it was the first week of December, there was no shortage of snow as he watched the small Russian villages appear and then disappear from view. After an overnight ride, the train approached the city of Perm.

Situated on the banks of the Kama River, Perm is in the European part of Russia near the Ural Mountains. Even at this stage in history, Perm was one of the most populous cities in all of Russia. Of critical importance to the Soviet Union, the Kama was the waterway which granted the Urals access to the White Sea, Baltic Sea, Sea of Azov, Black Sea, and Caspian Sea.

As Mikhail listened to the conversations around him, he got an uneasy feeling that two of the passengers were not railway workers at all. To him, they looked a lot like a couple of informants who were intent upon extracting information from those in the carriage. Time dragged on as the steel wheels of the train made rhythmic sounds as they passed over the steel rails. Soon, it was confirmed that the train would stop in Perm long enough to switch locomotives. Mikhail's daydream was suddenly interrupted when a member within the group loudly announced, *"Attention everybody. I am Serzhant Karpa. I am a special agent with the Red Army's Internal Affairs. Your credentials will be examined by our special officers."*

At first, it seemed as though no one had the courage to ask Serzhant Karpa about the reason for the search. However, after a long and nervous silence, someone did raise the question. The response from Serzhant Karpa was most revealing, *"During this time of uncertainty, the Soviet Government wants to make sure that it does not have a saboteur in its midst."*

With that, the 21 members of the railway crew were marched into an annex building near the railway station. Each member was required to present his identification before being interrogated by the Troika. Mikhail's mind was in overdrive. *What if they discover that I am operating under a false name? That they find out that I am a kulak deportee from Ukraine?*

"Name?"

"My name is Mikhail Baranov." At first Mikhail was about to add a few words of explanation, but decided against it.

"What is your place of birth?"

"I don't know my place of birth."

"You don't know your place of birth? How is that, you stupid bastard?"

Even Mikhail was surprised to hear his own response when he said, *"I am from the town of Novosibirsk. My mother abandoned me when I was a child. I was raised by my father."*

"Your father? What the hell is your father's name?"

"His name is our leader, Josef Stalin." But, even as Mikhail spoke those words, he noticed that the interrogator's assistant drew a pistol from a holster inside his jacket. There was a long silence on the part of the tribunal. Finally, one of them spoke up saying, *"Looks fine with me. His credentials are in order. We have nothing that would indicate that he should not continue on his journey."*

With that, the meeting was over for Mikhail. When he once again boarded the work car in a cold sweat, he counted only 16 workers. No one seemed to know what happened to the others. However, it was not out of the realm of imagination as to their fate. Once singled out for removal, there was little doubt as to what would happen next. Anyone refusing to obey a command was silenced one way or another as was evidenced by a shout from an NKVD guard, *"Don't let that son of a bitch get away. Shoot him!"* His command was immediately followed by a couple of shots, and then silence.

In a short time, a new locomotive was shuttled to the head of the train and with a loud blast of the train whistle, the train was once again en route to Kirov. By early morning one of the passengers announced that the agricultural town of Kirov was in view. Looking around, the scene was most serene with rolling hills embracing the Vyatka River, a navigable river that connects with the Volga a little ways downstream. *How peaceful and serene. Quite a contrast,* thought Mikhail, *to what had happened earlier right here in my railway carriage.*

Much like the city of Perm, Kirov is also situated west of the Urals and is considered to be a part of European Russia. The thought of being in a city considerably removed from Siberia and closer to his final destination of Moscow was not lost on Mikhail.

As Mikhail's work crew began work to repair two bridges spanning the River Vyatka, he was pleased, despite the extreme cold, to be in the capital city of the Kirov Oblast. Stretching along the Vyatka for several miles, the city was bustling with activity in engineering, chemical factories, woodworking, leather industries, and even a toy factory. Nearby, the rolling plains were partly covered with forests, marshes, and peat deposits. Seemingly to add balance to the economy, the region had iron ore deposits and several kolkhozes, two of them specializing in dairy farming.

During the one day each week that Mikhail was not required to work, he would often seek permission from Brigadir Rubashkin to spend some time visiting the main market in the city square, a freedom of movement not available to prisoners in labour camps. Many of the older buildings were constructed using interlocking logs with artistic grillwork on windows, colourful shutters, and decorative brick—all of which added charm to the city.

Perhaps as a harbinger of things to come for many of those with whom he toiled and who did not measure up, Mikhail observed a large NKVD poster prominently displayed in the market, *We will eradicate spies and diversionists, agents of the Trotskyite-Bukharinite Fascists.* These agents, according to Stalin, were the bitterest enemies of the state.

Despite the hardships encountered by those working to maintain the railway system, Mikhail worked doubly hard to ensure his new status as assistant to Brigadir Rubashkin. Still, he could not get out of his mind the interrogation at the hands of Serzhant Karpa, the Red Army's Special Unit on Internal Affairs. *Could it be,* reasoned Mikhail, *that Karpa is aware that I am operating under an assumed name?* However, to attempt to get at the right answers was out of question. In the midst of all of this uncertainty, the security in the railway work camp suddenly increased. As 1938 dawned, the number of armed guards with specially-trained dogs also increased. The movement of each worker was closely monitored.

With the crush of new prisoners, Brigadir Rubashkin assigned many of them to earthen dugouts called *zemlyanki*. This, in itself, presented a problem as the survival rate suddenly declined. Over time, many simply froze to death. Others froze their extremities and were rendered useless. No longer able to work, their food rations were cut and their demise assured. Little wonder that the large sign in the work camp which read *Work in the Soviet Union is a matter of Honour and Glory* would have little meaning for those who suddenly perished. Those identified with malnutrition ended up in the hospital in Kirov. Few, if any, survived. Few, if any, wanted to survive. After all, more of the same awaited those who did survive. In the midst of all the misery, Mikhail took heart when he assisted those in his barrack with the decoration of a small holiday tree. *Perhaps*, thought Mikhail, *the New Year will bring me a bit more joy.*

During Stalin's Reign of Terror (1937-1938),
women were subjected to searches and sexual abuse.
Source: Gulag History Museum, Moscow.

Women were frequently subjected to **physical searches and sexual abuse.**
Source: Gulag History Museum, Moscow.

April showers and the warm gleams of sunshine enticed Mikhail
to put away his winter clothes in favour of summer work clothes.
However, even the appearance of spring flowers in 1938 could not bring
joy to his heart. Communication with others in the work crew was next
to impossible, especially in light of Stalin's Reign of Terror, which
continued to increase in its intensity. The task was to live through each
day, to stay alive, not to get sick, to work less, and to eat more. Like
so many others, it seemed as though he was saved by his youth, health,
physical strength, and the maintenance of positive working relationships
with everyone.

The NKVD makes an arrest of a kulak family.
Source: Gulag History Museum, Moscow.

All around him, Mikhail found that men developed their survival techniques by embracing evil deeds, something that they would never engage in otherwise. Stealing food from others became a game of cat-and-mouse. Others made up lies about fellow-workers and then snitched on them in order to gain favour with the Brigadir and perhaps receive a bonus in the form of additional food rations or a few rubles. However, Mikhail vowed to raise himself above the conduct of these prisoners and the swarming mass of starving zeks who seemingly adhered to the principle of, *You can die today, I'll die tomorrow.* On reflecting on the conduct of the zeks, a railroad worker was heard to muse *"These are troubled times where man is wolf to man."*

As for the new arrivals to the railway work camp, after three or four weeks, most of the prisoners were broken men, obsessed with nothing more than eating and sleeping. They behaved like animals, disliked and suspected everyone, seeing in yesterday's friend a competitor in the struggle for survival. If nothing else, camp life taught one to harden, to learn how to lie effectively, and to be hypocritical in various other ways.

The closest that Mikhail came to hearing anything negative about any decision emanating from Stalin's Regime was on the first day of spring when Brigadir Rubashkin, in viewing a batch of new arrivals, was heard to say, *"From the iron broom of Soviet justice, sweeps only rubbish into our camps."*

As expected, there was no response from Mikhail. And yet, Mikhail made an important discovery. It would be the hard-core criminals dropped into the camp's midst who had the best chance of survival. Somehow, they were able to develop an informal communications link among each other, and even though they did not overtly support one another, they did not try to destroy each other either. Despite this discovery, it was difficult to say that there was a complete absence of morality in the camp, that no kindness or generosity existed.

This was really evident when, right out of the blue, Brigadir Rubashkin called Mikhail aside saying, *"From now on, Baranov, you will be the Foreman on my work crew."* No discussion and no directives as to expectations. One thing was now clear, his new posting provided him with a chance to remain alive. Suddenly, his work ethic was being noticed by the Brigadir. The work camp was not a black-and-white world where the line between masters and slaves was clearly delineated and the only way to survive was through cruelty. Not only did the inmates, free workers, and guards belong to a complex social network, but that network was always in a state of continuous flux.

Perhaps the most difficult decision for Mikhail was about to unfold when word came back to the barracks that Brigadir Rubashkin had fallen ill and was admitted to a hospital in Kirov. Meanwhile, an NKVD agent showed up at the camp with Czosnowski, the new brigadier. Czosnowski had a startling message for the work crews, *"Hard work will make you free. According to NKVD administration for the Kirov Oblast, we must fulfill higher norms set by the central planners in Moscow. I want everyone in this camp to redouble their efforts."*

Despite the best of intentions, Mikhail found that an evolving Communist axiom seemed to operate, *they pretend to pay us and we pretend to work.* Since the work on the railway not only required hard work but also an understanding of railway technology, made it necessary to retain the best workers and to pay them a small salary. However, Mikhail knew full well that a form of *tufta* (bribes) permeated virtually every aspect of work, ranging all the way from assignments to work organization and work accounting. A broad range of bribes in the form of rubles, favouritism in assigning labour duties, and even sexual favours became more and more prevalent. Recognizing this, Mikhail approached the newly-appointed Brigadir.

"Brigadir Czosnowski, may I discuss an important matter with you?"

"Da, what is it?"

"Before his illness, Brigadir Rubashkin asked me to join the railway crew in Kazan."

"A railway crew in Kazan? What the hell is all that about?"

"Brigadir Rubashkin said that they needed additional railway workers with experience."

"And, what was your response, Baranov?"

"Well, I said that I would abide by his decision."

"In that case, I will have to see Brigadir Rubashkin."

That evening, just thinking about the next leg of his journey to Ukraine, made it difficult for Mikhail to hold down the cabbage soup he had eaten. He knew well the risk. Should he be found out, his next stop would not be Kazan, but rather a shallow grave or the White Sea Canal Project. By the end of April, there was still no word from Brigadir Czosnowski. Not wanting to wait any longer, he once again approached the Brigadir, *"What did Brigadir Rubashkin say about my transfer?"*

"Rubashkin? Well, I tried to see him, but there is a problem."

"There is a problem? What kind of a problem?"

"Comrade Rubashkin is dead."

Nothing further was said until the following Monday when Czosnowski called him into his office. *"Baranov, your request is unusual. I checked with the Regional Office of the NKVD. They heard nothing of the directive from Rubashkin. So, I have personally prepared the transfer papers for you."*

"To whom will I report in Kazan?"

"To Commandant Korilov."

As Mikhail boarded the train bound for Kazan with transfer papers in hand, nothing seemed to make sense. He knew that if Brigadir Rubashkin were alive, he would have had to pay for those transfer papers. How did all of this come about? Why didn't Brigadir Czosnowski seek payment for the transfer papers? Was he not in the loop or was this some sort of a trap? He could not get out of his mind how circumstances conspired to make this move possible. At the same time, he had to admit that despite the unfairness of the arrests that he had witnessed, many remained true believers of the Soviet system of government.

This point was once again driven home when Mikhail discovered that several passengers in a cattle car had served their time and were now returning home to Moscow and other regions of Russia. Many even looked as though they were returning home against their will. Even though he knew that loose talk can be dangerous, Mikhail let it be known that he had served the Trans-Siberian Railway in Omsk. He hoped that someone from the Omsk Oblast might have some information about the status of the kolkhozes in the region. Unfortunately, no such luck.

Kazan is located on the confluence of two major rivers, the Volga and the Kazanka, nearly 800 kilometers east of Moscow. It has a proud history and even in 1938, with a population approaching 400,000, it was considered to be the capital of the Republic of Tatarstan. Conquered in 1552 by Ivan the Terrible, its residents were massacred and replaced with Russian farmers and soldiers. All were forcibly Christianized. As early as 1708, the city became a ship-building base for the Caspian Fleet.

By 1920, after the Bolshevik Revolution, Kazan became a center of Tatar Autonomous Soviet Socialist Republic. Unfortunately, Stalin's Regime destroyed most of the churches and mosques during the 1920s and 1930s. With the dawning of an automotive and aircraft industry, the upkeep of the railway system in Kazan became crucial to the Soviet Regime. As well, the city was gaining in its reputation for chemical, petrochemical, woodworking, carpentry, and food industries. The local bazaars were well known for marketing potatoes and mushrooms, in great demand by local residents as food staples.

When Mikhail arrived in Kazan, he was informed by Brigadir Korilov, a burly moustached but pleasant Russian, that Brigadir Novikov had been transferred farther north. The talk turned to the proposed construction of an underground metro system in Kazan, similar to one recently completed in Moscow. Nothing further was said about Brigadir Novikov. If nothing else, the news of Novikov's re-location put a crimp in his plans to work in Kazan for a short period of time before seeking a re-assignment to Moscow. Feeling that his hand had been forced, he elected to make a study of the train schedule between Kazan and Moscow. To delay until winter would make the task all the more difficult. He had to act now.

Knowing that he needed written permission to be re-assigned to work in Moscow, Mikhail was left with two options: approach Brigadir Korilov in the hopes of getting re-assignment papers or do something completely illegal. Deciding on the latter route, he had to find someone to forge his transfer papers. Meanwhile, Korilov's statement, *"There are camp laws which may not be understood by those who live outside the zone,"* raised a red flag. After all, it was Korilov who decided which of his workers deserved better food and pay than others without any regard as to what they had actually achieved. Bribes, ethnic, and clan loyalties determined a prisoner's output. *All the more reason*, thought Mikhail, *to stay away from Brigadir Korilov and accelerate the date of my departure.*

As Mikhail gently held his re-assignment certificate for work in Moscow, he had to admit that it was not cheap. Perhaps the most difficult part had been in finding a reliable counterfeiter, a most risky process that required several clandestine enquiries. Any bonuses that had been paid him in Kazan were turned over to a master counterfeiter. Even the seal of the NKVD looked very real. What worried Mikhail, however, was that the NKVD had recently discovered that camp managers and accountants manipulated statistics to their benefit. Several of those in command stole food, money, and were even involved in speculation. The pervasiveness of lying and cheating shocked Mikhail. Yet, this turned out to be a blessing. After all, who would be able to vouch for the attendance of every labourer in the camp in light of these irregularities?

Mikhail Baranov's plans to leave Kazan were further delayed when he sustained an injury while working on the railway. The freak accident happened while he was replacing a section of railway ties. Unlike the earlier days of railway construction, Mikhail's crew had the advantage of extracting and replacing railway ties with specialized machinery. While supervising the operation, a small wood chip broke off from a railway tie and punctured his scalp near his right eye. His fellow crew members rushed to his aid and were able to stabilize the bleeding. However, they concluded that to extract the chip from his scalp might damage his eye.

As a result, he was rushed to the hospital in Kazan where a medical doctor surgically removed the wood chip.

"Baranov," explained the doctor, *"you are one lucky hui (prick). Two centimeters closer to your eye and you would have lost use of it."*

Mikhail was full of questions, *"Doctor, why do I need this large dressing? When will I be able to remove it? How long before I can go back to work?"*

"I stitched your wound. You will not be able to work for at least two weeks. Be sure to keep the bandages in place until the wound heals. A nurse will instruct you on how to care for the injury."

While in the nursing station, he was addressed by an attractive young nurse, *"Good day, Gospodin (Mr.) Baranov. My name is Darya Dominova. I am a student nurse in this hospital and will provide you with the medication and the procedures for the care of your injury."*

"What about the stitches, nurse? When will they be removed?"

"First of all, you must apply a cold compress every three hours when you get home to keep the swelling down. Get lots of rest and come back in three days. I want to examine the wound at that time."

Looking into the deep brown eyes of Darya, Mikhail was struck with the thought that coming back to see her would be reward in itself. Not only did she have an attractive appearance but she also had a gentle touch. Despite the pain of his injury, Mikhail felt lucky to have met so pretty a nurse. He looked forward to seeing her again.

It would not be until one week later that Mikhail returned to the hospital to have the stitches removed from his eye injury. The conversation between the two was cordial and Darya approached her tasks in a professional manner. Before releasing him from the hospital, Darya had a few words of caution for Mikhail.

"You can remove the small bandage from your eye in one week. Keep it clean and get lots of rest. If a problem develops, you must come back to the hospital for another examination."

Returning to the barracks, Mikhail imagined getting an infection in the wound just so that he would have to return to the hospital. Just as suddenly, his thoughts turned to the railway engineers, designers, mechanics, and geologists of the camp who were separated from the ordinary zeks. They slept in comfortable beds and were well fed. The zeks, on the other hand, were forced to sleep on the same multiple bunk beds, eat at the same table, undress in the same bath, and put on the same underwear in which they worked and sweated for days on end.

The next morning, Mikhail tended to his injury and had a late breakfast. By this time, the labourers who worked in the camp's workshops had completed their skimpy breakfast. Looking around, it was obvious that it was the management of the camp who had the power to decide what sort of work ordinary prisoners were to do, how much food they were going to receive, and whether they would receive medical treatment if and when required. In other words, it was management who decided whether you lived or died. This made him very angry.

After the one week set aside for recovery, Mikhail resumed his work schedule. He was glad to have his transfer documents in order. A fellow labourer must have had similar thoughts when he raised a question of no one in particular, *"Where could a zek go without papers or money in a territory packed with concentration camps and scattered with control points? Where there is a bounty on his head of up to 300 rubles?"*

"You know all of this?" interjected Mikhail.

"Know of this? Let me tell you this, you scoundrel. I was one of those sent back when I was turned in. It got me an additional two years of exile."

Nothing further was said. Deep in thought and with images of what the stopover in Nizhny Novgorod, the mid-point between Kazan and Moscow, would be like, Mikhail, for whatever reason, could not get Darya Dominova, the diminutive dark-eyed nurse out of his mind. She exuded a measure of self-assurance that was unusual in Siberia. He recalled Darya telling him, *"Da, my father is in the service of the Party. As for me, I am so happy to be working toward a degree in medicine in the University of Perm."*

Recalling how he held Darya's hand for a moment as he left the hospital in Kazan, while breathing deeply the scent of her light perfume, Mikhail thought about the mystery of love. Those earlier romances in Zarya Kolkhoz, he realized, were no more than passing fancies. Darya had sensed his reaction, saying to him, *"I am a nurse at this hospital. My work is to help you get better soon and not to search for or encourage a romance."*

But, despite her admonition, Mikhail believed that the gentle manner in which she treated his injury spoke volumes. Darya's comment that she was not looking for romance had the opposite effect. It did not stop him from experiencing a sudden rush of testosterone and imagining himself embracing her and then planting a kiss, first on one rosy-red cheek and then on the other. He even imagined making love to her in a haystack in Horodok.

Instead of daydreaming about Darya, Mikhail would have been better off seeking more up-to-date information about international affairs. He might have become aware that 1938 marked the start of Stalin's Third Five-Year Plan and that the Soviet economy was once again on a war footing. Russia was devoting massive amounts of resources to the military sector in response to the rise of Nazi Germany. He was not even aware that the geographic area surrounding Moscow was being cleared of German settlers in preparation for what surely would become an armed conflict between the Soviet Union and Nazi Germany. How could he have been aware that on September 30, 1938, the Munich Agreement would cede Sudetenland, the northwestern region of Czechoslovakia, to Germany? That the residue from this action would suddenly change many things for Stalin and eventually for him?

That Sunday morning, an NKVD official appeared in his barrack, *"Are you Baranov?"*

"Da, I am Mikhail Baranov."

"The Brigadir wants to see you in his office immediately."

When Mikhail received the order, somehow he knew that the news would not be good. Brigadir Korilov did not mince his words. *"Baranov, here are your transfer papers. You are being assigned to Novosibirsk."*

"Novosibirsk? What kind of shit is this? To do what?"

"The order came directly from NKVD headquarters. I do not seek an explanation for any transfer. That is Party policy."

"Party policy? You didn't have the power to appeal my transfer?"

"The only power I have is to carry out Stalin's orders."

"Am I being assigned to a work camp?"

"I do not think so."

"Brigadir Korilov, you don't think so? How is that?"

"Because, you will be reporting to a Colonel Zenon Czarski, and he is on a special NKVD assignment. That is all I know."

Mikhail was in a state of shock. Suddenly, the plans he had made to return to Ukraine came tumbling down around his feet. He would soon find out why there was a sudden reversal in his fortunes.

PART 4

THE GREAT PATRIOTIC WAR

Chapter 14

NOVOSIBIRSK

This railway is Russia's window on Asia

It took Mikhail Baranov the longest time to come to grips with this sudden turn of events. So close to his final destination of Moscow and now forced to retrace his steps to Siberia made the pain almost unbearable. That many others may have been in the same boat did not lessen the pain. Try as he might, he simply could not unravel which of his several contacts had been complicit in his transfer to Novosibirsk. In the end, it didn't seem to matter.

As the train left Kazan winding its way once again in an easterly direction towards the Urals and back into the heart of Siberia, Mikhail intently listened to the conversations near him. He soon concluded that those around him were no ordinary Russians. There was no mistaking that this particular railway car was filled with NKVD officials and Red Army military personnel. Try as he might, while at all times being discreet, he was not able to eavesdrop on any conversation that would give him a clue as to the destination of his fellow passengers. What made the task more difficult was that everyone in the carriage strictly adhered to an unwritten code: do not ask any questions dealing with Soviet government decisions and do not provide any information, particularly to strangers, unless that person has a right to that kind of information.

Mikhail knew that in his pocket he carried his transfer papers and that the Serzhant in charge of the personnel in his passenger car was a military man. He knew this because at the moment the train was leaving the train station, the tall meticulously-dressed military officer addressed those in the railway carriage, "*My name is Serzhant Fitisev. I am in charge of this operation. Behind us, this train has a number of carriages transporting a criminal element to various labour camps. I have been assigned an army brigade to take charge of security. Any criminal causing a disturbance or attempting escape during the journey will receive a bullet in the back of his head.*"

"*Serzhant,*" was Mikhail's guarded question, "*is this criminal element in this car?*"

"*Are you a criminal?*"

"*I am not a criminal and I have never been one.*"

"*In that case, you have your answer.*"

As Mikhail looked around at the passengers in his carriage and digested the message, he had his answer. Serzhant Fitisev left little doubt that most of the personnel in his carriage served in the Russian Red Army and were there for only one purpose, and that was to ensure that those being transferred arrived at their respective destinations. As was the case with any re-location, a person had to consider whether he was being deported, exiled, or assigned to a special task by the NKVD. The distinction was not only important, but also a clear predictor of one's chances of survival in the next labour camp.

If nothing else, Mikhail had plenty of time to observe those who occupied his railway carriage as well as the other carriages during the two thousand kilometer journey to Novosibirsk. Viewing the extent of the train as it wound its way through the Urals, he was able to count no fewer than 35 carriages, in addition to the two lead carriages. The windows in all of the trailing carriages were barred shut and under heavy guard by military personnel located in the two lead carriages. From this, Mikhail concluded that his transfer papers were prepared for purposes other than for a labour camp in Novosibirsk. *What is the possibility of escape, thought Mikhail, during one of the train stops along the way?*

In all of this, Mikhail had to calculate his chances of success and the penalty for failure. Unlike his earlier transfers from Omsk while en route to Kazan where he seemingly had plenty of support, he was now on his own. Perhaps the final nail in his plans occurred with the death of Brigadir Rubashkin in Kirov. Somehow, the orderly sequence of transfers that he had so carefully planned in Omsk was now broken. Stripped of his special status and feeling like an ordinary zek, his very survival was now in doubt.

To complicate matters, Mikhail realized that travelling under an assumed name was a double-edged sword. Had he retained his given name, he might have been able to approach Serzhant Fitisev seeking permission to visit his family in the Omsk Oblast. However, this was not to be. Still, he decided to approach the NKVD guard, *"Serzhant, would it be possible for me to spend a couple of days in Omsk?"*

"A couple of days in Omsk? Are you out of your stupid mind? Your transfer is an order by the Party. You have special work to do in Novosibirsk."

"Da, I know that. In that case, would it be possible for me to stop in Omsk for a couple of hours and then take the next train. Omsk is a town where I spent some time working on the railway crew. I want to say hello to some of my comrades at the station."

"We will be stopping in Omsk for 30 minutes. Maybe you can make your enquiries during that train stop."

Between the Tyumen and Omsk railway stations, Mikhail thought about his plight. *Should I do something risky or should I blend into the morass of humanity being relocated?* He knew that any kind of a misstep along the way would bring disaster to his door. He concluded that his transfer status could suddenly change from one being assigned to special duty to that of a prisoner assigned to a hard labour camp.

Arriving at the Omsk train station, he sought out the station master.

"Excuse me, can you tell me what is new in Omsk?"

"You want to know what is new in this region of Siberia?"

"Da, how are the local kolkhozes doing? Have they met their production plans?"

"Fine, the kolkhozes are doing fine. All have met their first Five-Year Plan to collectivize agriculture."

"What about Comrade Stalin's second Five-Year Plan? The industrialization plan?"

The second Five-Year Plan was completed last year."

"They completed their first Five-Year Plan in 1933 and the second one in 1937?"

"Da, of course. Where have you been, hiding under a rock? Why do you think the kolkhozes in this region all have new tractors?"

"My work is with trains, not with tractors. Who do you think has kept these trains running? Father Frost? My only question is about the local kolkhozes, that is all."

"You know of the kolkhozes here?"

"Da, a little bit. I worked here three years ago and got to know a girl that lived here. I believe that she was from the Zarya Kolkhoz."

"All I can tell you is that the local kolkhozes lost all of their experienced labourers. Most were kulaks from Ukraine. Perhaps they have served their sentences and their education is now complete. Some have been re-assigned to other kolkhozes. Who knows, some of them may have been sent back to Ukraine."

"Are the kolkhoz labourers being replaced with new arrivals?"

"Da, of course. There seem to be more replacements coming in than those leaving, mostly from Poland and Ukraine."

"Do you know anything about the Rodina and Iskra kolkhozes?"

"Nyet, I know nothing about them."

This information stopped Mikhail in his tracks. The short whistle from the engineer of his train brought him back to reality. Under the watchful eye of the guards, he slowly made his way back to his carriage. *What of my family? Where are they now?* As he looked up, Serzhant Fitisev was intently looking at him. It seemed as though the Serzhant had read his mind. If the information from the station master was correct, it could well be that his family was no longer in Siberia. *Was my family returned to Ukraine in advance of my grandiose plan to escape the Gulag? Could it be that all the risks I took were for nothing?* Back in his carriage bound for Novosibirsk, Mikhail realized just how difficult it was to establish any kind of contact with one's family scattered all over western Siberia. Just asking an innocent question about a family member had its own risks.

If new exiles, prisoners, and deportees were arriving in Omsk, who were they? After all, from an historical perspective, by 1935 Stalin's henchmen had cleansed most of Soviet Ukraine of kulaks. More recently,

Stalin had turned to a program of assigning the status of *special re-settler* to all new deportees. With the dawning of 1938 and the menace of Nazi Germany in the background, Stalin embraced a policy of cleansing measures targeting socially dangerous elements in central and western regions of Russia. Included in this group were German settlers within the Ukrainian frontier zone who, in any future conflict, might be sympathetic to Hitler.

Slave labourers were frequently required to construct and live in straw-mud huts called zemlyanki.
Source: Gulag History Museum, Moscow.

By July 1, 1938, nearly 2,000 labour settlements were registered by the NKVD at the Department of Settlements in the Soviet Union. The population of the settlements comprised almost one million labour settlers, equalling an average of 373 persons per settlement. Of this group, nearly 200,000 were destined for the Novosibirsk region. In a number of cases, the Novosibirsk Oblast could not accommodate these numbers. As a result, many were entrained to Karaganda, Kazakhstan, where very soon over 70 percent of the inhabitants would be ethnic Germans and Ukrainians.

As was the case with the Kozlov family when they first arrived in Omsk, the families of the deportees who ended up in Novosibirsk and Karaganda were not separated. In cases where a family had teenagers, it was not unusual to find instances of romance, casual sex, marriage, and even the birth of children in these work camps. Despite their political status, the resettled target groups were not deprived of their citizenship rights. They retained the right to move around, but only within the boundaries of the destination administrative district. Their destination followed the pattern of the existing labour settlements where the NKVD was in charge of arranging their housing, providing employment in agriculture, and ensuring that each person was provided with the bare essentials. Where possible, the provision of essentials included the re-settlers' own financial contributions.

At their destinations, the re-settlers were provided with collectivized land, livestock, and equipment for establishing tractor stations in newly-created kolkhozes. The tractor stations were a state enterprise for the ownership and maintenance of agricultural machinery to be used in the kolkhozes. First introduced in 1928 as a shared resource of scarce agricultural machinery and technical personnel, the main units were tractor and automobile brigades which existed as an independent, inter-kolkhoz service. Agricultural cooperative associations were formed, exempted from taxes, their production goals set, and delivery plans put into place for a three-year term. In many cases, the NKVD allowed deportees to bring privately-owned livestock to Siberia from their home village.

In accordance with a 1937 resolution on *Re-settlers from Ukraine,* put into place by the *Central Committee and Council of People's Commissars of the Republic of Kazakhstan,* over 5,000 families ended up in the Karaganda Oblast. The economic objectives that were pursued by this project included the expansion of areas used for sugar beet and tobacco harvesting, and the development of the sugar industry. In all, over 59,000 Polish, Ukrainian, and German deportees ended up in North Kazakhstan. However, in the midst of outbreaks of scarlet fever, measles, and typhus, just to survive the trip was a challenge. Even though the NKVD took decisive measures aimed at reinforcing prevention procedures at the places of departure, during transportation, and at their destinations, thousands died during the deportation journey.

During this particular period in the development of southern Siberia and Kazakhstan, the Soviets required additional manpower for the collective farms in Novosibirsk and Karaganda. This was immediately borne out when Mikhail reported to Brigadir Czarski in Novosibirsk. His orders for Mikhail's new assignment were brief, *"Baranov, your work will be with the railway crew between Novosibirsk and Karaganda, Kazakhstan."*

"The railway to Kazakhstan? What about my residential and work credentials? Will I be allowed to work in that Soviet Republic?"

"Kazakhstan is a part of Soviet Russia, you dummkopf! The Turkestan-Siberian Railway is a branch of the Trans-Siberian Railway."

"I should know all of this?"

"Da, you should know this. The railway was completed in 1931 and it is Mother Russia's window on trade with Asia. It is important that this railway be operational all year round. Don't ask me any more of these stupid questions."

The railway line was constructed during Stalin's First Five-Year Plan by Gulag prison labour. Soon, Mikhail would join a railway repair crew headed up by Brigadir Polarski. Stationed in Novosibirsk, there was no shortage of hushed talk about deportees and the criminals among them who frequently attacked, shot, and suffocated armed guards. If Soviet workers or local residents got in the way, they, too, were harmed.

There were also stories about successful and unsuccessful escapes from labour camps. One story that made the rounds involved cannibalism where pairs of criminals would agree in advance to escape along with a third man who, without knowledge, was destined to become the sustenance for the other two on their journey. It was these kinds of stories that made Mikhail ever vigilant about any strangers or interlopers in the midst of the railway repair crew. Unlike his earlier experiences where prisoners would attempt escape to Europe via a northern route, most in the Novosibirsk region preferred escape through Kazakhstan,

Afghanistan, or Persia (Persia and Iran, *Land of the Aryans,* are often used interchangeably).

Assigned to workers' barracks, it was not unusual for railway workers to talk about the possibility of escape. With the long winter days, this would somehow become a means of therapy. After all, everyone involved in these discussions believed, deep down, that their preparations for escape were futile. If escapes were not possible, rebellion was unthinkable. Most were incapable of even thinking ill of the Soviet regime, let alone organizing against it. The humiliating experience of interrogation, prison, and deportation had robbed many of them of the will to live. Not only that, but the railway workers were well aware of the importance of their work. So was Brigadir Polarski. Consequently, Polarski was able to conduct frequent work stoppages knowing that authorities would be reluctant to punish his work crews.

By summer's end of 1939, Mikhail had spent nearly one year labouring on the railway between Novosibirsk and Karaganda. Despite the relative isolation of his work, the railway crews heard the news that Germany had invaded Poland and that most of the Commonwealth countries in the British Empire had declared war on Germany.

Becoming ever more aware of recent developments on the world stage, the railway workers wanted to know if the stories of Adolf Hitler's unsuccessful attempt to overthrow the German government in 1923 were true. *And, another thing,* thought Mikhail, *how was Hitler able to abolish democracy and become the Chancellor of Germany in 1933?* Other railway workers likely concluded, in secret, of course, that Hitler's rise to power mirrored that of Josef Stalin. Few, if any, wanted to engage in any exhaustive discussions of politics. The penalties for doing so were severe. *"It will not be long,"* stated Brigadir Polarski, *"before that mad bastard Hitler will dream of attacking our*

Motherland. Well, our esteemed leader, Stalin, will have something to say about that."

In September of 1939, the Red Army occupied the eastern provinces of Poland, declared them to be the western territories of Soviet Ukraine and Belarus and began extensive cleansing operations on these territories. This time it was Polish, Ukrainian, Jewish, and other nationalists who were targeted for deportation, pursuant to the Molotov-Ribbentrop Pact, and as part of the continued vision of nation building by the Communists.

At first, the German soldiers and officers taken prisoner by the Soviets were transferred to Siberia. This was followed by the deportation to Siberia of oblast governors, public officials, members of local police forces, land proprietors, industrialists, traders, forest rangers, railway workers, prisoners, and the socially alien elements who failed to hide in time. Stalin wanted to make sure that with the outbreak of hostilities none of these groups would take up arms against the Soviet Union. All potential deportees were quickly prosecuted by Troikas and sentenced, under *Articles 54 and 58* of the Soviet *Criminal Code* to prison terms of eight to twenty years.

The information about these deportations was communicated to the NKVD authorities in Siberia as early as November, 1939. However, it would not be until 1940 that the wheels of mass banishment would begin to turn and last until 1941. In a communiqué from Lavrentiy Beria to Stalin, the first group of Polish and Ukrainian deportees, deemed to be the bitterest of enemies of the working people, took place in December of 1939. The Ukrainian and Polish *osadniki* were listed as *special re-settlers*, which specifically included former military service members who distinguished themselves in the Polish-Soviet war of 1920. Nearly 1.7 million Poles, Ukrainians, and Belarusians living near the Soviet border prior to the outbreak of World War II were considered to be a threat if they should take up arms against the Soviet Union on the side of Germany. As a result, in a major re-settlement initiative, Stalin moved thousands to Siberia. To accomplish this massive deportation, the Soviet government readied thousands of carts driven by local coachmen, and hundreds of trucks, and railway carriages.

Many of the re-settlers ended up in timber-harvesting locations along the Trans-Siberian Railway, while others found themselves in camps and prisons rather than in special settlements. Added to this group were the liberated Poles: police officers, state employees, kulaks, teachers, petty traders, prostitutes, land proprietors, industrialists, and members of insurgent organizations who were assigned the category of *administratively exiled.*

The process for the arrests had not changed much from that which involved the Kozlov family in 1930. There was the customary knock on the door, an identification of all residents, and the confiscation of passports. It was not unusual for the soldiers to assist the deportees with the packing and loading of a maximum of 100 kilograms of belongings per person.

The general feeling of the Soviets was, " . . . *you could convert a Pole to Communism, but not the present generation. All of them are our enemies, no matter how many of them there are.*" For the most part, the deportees were Polish citizens, 85 percent of whom were Jews fleeing east from the advancing Nazi Wehrmacht in western Poland. Considered to be refugees, the Germans refused to accept them within the annexed portions of western Poland, a decision which may have saved numerous Jews from certain death in extermination camps.

Years later, the citizens of the Soviet Union would learn that during the Soviet invasion of Poland in 1939, over 23,000 Poles were arrested and murdered in the Khatyn Forest massacre near Smolensk, Russia. Among that group were more than 8,000 military officers, 6,000 police officers, and the leading members of the Polish intelligentsia. The order for this dastardly deed came directly from Stalin.

As a result of this horrific action, the Soviet Union felt confident that the Polish administration, army, and intellectual sector ceased to exist. However, Stalin's attitude towards the 380,000 Poles deported to Siberia changed when the Nazis attacked Russia. By agreement between the Soviet and Polish governments on June 30, 1943, an amnesty was extended to all former Polish citizens on the territory of the Soviet Union, after which another Polish army was gradually established on Soviet territory.

In addition to the deportation of all those living in the border region of Russia, some 21,000 counter-revolutionaries and nationalists were banished from Ukraine in May of 1941. Their destination was Omsk, Novosibirsk, and the Karaganda Oblast in Kazakhstan.

Things really began to change the moment the Nazis crossed the River Bug in Ukraine on June 22, 1941. On that day the total preventive deportation of Soviet Germans was born. One of the first actions by Stalin was to establish a 25-kilometer combat operational zone in advance of the Nazi attack where all settlements, without exception, would be destroyed lest the enemy use them. All residents were moved eastward out of harm's way.

Yet, this plan did not have complete success when the Nazi occupying forces quickly impacted 65 million people. More than one million of them actively collaborated with the occupying forces. Many individuals living in Ukraine and Russia betrayed their own families by joining the occupying forces. Branded as traitors after World War II, many were subsequently punished by the Soviet Regime.

The first pre-war deportation action came with the round-up of Soviet Germans who were regarded as potential collaborators. This operation netted over 1.5 million Soviet Germans who were subjected to resettlement. Living in cities and villages throughout Ukraine and Russia, they were earmarked for deportation to Kazakhstan, the oblast of Omsk, and the Altay oblasts. However, there was a delay in the deportations in 1941 due to the need to bring in the harvest.

The situation became critical when Ukrainians and Russians reported that the ethnic Germans living in Soviet Ukraine shot at the withdrawing Soviet troops from windows and vegetable gardens. Some ethnic Germans even greeted the advancing German troops with the traditional greeting of bread and salt. Stalin's reaction was instantaneous and his communiqué to Beria was straightforward, *"We must smash into oblivion the pockets of ethnic Germans living in Soviet Ukraine."* As a result, in August, 1941, the deportation of ethnic Germans from Soviet territories took place. Once again, it would be the executive Troikas established by the NKVD in each oblast who would put the deportations into operation.

The Soviet Union was finding it increasingly difficult to feed all of the deportees. As a result, the departing Germans were allowed to take personal belongings, small items of agricultural and domestic equipment, and a one-month food supply. The total weight of their luggage, however, was not to exceed one ton per family, regardless of the number of members in the family. Stalin was of the view that the Germans would put the basic farming implements to good use. The time allotted for packing was extremely short. Re-settlers had an opportunity to prepare only a minimal food supply. Some went so far as to slaughter their livestock, make sausages, and bake bread for the impending journey.

The ethnic Germans were banished from almost everywhere within the western part of the Soviet Union, from areas where they had resided for many years and from areas where it was possible to reside under war-time conditions. In this way, the entire German population, with the exception of those who fell into the hands of the advancing Nazi troops, was forced to entrain to Siberian oblasts east of the Urals. By October, 1941, fully 870,000 Germans were deported. This figure increased to well over one million by February, 1942. Nearly one-third of these special settlers ended up in Kazakhstan on collective farms.

The expulsion of entire peoples from their homelands destroyed their centuries-old way of life in terms of economy and social relations. One can only imagine the experiences that the kulaks, Poles, and ethnic

German deportees had to go through in an alien climate and hostile political and social environment to assimilate into the new economic reality. Those not able to adapt to destinations that centered round such industries as timber harvesting, coal mining, and other mining operations, soon perished.

With the arrival of thousands upon thousands of deportees in Novosibirsk, a labour army started to be formed by the NKVD. Construction battalions were molded into units of workers stationed in barracks. Those Germans withdrawn from active duty were registered as *special settlers* and then drafted into the labour army, which combined the characteristic of military life with that found in labour employment.

With the deportation of ethnic Germans to the oblasts of Novosibirsk and Karaganda, Stalin was able to assign many of them to kolkhozes. It was his intent to augment the agricultural labour force to a level necessary to improve the economic profile of the newly-adopted lands. However, the removal of ethnic Germans from Ukraine and Russia to Siberia created another problem. Soviet authorities found it necessary to re-settle the vacated areas, often by almost equally forceful measures. Belatedly, Stalin realized that his experiment had turned out to be an utter failure.

The Nazis, under the code name of Operation Barbarossa, launched their attack on Russia on June 22, 1941. This turned out to be the largest military offensive in history and lasted almost a full year. Stalin's reputation contributed both to the Nazis' justification of their assault and their faith in success. During the Great Purge of 1937-1938, Stalin killed or incarcerated millions of Soviet citizens. The loss of so many competent and experienced military officers in the Red Army left the Soviet military weakened and leaderless.

The Nazis often emphasized the Soviet Regime's brutality when targeting the Slavs with propaganda claiming that the Red Army was preparing to attack them. From this and from the Nazis' early war success in France, Hitler told his generals that it was time for a showdown with Bolshevism. Hitler envisioned success in a conflict with Russia. This, thought Hitler, would relieve the labour shortage in Germany, while at the same time realizing a reliable source of agricultural products from Ukraine.

As the casualties of World War II began to mount, Ukrainians realized just how negative was the impact of Soviet de-nationalization policies implemented in the 1930s. Those wayward policies led to the implementation of collectivization, the Ukrainian Famine of 1932-1933, the Reign of Terror of 1937-1938, and the massacre of Ukrainian intellectuals after the annexation of Western Ukraine in 1939. Perhaps this explains why the population of whole towns, cities, and villages greeted the Germans as liberators. This also helps to explain the unprecedented rapid progress of the German forces in the occupation of Ukraine.

Even before the Nazi invasion, two battalions of ethnic Ukrainians were set up and trained as Ukrainian battalions in the German Wehrmacht, thereby becoming a part of the initial Nazi invading force. With the change of regime, ethnic Ukrainians were allowed, and even encouraged, to work in various administrative positions in the proposed Reichskommissariates.

When Operation Barbarossa was launched, Hitler had at his disposal 3.9 million forces, including 29 armored and motorized divisions. The Nazis attacked the Soviet Union along a 1,200-kilometer front. At the same time, the Red Army numbered 6 million troops. The Nazi attack was two-pronged: Army Group North was to attack Russia en route to Saint Petersburg, while Army Group Center was to take a route directly towards Moscow.

The invading Nazis took note that Soviet citizens had a page in their internal passports with information regarding their ethnicity, party status, military rank, service in the Soviet Army reserve, and information as to where they were to assemble in case of war. These documents also contained a citizen's social status and reliability. When taken as prisoners of war, these documents were carefully reviewed by the Nazis. Those taken prisoner and showing anti-Soviet tendencies were quickly released from the prisoner of war camps. They were frequently offered administrative and clerical positions or encouraged to join local police units. Some were trained as camp guards, while others were forced to enlist in the Wehrmacht.

At this point, things were not going so well for the Red Army. Moscow at first failed to grasp the dimensions of the catastrophe that had befallen the Soviet Union. Marshall Timoshenko ordered all Soviet forces to launch a general counter-offensive, but with supply and ammunition dumps destroyed and a complete collapse of communication, the uncoordinated attacks failed.

Meanwhile, Marshall Zhukov had earlier signed the infamous *Directive of People's Commissariate of Defence No. 3,* which ordered the Red Army to start an offensive. Zhukov commanded the troops to encircle and destroy the enemy grouping near Suwalki, Poland, and Brody, Ukraine. This manoeuvre failed and the disorganized Red Army units were soon destroyed by the German Wehrmacht forces. In short order, the German armies advanced deep into Russia. By early fall in 1941, the Nazi armies were within striking distance of Russia's two major cities, Leningrad and Moscow.

But, all was not doom and gloom for the Soviet Union. At the start of Operation Barbarossa, Soviet exports of raw materials to Germany proved vital to the initial success of the Wehrmacht. Suddenly without Soviet imports, German stocks began to run out by October, 1941. Without major Soviet deliveries of rubber, manganese, oil, and grain,

Germany experienced critical difficulties in completing its attacks on Leningrad and Moscow.

As if by some stroke of genius, Stalin was able to marshal many of his available human resources which ended up in Siberia under very different circumstances. In mid-November of 1941, Mikhail was approached by a Red Army recruiting officer, *"Is your name Baranov?"*

Mikhail, suspecting something ominous was about to happen, didn't hold back his retort, *"Why are you asking me a stupid question when you already know the answer?"*

"Baranov, you are ordered to appear at the Regional Recruiting Office in Novosibirsk."

Mikhail's reaction was swift and predictable, *"The Regional Recruiting Officer in Novosibirsk? What kind of bullshit is this? Is this some sort of a stupid joke?"*

"This is not a joke. You are needed in the Soviet military."

"The Soviet military? The hell you say!"

Mikhail Baranov's life was about to take another u-turn.

Chapter 15

THE RED ARMY OR NORILSK

Baranov, the choice is yours

With the coming of unusually early and severe winter weather in 1941, Operation Barbarossa was brought to a standstill. However, even though the Germans had failed to take Moscow outright, they held huge areas of the western Soviet Union, including the entire regions of what are now Belarus, Ukraine, and the Baltic States. The occupied areas were not always properly controlled by the Germans and underground activity rapidly escalated. Due to directives issued by Adolf Hitler, German Wehrmacht occupation was brutal from the beginning. To their ultimate regret, the Nazis considered the Slavic peoples to be an inferior race.

This attitude held by the Germans alienated Ukrainians and Russians. As a result, anti-German partisan operations intensified as Red Army units, after major defeats, dissolved into the country's vast uninhabited areas. This pause in the fighting gave Stalin sufficient time to offer support for the partisan groups and to organize his troops beyond the Ural Mountains.

With the words of Brigadir Pilarski ringing in his ears, Mikhail wanted to know the reason for the order to appear before the Regional Recruiting Officer in Novosibirsk. Pilarski's answer was predictable, *"I do not question the wisdom of the Red Army. But, if I were to make a guess, I would say that you are needed elsewhere. Maybe it's the Red Army to protect our Motherland."*

If Mikhail was waiting for a definitive reply from Brigadir Pilarski, none was forthcoming. When he arrived at the Red Army Recruiting headquarters in Novosibirsk, the first question posed to him by the Kapitan in charge of the recruiting office was, *"Baranov, Mother Russia needs you in the Red Army. But, you do have a choice. You can select service in the Red Army to help defeat those German dogs or a Norilsk labour camp."*

"Norilsk? Why Norilsk? Isn't that a work camp for criminals?"

"That could be. But, it is also a mining and metallurgy complex critical for the defense of Mother Russia."

Mikhail did not have to ask where Norilsk was located. Every prisoner knew that it was in Far East Siberia, a mining operation in which few forced labourers survived for any length of time. He could tell by the Kapitan's demeanor that he wanted an immediate answer. In the final analysis, Mikhail knew that he had no choice. Still, there was no harm in asking, *"You say, Kapitan, the Red Army or Norilsk?"*

"Is there something wrong with your hearing? Do you want a swift kick in your fat ass or a bullet in the back of your head? I need your decision immediately."

In a flash, Mikhail's fate was sealed with his own words, *"I choose the Red Army."*

In short order, Mikhail would become a recruit into the Red Army. But, he would not be the only recruit. He would soon be joined by thousands of other exiled kulaks, ethnic groups, and criminals who had recently been banished to Siberia. These deportees were now being commandeered to help with the attack on the Nazi positions. *"Soon,"* Stalin declared from his perch in headquarters, *"the German Wehrmacht will have to contend with much more than just freezing their asses in a Russian winter."*

Mikhail Baranov was drafted into the Russian Army, not at the lowest rank of *ryadovoy* (private) but rather as a *yefreytor* (senior private). After two months of basic training in Novosibirsk, he was selected by the Commanding Officer to begin training for a secret parachute jump from a military aircraft. At the time, he was not certain of the reason for the development of this special squadron, yet he knew that had he refused he might well have been transferred to a labour camp. Although Mikhail would not be a part of the Soviet Union's first parachutist squadron, his mission would be an important one. By the time Germany attacked Russia in 1941, the Soviet Union already had five airborne corps.

The initial training for the airborne squadron consisted of a series of mock jumps using a parachute from a height of 40 meters. This was followed by several practice jumps from an aircraft. During the intensive training, attention was given to the proper exit, checking body position, and counting up to a predetermined number before deploying the parachute. Once the parachute was deployed, the parachutist would be required to check the canopy, gain control of his descent, and keep a sharp lookout for all other jumpers. By properly turning into the wind during the final stage of the descent, a soft landing would be assured. Mikhail quickly realized that improper techniques could be tragic when two recruits were lost during training.

Following some intensive basic training, the special squadron was ordered to prepare for the next phase of their preparation for a special mission. After a flight from Novosibirsk to Moscow, Mikhail joined a paratrooper training squadron near Moscow. *"You will be on a special mission named Hawk"* explained the Commanding Officer. *"Our tank forces are having a hell of a time with those Nazi bastards in the Battle for Moscow. Because we are at a standstill, Soviet paratroopers will land behind the German tank lines and attack them from the rear. In this way, we will be able to enter the war while evading fortifications that are in place."*

The paratroopers continued their training using parachutes of a round canopy design which could be steered by pulling on the risers and suspension lines attached to the canopy. Mobility of the parachutes was deliberately limited to prevent the scattering of the paratroopers. Based upon the urgency of the plan, the training for active duty was relatively short, often in questionable weather conditions, and with the use of equipment that was nothing short of primitive.

A woman and child on a soviet poster pleading to be saved from Nazi tyranny by the Red Army. Meanwhile, Stalin was very aware of the importance of bringing into the world more children who would eventually serve in the Soviet Military.

On December 5, 1941, supported by new T-34 tanks and Katyusha rocket launchers, the reinforcements attacked the German lines near Moscow. The specially-trained Soviet troops, including several ski battalions, were well prepared for winter warfare. By January of 1942, the exhausted and freezing Germans were routed and driven back, 200 kilometers west of Moscow.

Even at the earliest stages of Operation Barbarossa, Stalin recognized that the Russian resistance movement by the partisans was having a major impact on the course of the war on the Eastern Front. Earlier,

265

many Ukrainians had looked upon the Germans as liberating them from the tyranny of Stalin. However, with the Nazi attacks on Leningrad and Moscow, they suddenly changed their minds. Countless Ukrainians turned to the resistance movement as a way to help defeat Germany. The partisans invariably fought in terrain that the Germans found impossible to patrol and control. Many thousands of Russians joined the partisan groups in the marshes and attacked the Nazi Army in the rear as it advanced in an easterly direction.

The battle for Moscow had earlier moved to a critical stage in November of 1941. This caused Stalin to order his Central Staff to direct the activities of the partisans in an effort to damage Nazi military property, communication lines, and supply depots. This strategy had its effect. As the German Army retreated in their battle for Moscow, several Nazi brigades found themselves in the stronghold of the partisans which, by the spring of 1942, had swelled to over 142,000 individuals. Attacked by the Red Army in the rear and partisans in front of them, the German Army had a fearful time as it retreated. In the end, this battle cost Germany 300,000 soldiers.

Mikhail Baranov entered the conflict in March, 1942, as part of a Soviet parachute drop on German-held Dorogobuzh, a historic town straddling the Dnieper River, in the oblast of Smolensk. Regrettably, the parachute drop proved to be a disaster. Unfortunately for the Red Army, the paratroopers had been dropped off too close to the retreating German Army. As a result, most of the paratroopers were picked off like clay pigeons. The paratroopers who survived the jump had to escape to the partisan-held areas.

Mikhail managed to hide out with two other paratroopers behind the German lines on the outskirts of Dorogobuzh. It was their good fortune to find safe haven with a Russian villager who provided them with information about the conduct of the war in Stalingrad, Moscow, and Leningrad. But, their good fortune did not last long. The Soviets once again attacked the German positions from the east. While hiding out in the barn of a villager, the retreating Waffen-SS came looking for them. Not willing to reveal the hiding place of the three paratroopers, the stubborn villager was shot.

Realizing that they were in peril in their hiding place, the three paratroopers were compelled to make a decision—stay and try to shoot their way out or attempt an escape to points farther west in the hopes of joining a partisan group. Mikhail sought the advice of the other two survivors. *"It is impossible for us to escape as a group of three,"* whispered Mikhail. *"What do you think, Serzhant? Should we split up and increase our chances of survival?"*

The Kursk tank battle, 1943.

Soviet Victory, Kursk tank battle, 1943.

Soviet paratroopers deployed in the Battle
for Moscow, 1943.

Soviet Paratrooper Insignia.

Captured Nazi soldiers being marched to Siberia
during World War II.

"Nyet, I do not agree with that. I think that we should stick together. What about you, Mladshiy Serzhant? What do you think?"

"I agree with you, Serzhant. We should stick together. If we are to perish in this war, it is best that we perish together."

Fear gripped the three paratroopers as they planned their escape into the forest. They were well aware that the German soldiers must be nearby looking for them. With the decision to simultaneously make a run for the nearby forest, but in three different directions, they burst out of the barn. The German soldiers must have guessed correctly that they would attempt an escape, shouting, *"Achtung. Achtung. Stop oder ich werde schießen* (Stop or I will shoot). *"*

Although Mikhail made it to the woods with a shoulder wound, his two comrades never made it. In a flash, three German soldiers were at his side yelling, *"Hände nach oben!"* (Hands up.) Bleeding from the shoulder, Mikhail had no alternative but to give himself up. To do otherwise, he would also be a casualty of the war.

"Geben Sie mir Ihren Namen und Rang (Give me your name and rank), *"* was the command from the German officer.

"I speak no German, " was the response from Mikhail. At that point, he was certain that that the end was near. However, he soon realized that he would be of more value alive than dead. After all, they would certainly want to pump him for information about the parachute jump. To his surprise, the Germans applied a dressing to his shoulder wound and made preparations to escort him, under guard, to the Nazi temporary field headquarters on the outskirts of Dorogobuzh. Here, he was vigorously interrogated by the Nazis.

As expected by Mikhail, the Germans wanted to know the number of paratroopers taking part in the parachute drop and the strength of the Red Army. During the interrogation, Mikhail, through an interpreter, confessed that his birth name was not Mikhail Baranov but Konstantin Kozlov. He reasoned that were he able to convince the German interrogator that his service in the Red Army was not of his own choice might improve his chances of survival. Unfortunately, with the death of his two comrades, the Germans were not able to confirm anything that Mikhail told them. Yet, they were likely aware that Stalin had deported thousands of Ukrainians and ethnic Germans from this region to Siberia before the outbreak of the war.

Fortune smiled upon Mikhail when one of the Nazi officers interrogating him spoke Russian. In assessing the reason for the failure of the parachute drop, Mikhail concluded that the paratroopers were too hastily organized and the careful preparation required was simply not there. Moreover, most of the parachutists had never jumped out of an airplane before. Their only training was a jump or two using a parachute harness from a training tower. The parachute jump lacked transport aircraft, the pilots didn't have much experience, and the German flak was alert and effective. To avoid the risk of German fighters, the drop was done at night but this just added to the muddle. His thoughts were interrupted when the Russian-speaking Nazi officer asked a most unusual question, *"Tell me, what do you think of Marshal Stalin?"*

"What do I think of Stalin? I hate the tyrant. He was responsible for deporting my whole family to Siberia in 1930. I have been a prisoner of Bolshevism for eleven years."

"Gut. Das ist schon. (That is good.) *We are gathering those Russians and Ukrainians who want to travel to Germany, to work in Germany in the hopes of defeating Stalin. Do you want to join that group?"*

Mikhail did not have to think too long to make a decision. To do otherwise, he felt that he, too, would become a prisoner of war and eliminated by the Waffen-SS as the German Army prepared to retreat from the merciless pounding by the Red Army.

"Go to Germany? What would I do in Germany?"

"Each day we have three trains that leave Smolensk for Germany after dropping off supplies for our troops. You will take the next train to Hamburg where you will be registered as a prisoner of war. We will send a recommendation that you be given the option of working for Germany. We need more workers to win this war against these Bolshevik murderers."

Under guard, Mikhail was taken to Smolensk and placed on a train bound for Hemer, Germany, a journey that took three days. The fact that the Nazis transported many prisoners of war to this destination was not a surprise. In 1934, Hemer, a town about 30 kilometers from the German city of Dortmund, became a garrison town. The Nazis decided to build three barracks in neighboring Iserlohn to be used as a military training area and as a military hospital.

When World War II broke out, the buildings were set aside as a prisoner of war camp. The first Polish POWs arrived in October of 1939 and had to sleep on the floor as the beds were not finished. Inadequate equipment remained a problem throughout the whole of the war, both because the materiel was needed at the front and also because the camp was permanently overpopulated. At first, the inmates were mostly from Poland and France. After the outbreak of the war with the Soviet Union in 1941, Soviet POWs quickly became the majority.

Most camps in Hemer were simply open areas fenced off with barbed wire and watchtowers but with no housing. The meager conditions forced the prisoners to live in dugouts, completely exposed to the elements. Beatings and other forms of abuse by the guards were common, and prisoners were malnourished, often consuming only a few hundred calories each day. Medical treatment was non-existent and a Red Cross offer to help was rejected by Hitler. Yet, Mikhail, even though he was processed by the Wehrmacht and sent under guard to Hemer in an open railcar, had to admit that his time in the Gulag prepared him well for the conditions in Germany. After just one week in Hemer, Mikhail was ordered to appear before the Camp Commandant, *"Baranov, were you taken to Siberia against your will in 1930?"*

"Tak, I was."

"Were you a soldier in the Red Army when captured in Smolensk?"

"Tak, I was, but against my will."

"Against your will? How is that?"

"Well, I had a choice, the Red Army or a labour camp in Far East Siberia."

"Are you opposed to the policies of Stalin?"

"Tak, I am."

"Are you prepared to work in Germany as an Ostarbeiter?"

Noting the degree of starvation around him and the fact that once a week the sick inmates were being shot, Mikhail made a decision to go to work for the Germans. In this way, he felt that he might be able to escape death from dysentery, typhoid fever, or malnutrition. The Gestapo conducted an ongoing weeding-out program. Communist Party officials, commissars, academic scholars, Jews, and other undesirable or dangerous individuals were transferred to concentration camps. Most were put to work, while others were immediately and summarily executed. This made Mikhail's decision somewhat easier.

From 1941-1944, about 10 percent of all Soviet POWs were turned over to the Waffen-SS, a multi-national military force of the Third Reich composed of foreign volunteers and conscripts. Known as the *Einsatzgruppen*, these infamous German death squads were responsible for the mass killings of political prisoners, Jews, Romas (Gypsies), Jehovah's Witnesses, homosexuals, and those afflicted with mental illnesses. During the war, millions of Red Army prisoners of war were also taken. Some were arbitrarily executed in the field by German forces. Others died under inhumane conditions in concentration camps.

Most of the deaths took place between June, 1941 and January, 1942, when the Germans killed an estimated 2.8 million Soviet prisoners of war primarily through starvation, exposure, and summary execution. By comparison, between 374,000 and one million German prisoners of war died in Soviet labour camps.

Considering these statistics, Mikhail was one of the lucky ones. He did not take an active part in the war until the spring of 1942, at which point the Nazis realized that unless they recruited foreign workers, mostly through coercion, their war-oriented factories back home would suddenly come to a halt.

When Mikhail was taken prisoner, he was stripped of his supplies and clothing by ill-equipped German troops and left with nothing more than the shirt on his back. The camp to which he was initially assigned in Hemer was especially reserved for Russian POWs. Mikhail, along with other Russian and Ukrainian soldiers, was kept separated from the prisoners of other countries. The Allied regulars were usually treated in accordance with the 1929 Geneva Convention, which had been signed by Germany but not by the Soviet Union.

In January of 1942, Hitler authorized better treatment of Soviet POWs because the war had really bogged down. As a result, German leaders decided to use prisoners for forced labour. The number of prisoners of war forced into labour increased from barely 150,000 in 1942 to a peak of 631,000 in the summer of 1944. Like Mikhail, many were dispatched to the coal mines. Others were sent to Krupp, Daimler-Benz, or countless other companies where they provided labour for the war effort while being slowly worked to death. The largest employers were in mining, agriculture, and the metal industry. In all, about 200,000 prisoners died during this period of forced labour.

Use of forced labour in Nazi Germany during World War II occurred on a large scale. It was an important part of the German economic exploitation of conquered territories and the extermination of populations of German-occupied Europe. In all, the Germans abducted about 12 million people from over 20 European countries, about two-thirds of whom came from Eastern Europe. Hitler's policy of *Lebensraum* (additional living space) strongly emphasized the conquest of new lands in the East.

In reality, Mikhail was forced into labour as a Russian POW. However, the Nazis considered him to be a volunteer POW based mainly upon his family being deported from Ukraine to Siberia in the first instance. Having survived a decade in the labour camps of the Gulag, Mikhail found himself to be in a better position to survive his tenure in forced labour in the mines of Germany than did other less informed slaves.

Although most Ukrainians fought alongside the Red Army and Soviet resistance, some elements of the Ukrainian nationalist underground created the Ukrainian Insurgent Army in northwestern Ukraine in 1943, which at times engaged the Nazi forces. They continued to fight the Soviet Union after the war. Using guerilla war tactics, the insurgents targeted for assassination and terror those who they perceived as representing or cooperating at any level with the Soviet state. At the same time, another nationalist movement fought alongside the Nazis. In total, the number of ethnic Ukrainians who fought in the ranks of the Soviet Army is estimated to be between 4.5 and 7 million. The pro-Soviet partisan guerilla resistance in Ukraine is estimated to number 47,800 at the start of occupation to 500,000 at its peak in 1944, with about 50 percent of them being Ukrainians.

The vast majority of the fighting in World War II took place on the Eastern Front where Nazi Germany suffered 93 percent of its casualties. The total losses inflicted upon the Ukrainian population during the war are estimated to be between 5 and 8 million, including over half a million Jews killed by the Einsatzgruppen, sometimes with the help of local collaborators. Of the estimated 8.7 million Soviet troops who fell in battle against the Nazis, 1.4 million were ethnic Ukrainians.

One of the conclusions of the Yalta Conference, February 11, 1945, was that the Allies would return to the Soviet Union all Soviet citizens who found themselves in the Allied zone. The prisoners of war and civilians were kept in separate camps until they were handed over to the Soviet or United States authorities. It was the plan for each nation's military authorities to report those military or civilian personnel liberated in the reclaimed countries of Ukraine, Poland, and Germany. This immediately affected the Soviet prisoners of war liberated by the Allies. On March 31, 1945, Josef Stalin, Winston Churchill, and Franklin D. Roosevelt concluded the final form of their plans in a secret codicil to the agreement. Outlining the plan to forcibly return the refugees to the Soviet Union, this codicil was kept secret from the American and British people for over fifty years.

By the end of the war, Mikhail had completed more than two years as a slave labourer in a German coal mine. On numerous occasions, his thoughts had turned to the nurse he met in Kazan. These romantic thoughts made the days seem shorter and the work less strenuous. It did not take long for word to reach him that all Soviet POWs would be held in a camp in Hemer until such time that all paperwork could be completed. Common to all of them was an absolute dread of returning to the Soviet Union. They were certain that they would be killed or at the very least sentenced to the unspeakable horrors in labour camps.

This strong resistance to be returned to the Soviet Union mattered little when Winston Churchill confirmed that all Russian POWs must be repatriated, forcibly if necessary. The early debate over the disposition of the Russian prisoners had been won on the insistence of British Foreign Minister Anthony Eden in order that British POWs liberated in Russian-controlled zones would be safely returned to the United Kingdom.

Although the Americans objected to the forced repatriation, it is also noted that their objection was based upon the provisions under the Geneva Convention and not on the agreement between the British and the Soviets. When the war ended in May of 1945, all Russians liberated in Germany were simply handed over to Soviet troops for repatriation to the Soviet Union.

Altogether some 2.75 million people were repatriated. Most did not have to be physically forced—all their lives they had been accustomed to following the orders of the state. Besides, Stalin did broadcast that all Soviet troops and forced labourers would receive a general amnesty. However, this declaration of an amnesty did little to dissuade those being held in the camp from mounting, in many cases, a brutal resistance to repatriation to the Soviet Union. Several Soviet POWs hung themselves from their bunks in the barracks rather than being forced back to the Soviet Union. In other cases, POWs repeatedly stabbed themselves to avoid being taken into custody. These self-inflicted injuries were quickly patched up by doctors and those being repatriated sent on their way. Others had to be beaten practically senseless by the guards, who used rifle butts, pick-ax handles, and even bayonets, before the prisoners could be put onboard a train.

Many of those being repatriated after the war refused to go back to the Soviet Union. They knew that they would be marched to a filtration camp where they would be processed and sentenced to years of hard labour in Siberian concentration camps, regardless of whether they had fought for or had been taken prisoner by the Germans. Eventually, most were shoved onto east-bound trains without many formalities. On their way to the collection points that would put them into the hands of the Bolsheviks, many committed suicide. Those loaded onto transport vans were provided only a bucket of water to drink and another bucket to use as a lavatory. With the doors locked, the officials discovered that many were dead upon arrival at the transfer points.

During the war, Stalin created SMERSH, a counter-intelligence agency under the control of the NKVD. Its main task was to secure the Red Army's operational rear from partisans, saboteurs, and spies, and to investigate and arrest conspirators and mutineers, traitors, deserters, spies, and criminal elements at the combat front. As the war wound down, the activities of SMERSH turned to filtering the soldiers and forced labourers recovered from captivity as well as the capture of Soviet citizens who had been active in anti-communist armed groups fighting on the side of Nazi Germany. SMERSH was disbanded in May of 1946 and one year later, Operation East Wind handed over its final contingent of repatriates, bringing the long and sad story of forced repatriation to a close.

At the end of World War II, there were approximately 3 million surviving Ukrainian displaced persons. By the autumn of 1945, all but 200,000 were repatriated to the USSR. Most of the 2.8 million Ukrainians were forcibly repatriated against their will and contrary to the provisions under the Geneva Convention. Under Stalin's orders, hundreds of thousands of repatriated Ukrainians were killed. Others were transferred to Gulag concentration camps where many were tortured or worked to death.

Realizing that thousands resisted repatriation to the Soviet Union, Stalin launched a propaganda campaign falsely smearing Ukrainian refugees as Nazi war criminals.

As Mikhail awaited his fate in a holding camp in Hemer, he tried to convince the Americans of how his family was deported to the Gulag in 1930 and that he did not wish to return to the Soviet Union. Unfortunately, the Americans knew precious little about the forced labour camps in Siberia. In the end, and even though the Americans did place him in the category of disputed, he was cleared for repatriation to the Soviet Union. This decision was taken, in part, because throughout the summer of 1945, no provisions existed to determine the future of disputed soldiers or citizens.

Most displaced persons were housed in schoolhouses and barns, usually with common sanitary facilities. As a prisoner of war and a former Ostarbeiter, Mikhail developed a defensive attitude as protection against German brutality. As well, he learned to steal to supplement the German starvation diet while at all times distrusting promises of the Soviets. His world revolved around food and shelter.

Soviet authorities described those who refused to return to the Soviet Union as being collaborators or idlers who preferred to live in the comfort of Western decadence rather than returning to their homeland. For those who had no knowledge of the Soviet Union, it seemed incredible that people would not want to return home.

As early as the autumn of 1944 and the spring of 1945, Stalin orchestrated a propaganda campaign to encourage repatriation aimed at non-returnees and Western public opinion. A new 30-page publication, *Home to the Motherland*, was widely circulated, filled with emotional images of the Motherland awaiting her children. Letters from relatives at home were often fabricated to convince people of safe conditions in the Soviet Union.

The issue of returning refugees became one of Stalin's main priorities in establishing a new postwar order. By the fall of 1945, the repatriation program was well organized, had the approval of the Allies, and gave Soviet leaders a legitimate context for conducting repatriation and a legal framework within which to advance their demands. To carry out these plans, Stalin created the Soviet Administration of the Plenipotentiary for Repatriation Affairs (APRA). APRA used both legal and covert methods of deception, kidnapping, bribery, and threats to repatriate Soviet nationals from Western officials, assist Western authorities in locating and identifying their charges, and safeguarding the rights of Soviet citizens under Western control.

Once the Russian liaison officers convinced the British officers at the Hemer camp that all refugees were Russians, the Soviet POWs and Ostarbeiters were given papers for transport to the Russian zone. Mikhail noted that there was a scurry of activity to complete the repatriation of Soviet citizens. At the same time, those POWs from Allied Forces held by the Russian Army were repatriated to the West in the form of exchanges.

The words of the Soviet Ambassador to France set the tone for repatriation to the Soviet Union, *"The Motherland would not be a mother if she did not love all her family, even the black sheep. Every man will be given a chance to redeem himself at home—if he is of military age, in the army; otherwise in a factory. There will be no judgment here. All are accepted here; all return home; all are considered sons of the Motherland."*

Against his will, Mikhail found himself once again in a cattle train headed in an easterly direction.

Even as the last POWs and Russian Ostarbeiters were being rounded up, Stalin's complaints campaign continued to claim that anti-Soviet Ukrainians were impeding repatriation. This prompted Western authorities to re-circulate the orders denying recognition of Ukrainians as a separate nationality. A very effective tactic of this propaganda campaign was to portray all refugees refusing repatriation as war criminals. The official Soviet newspaper, *Izvestiia*, published an article which claimed that *The only persons who do not wish to return to their country are traitors. All honest people taken from their homes by the Germans wish to return.*

After Nazi Germany's defeat, ten NKVD-run special camps were set up in the Soviet Occupation Zone of post-war Germany. The Soviet POWs, housed in the German Stalags, were used for work in coal mines, factories, quarries, agriculture, and railroad maintenance. In contrast, the German POWs in Russia's Siberia were kept in a separate camp system under the control of a separate administration.

During and after the war, freed POWs were sent to special Soviet filtration camps. By 1944, about 100 filtration camps were set up for repatriated Ostarbeiters, POWs, and other displaced persons. In May of 1945, as many as 2 million former Russian citizens were forcefully repatriated to the USSR. Many of these were treated as traitors under Stalin's *Order No. 270* which directed that any Commander or Commissar tearing away his insignia and deserting or surrendering should be considered to be a malicious deserter. This required superiors to shoot the deserters and subject their family members to arrest.

These filtration camps processed over 4 million people. By 1946, 80 percent of the civilians and 20 percent of the POWs were freed, 5 percent of the civilians, and 43 percent of the POWs were re-drafted, 10 percent of the civilians and 22 percent of the POWs were sent to labour battalions, and 2 percent of the civilians and 15 percent of the POWs were transferred to the NKVD. Those transferred to the NKVD ended up in the Gulag.

The KGB found 233,400 out of 1,836,562 Soviet soldiers who returned from captivity to be guilty of collaborating with the enemy and then sent to Gulag camps. To add further confusion as to the exact numbers, *The Black Book of Communism* provides different numbers. The *Black Book* concluded that 19 percent of the ex-POWs were sent to penal battalions of the Red Army, 14 percent to forced labour reconstruction battalions for a period of two years, and 360,000 people were sentenced from 10 to 20 years in the Gulag.

As summer days turned towards fall in the northern region of Germany, Soviet military officers were charged with the responsibility of repatriating POWs and Ostarbeiters to the Soviet Union. Each person in the barracks at Hemer was required to confirm their identity and was then provided with transfer papers for their final destination. The thought of escaping transfer back to the Soviet Union was always with each person being repatriated. However, each knew that escape was unlikely. After making a few stops along its route north of Berlin to the newly-occupied Soviet territory of East Germany, the repatriation train arrived in Szczecin, Poland.

Szczecin turned out to be a collection point for thousands of citizens to be repatriated to the Soviet Union. It is here that those being repatriated would witness the full devastation of war. Most shocking were the rumours of Nazi treatment of Soviet prisoners of war since 1941. They had become the first victims of Nazi policy of mass starvation. With time, their rations dwindled to 700 calories per day consisting of special Russian bread made from sugar beet husks and straw flour. In POW camps in Germany, Soviet POWs had often been left for months to vegetate in trenches, dugouts, or sod houses. In Belarus, structures with roofs but no walls were used to house prisoners. If death by starvation did not occur, then the long marches across hundreds of kilometers took their toll. In cases where a prisoner was not able to continue, he was immediately shot.

Mikhail's eastward journey took him from Szczecin to Warsaw where additional POWs and Soviet citizens continued to be added to those already on board. Throughout, there was no shortage of horror stories of what happened in the Nazi extermination camps of Auschwitz-Birkenau and Majdanek. But, the telling of these horrific stories did not end there. As the train chugged its way from Warsaw to Siedlce en route to the Polish border crossing at Brest, other stories about concentration camps located in Treblinka, Belzec, and Sobibor

STEVEN KASHUBA

surfaced. Stories about how millions of Soviet POWs, citizens, and Jews were exterminated in camps engineered by Heinrich Himmler. Of the thousands of Soviet prisoners of war brought to concentration camps in Poland by the Nazis, only a few hundred survived by the end of the war.

There was one other shocking rumour that came to light during the process of repatriation. Of the some 10,000 Soviet prisoners who were harnessed by the Nazis to build the Birkenau extermination camp in Auschwitz, only a few hundred survived. One such POW told Mikhail that in June of 1941, he was taken prisoner of war by the Nazis to a concentration camp behind the German lines where he and thousands of other Soviet POWs were kept corralled like animals and fed only on thin soup. *"But,"* commented the POW, *"when my comrades started to die of starvation, I survived. I survived because of my experiences on a collective farm."*

"You were a labourer on a collective farm?"

"Da, da. The average survival time for a Soviet prisoner in Birkenau," continued the POW, *"was two weeks. If you got something eatable, you ate it no matter if it was a dirty raw potato or carrot. In fact, it was not unusual to find instances of cannibalism. When it was time to get up in the morning, those who were alive moved, and around them would be two or three dead people. You went to bed alive and when you woke up in the morning, there was death everywhere."*

To explain the cause of death, the Nazis would frequently list heart attack or pneumonia.

As the train wound its way to Brest, Belarus, it was difficult, if not impossible, for Mikhail to think about anything except the devastation and pervasiveness of the war. However, in the midst of this, there was also talk amongst those being repatriated to Russia about the war and each person's experiences as a labourer in Germany. There was also

282

discussion about the countries of origin, home towns, and plans for the future.

Mikhail's ears really perked up when he heard a comment from a POW that aboard the train was a Russian repatriate by the name of Dominova. The very mention of Dominova brought back a flood of memories. *Could it be possible,* he thought, *that she is the girl I met eight years ago in Kazan? The nurse who wanted to be a medical doctor?* Suddenly, Mikhail was consumed with thoughts of Darya Dominova.

What were the chances that this woman is the very nurse who looked after me when I sustained a head injury? There was only one way to get at the truth. Mikhail was now determined to look into every carriage in the hopes of finding the truth.

All too soon Mikhail would have his shocking answer. In fact, he would have one additional startling answer to a question he had not even raised.

Chapter 16

REPATRIATION TO SIBERIA

Here are your transfer papers to your Mother Homeland

As the Soviet repatriation train crossed the Polish border en route to Brest, Belarus, Mikhail Baranov examined his repatriation papers and contemplated his fate. He had to pinch himself to make sure that all of this was real and not a dream. His most recent odyssey started in the Gulag, a hell-hole he tried so hard to escape and suddenly he was being forced right back to where he started. Rumours of the pain inflicted upon those being repatriated to Mother Russia seemed without end. It was not enough that so many young men and women were forced from their homes to work in Germany as Ostarbeiters, but the information that many females being returned to Russia were raped by the soldiers of the Red Army during their release from prisoner of war camps in Germany added to the horror. Terrible as were the rumours of rape, there remained a special quality to the suffering inflicted by soldiers on their own compatriots.

Earlier, Stalin had said that *"There are no Soviet prisoners of war held by the Germans, only betrayers of their Rodina-mat"* (Mother Homeland). This attitude could not have been expressed with more clarity than by the NKVD and Red Army units who arrived at the concentration camps in Poland. Instead of being welcomed back and allowed to resume their lives as Soviet citizens, many were interrogated for weeks. The standard question from the SMERSH investigators was, *"When did you join the German Army?"* The questioning would not stop, often ending with the admonition from the interrogator, *"Admit this, you are a spy. Your confession will set you free."*

Knowing that so many others had been branded as traitors, Mikhail felt that he was most fortunate to be repatriated without the stigma of betrayal. His circumstance would have been completely different had he taken up arms against the Red Army. Still, his circumstance was not without several introspective thoughts, *Just who am I, Mikhail Baranov or Konstantin Kozlov? Am I a citizen of Russia or a citizen of Ukraine? What have all these transfers done to me? How long will I have to continue with this deception?*

Repatriation train to the Soviet Union, 1945.

Work on the Trans-Siberian Railway in Tyumen, 1945.

Yet, despite all the questions, Mikhail felt some measure of comfort when he realized that he was not alone on this journey. Crowded in the smelly cattle car, he could tell from the conversations around him that although the destination of others was Siberia, the similarity ended there. Some were destined for Central Siberia, while others were being repatriated to Kazakhstan. Reflecting on the time he spent in the German coal mine working as an Ostarbeiter, this transfer was a welcome break. Despite earlier deprivations, most seemed happy that the war at last was over. Those around him were in a celebratory mood even though they were uncertain of what lay ahead of them. Listening to the cacophony of sounds emanating from those around him, he could discern that some of the fellow-repatriates were from Ukraine, while others were from Poland, Belarus, the Baltic States, and Russia.

The devastation of the Polish countryside did not escape those being transported. The artillery and bombs had done their dirty work in the countryside and on many sections of the railway which showed the scars of recent battles. The day was very hot and soon the air in the cattle car became rancid with the smell of sweat and excrement from the bucket in the corner. This was made all the more stark by the relatively slow pace of the train, thereby giving the political prisoners plenty of time to reflect. The wait for the railway crew to repair a bridge over the River Bug near Brest was inordinately long. Just thinking about what happened to the Poles and Ukrainians in this region sent chills running up and down Mikhail's spine.

Putting aside those horrible images of the war, somehow Mikhail's thoughts once again turned to Darya. Under the watchful eye of Soviet soldiers, the deportees were allowed to disembark and stretch their weary legs. This gave Mikhail an opportunity to mingle with POWs and citizens from other railway cars. Approaching a POW in the forward car, he felt compelled to ask, *"Excuse me, I am looking for a Russian nurse. Could she be a passenger in your carriage? Is there such a woman in your car?"*

"Could be. There are several women in our car."

"Several women? Where are these women?"

"Over there. They were permitted to take a break in the woods to relieve themselves. But, one of them is ill. She is still in the railway car being tended to by a Russian nurse."

When the order came from the Soviet officer to board the train, Mikhail discreetly gathered up his gunny sack from his railway car and promptly boarded the carriage that housed the Russian nurse. He was not surprised to note that his move seemed not to be detected by the military guards. As the train lurched forward, Mikhail carefully examined the face of each passenger in the railway car. Although a number of POWs and citizens sat on the two benches along the perimeter of the car, all others remained standing, perhaps taking turns sitting on one of the two benches.

As his eyes grew accustomed to the darkness in the car, he noticed three women huddled in the far corner. Like so many POWs and citizens being transported, it was difficult to guess the age of any of the three. Most everyone in the railway car looked like they could do with a change of clothing and a bath. Approaching the three women, Mikhail quietly asked, *"Excuse, me. I am looking for a nurse by the name of Darya. Darya Dominova. Might one of you be named Darya?"*

The answer to his question was slow in coming. Perhaps there was a reason for it. Other than responding to officials, it was obvious that the women were reluctant to give out any information to anyone, especially a stranger. Finally, a response came from what appeared to be the youngest of three, *"Da, I am Darya. Should I know you?"*

Looking intently at Darya, Mikhail thought back to the time he sustained a head injury while working for the Trans-Siberian Railway near Kazan. Despite the darkness in the carriage, there was no mistaking that this was the young woman who tended to his injury. Mikhail was struck by the gentleness of her facial features, as if the hardships of the war only helped her mature as a woman. The teenage girl he had met in Kazan, despite the raggedy clothes she was wearing, had gone through quite a transformation.

Finally finding his voice, all Mikhail could do was answer quietly, *"Do I know you? Maybe, I worked on the railway crew in Kazan. Were you in Kazan in 1937?"*

As Mikhail awaited a response from Darya, a thousand questions popped into his mind. Could it be that the terror and brutality of the Gulag gave him an opportunity to first meet Darya eight years ago and World War II another chance to find out who she really was? Was she, in 1937, a university student or was she a member of the Komsomol under the employ of the NKVD? What did she know of his past? Mikhail's thoughts were suddenly interrupted when he heard Darya say, *"What did you say your name was?"*

"Mikhail. Mikhail Baranov. I worked on the special railroad detail in Kazan. Were you the university student registered at the University of Perm when we met in Kazan? Did you treat my head injury?"

"Da, it was me," was Darya's response. *"However, the war interrupted my medical studies. As a result, I served my country as a field nurse."*

"A field nurse? How then did you end up in Germany?"

"I served on the Eastern Front as a nurse with a medical evacuation unit during the defense of Moscow. I was taken prisoner in 1942 and forced to work as an Ostarbeiter for the Nazis until now."

"Where did you work in Germany?"

"In Hamburg."

For the longest time Mikhail Baranov seemed lost in thought as he contemplated the journey by train from Minsk, Belarus, to Tyumen, Siberia. There was no shortage of movement of trains, heavily loaded and headed for the interior of Russia. Mikhail was not surprised to learn that Darya was also being repatriated to Russia. According to the NKVD, Darya, like so many other Ostarbeiters, may have picked up some bad habits in Germany and developed an anti-Communist sentiment. To them, this would have been sufficient reason to schedule Darya for remediation so that she might once again embrace the ideals of Communism. Only then could she realize the dreams that she had for herself that were so rudely interrupted by the war.

Despite the primitive conditions in the train, Mikhail wanted to find out more about Darya, especially about her role while she worked in Kazan. But, try as he might, no significant information was forthcoming other than her treatment at the hands of the Nazis. However, there was one bit of information that caught Mikhail Baranov off guard.

"Mikhail," Darya enquired, *"did you say that your family was deported to Omsk in 1930? That they were from Ukraine?"*

"Da, we were deported from Ukraine to the Omsk region. I spent seven years in a labour camp before getting work on the Trans-Siberian Railway system. Why do you ask?"

"I ask this question because when I worked as a nurse in Hamburg, I treated a prisoner of war who came to the clinic with a back injury. He told me that he was from Ukraine and that at the age of eighteen he joined a partisan group in Zhitomir, Ukraine. He said that his first name was Pyotr. But that would be of no interest to you."

"No interest to me, Darya? How is that?"

"Da, that is easy, Mikhail, his family name was not Baranov."

"What was his family name?"

As Mikhail Baranov waited for Darya to respond, he felt as though he had been struck by a bolt of lightning. In a world war that involved millions of combatants, is it possible for a Russian nurse serving as a caregiver to come in contact with two brothers who had not seen each other for fifteen years? Noting that a response was not immediately forthcoming from Darya, Mikhail asked, *"What does he look like?"*

"He is a strong-looking lad, about your height. In fact, he looks a lot like you. I recall him saying that his family members were deported to Siberia when he was eight years of age."

"Would his family name be Kozlov?"

"Kozlov? No, that name does not sound familiar."

"If his family name was not Kozlov, do you remember it?"

"Not really. However, I believe that the name had the sound of 'dukh' in it, the Russian word for spirit."

"Dukh? Could the full name have been Dutkewycz?"

"Good Lord, I do believe that it was Dutkewycz! How did you ever come up with that name?"

"Just a thought, that's all."

Suddenly, Mikhail had another challenge on his hands. Finding Darya Dominova on the same train bound for Siberia was a minor miracle. Could it be that another miracle was about to unfold? What might be the chances that his younger brother Pyotr was on the same train? He knew that he could not undertake the task of searching for him on his own initiative without raising the suspicions of the NKVD. Darya would have a better chance of finding Pyotr if, indeed, he was on the train. After all, it was Darya who had nursed Pyotr back to health and it would be Darya who would be able to recognize him. In making the request, Mikhail did not tell Darya that Pyotr might be his younger brother, a brother that he had not seen since 1930. Besides, his passport now said that he was Mikhail Baranov, a soldier in the Red Army.

Darya's challenge of searching for Pyotr was made all the more difficult as there was no assurance that he was on this or any other train bound for Siberia. All Darya knew is that she did catch a glimpse of an Ostarbeiter getting on the train in Hamburg who looked a lot like Pyotr. That Darya was herself under suspicion by the NKVD, who believed that she may have been involved in some sort of anti-Soviet activity, did not deter her from pursuing this new challenge. In a strange way, her search for Pyotr was aided and abetted by the shabby condition of the railway system and the frequent stops at locations where the railway tracks were under repair. This provided her with sufficient time to look for Pyotr.

The search for Pyotr did not come without difficulties. First of all, it was the expectation that all POWs and citizens would continue their respective journeys to the USSR in the railway car assigned to them. However, the maintenance of any records as to who occupied a particular railway car were scarce and in some cases non-existent. In all of this, it was the main task of the NKVD to ensure that those aboard did not abandon or escape their eastward journey.

The next major problem stemmed from the realization that Darya could not put out the word that she was looking for anyone. To do so would have raised serious questions. With over 50 railway cars in the transport train, Darya decided to first undertake a search of all railway cars towards the rear of the train.

Darya discovered that several cars which carried political prisoners were under constant guard and surveillance and, as a result, out of bounds to all but authorized officials. According to information from one NKVD agent, this surveillance became necessary because the cars contained prisoners who were apprehended while wearing Nazi uniforms. This led the NKVD to conclude that they were traitors because they elected to enter the conflict by switching sides. This brought out the question, *what if Pyotr happened to be identified as a person who switched sides thus being branded as a traitor and located in one of these railway cars?* Without any access to these cattle cars, it would not be possible to locate Pyotr.

It would not be until the train reached the railway siding in Nizhny Novgorod, some 400 kilometers east of Moscow that Darya felt certain that the passenger she spotted in car 43 looked like the patient she nursed in Germany. Making sure that she would not raise any suspicions, she approached him quietly, *"Excuse me, is your name Pyotr?"*

"Is my name Pyotr? Why do you ask? Are you an NKVD agent?"

"My name is Darya. Would I be the nurse that looked after you in Germany? Do you remember me?"

"Remember you? Let me have a closer look at you. Of course, I remember you. You are the nurse who saved my life. What are you doing here?"

"I am going back to Mother Russia. Back to where I was born. Back to Tyumen."

"Tyumen? In Siberia? Are you on the NKVD's list for repatriation?"

"Da, to Tyumen in Siberia. What about you? Where are you being transferred to?"

"I don't know my final destination. However, the NKVD will direct me when I arrive in Novosibirsk."

"Why is your destination Siberia? Are you not from Ukraine?"

"Da, but I joined a partisan group while in Ukraine and was taken prisoner by the Nazis in 1942. During the balance of the war, I worked in Germany as an Ostarbeiter."

"Do you know a person by the name of Mikhail Baranov?"

"Baranov? Did you say Baranov? Nyet, I know no such person."

"Do not leave your carriage. I will bring Baranov to meet you just as soon as I can."

Under the watchful eyes of the NKVD, Darya made her way back to her railway car. Once she was certain that she would not be overheard, she whispered to Mikhail, *"Da, he is the soldier I nursed back to health in Hamburg. At first, he did not recognize me. It was not until I told him about his injuries that he recalled meeting me."*

"What does Pyotr look like? Is he tall or short and stocky?" asked Mikhail.

"To tell you the truth, he looks like your typical Ukrainian or Russian. It's his hair, though. His hair looks much like yours, maybe a little wild and all over the place. Well, as I look at you, I would say that he could even be related to you."

"You mean he looks like me? Strange, very strange."

It would not be until the train reached the city of Perm that Darya and Mikhail would risk making their way to carriage 43 and a meeting with Pyotr Dutkewycz. As was the case with every train stop, there was no shortage of NKVD and Red Army guards. Security was tight and those entrained to points farther east knew that escape would not be possible. There was a limited area of movement on the platform of the train station but in the hustle and bustle of repatriates bargaining for a morsel of food it was easier for Darya and Mikhail to make their way to carriage 43.

When Darya singled out Pyotr, she quietly introduced him to Mikhail Baranov. Looking Pyotr over from head to foot, Mikhail had a burning question, *"So, your name is Pyotr? What is your family name?"*

"My family name is Dutkewycz."

"Dutkewycz? Do you mean to tell me that your father's name is Dutkewycz?"

"Nyet, it was not Dutkewycz."

"Not Dutkewycz? What then is your family name?"

"I grew up with my aunt and uncle. My father's name is Alexei Kozlov."

"God Almighty, do you mean that? Your father's name is Alexei Kozlov? What happened to him?"

"My whole family was taken to Siberia when I was a small boy."

"To Siberia? Where are they now?"

"I don't know. When father returned from Siberia in 1938, he found work on a kolkhoz in Zhitomir. I have not seen him since 1942."

"So, you took the name of your aunt's family, did you?"

"Da, my uncle did that. He said that he didn't want the NKVD looking for me and then deporting me to Siberia."

Any kind of a prolonged conversation, always under the watchful eye of the NKVD and fellow deportees, was not without risk. As a result, Mikhail and Pyotr had to wait until such moments that conversation could take place without being overheard by others. *"Pyotr,"* whispered Mikhail, *"this is God's miracle!"*

"God's miracle? Why do you say that?"

"Because my christened name is not Mikhail Baranov, it is really Konstantin Kozlov. And, your birth name is not Pyotr Dutkewycz, it is truly Pyotr Kozlov!"

"Do you mean to say that you are my brother?"

"Tak, tak. When we were deported to Siberia, I worked in a lumber camp, a kolkhoz, and finally the Trans-Siberian Railway before I decided to escape Siberia forever."

"You say that you escaped from Siberia?"

"Nyet. Before I could accomplish the final phase of my escape, the NKVD may have been aware of my deception, arrested me, and transferred me to Novosibirsk where I was forced to join the military."

"So, you served in the Red Army?"

"Tak, but against my will. I participated in a parachute drop for the Russian Air Force near Smolensk in 1942. I was captured by the Nazis and sent to Germany as a prisoner of war."

"Good Lord, how did you survive as a Nazi prisoner of war?"

"The Nazis gave me an option. I could choose the status of a prisoner of war or that of an Ostarbeiter."

"And you chose to work for those butchers?"

"Tak, it was that or the death penalty. The NKVD must see me as a traitor to Mother Russia. They are sending me to Tyumen for some restructuring. What about you, Pyotr? How did you end up in Germany?"

"When I was 17 years of age, the Germans occupied Ukraine. I joined a Ukrainian partisan group in Lutsk. We all wanted a free and independent Ukraine. I was captured by the Germans in 1942. It was either get shot or be sent to a prisoner of war camp in Germany. When I arrived in Hemer, I could either rot in a prisoner of war camp or go to work for the German Wehrmacht."

"What is your destination in Siberia?"

"My destination is a place called Novosibirsk, Siberia. The NKVD believes that I am a traitor and should be punished. My transfer papers say that I will be assigned to a kolkhoz somewhere in the Oblast of Novosibirsk."

What little time they had together, Pyotr told Mikhail about the repatriation of Alexei Kozlov to Horodok in 1938 and their brief time together before Alexei joined a kolkhoz in Zhitomir. *"What about Katusha and Nikolashya, did they not return with father?"* asked Mikhail.

"Nyet, Katusha and Nikolashya did not return to Ukraine. When father left the kolkhoz in Siberia, he was told that our two sisters were re-assigned to another camp. He was repatriated to Ukraine without them. Sadly, that is all I know."

Mikhail, in an attempt to prepare Pyotr for the living and working conditions in the camps in Siberia, cautioned him, *"As you will learn, the working conditions in the camps vary significantly across time and place."*

"Each camp is different?"

"Tak, depending upon, among other things, the impact of broader events such as the war, country-wide famines and food shortages, waves of terror, sudden influx or release of large numbers of prisoners."

"You worked in more than one camp?"

"Tak, no matter where I slaved for those damn Bolsheviks, there were food shortages and food rations, inadequate clothing, over-crowding, poorly insulated housing, poor hygiene, and inadequate health care. We were all compelled to perform harsh physical labour."

"What about the mechanization of labour? Did you not have tractor farms?"

"Tak, tak. But, in most Soviet periods and economic branches of government, the degree of mechanization of work processes was significantly lower than in the civilian industry. Tools were often primitive and machinery, if existent, was short in supply. Work hours were longer and days off were fewer than for civilian workers. All of this hard labour was performed without pay. However, even this varied from camp to camp."

"My dear brother, shall I call you Mikhail or Konstantin?"

"I think it best that we refer to each other as listed on our repatriation papers. To do otherwise could lead to unnecessary problems."

"You say, Mikhail, that you experienced all these terrible things in Siberia?"

"I have suffered through all of these things. But, I have survived through hard work and lots of good luck. I listened and kept my mouth shut. My biggest advantage was working on the railway. I saw with my own eyes what was happening in all of Siberia."

During their conversation Mikhail pointed out that every labour camp in the Gulag was unique and that NKVD officials behaved in a variety of ways. *"In fact,"* continued Mikhail, *"some NKVD officials do have some human characteristics, while others act like savages. In some cases*

I have even known of an NKVD official to undergo a change in his own behaviour."

"Those criminals were capable of change?"

"Tak, they were. Some lost their positions of privilege and became zeks, labourers. In many cases they did not survive long. I have learned that human beings can become different people according to extremes of circumstances or the directives from Stalin," explained Mikhail.

"Do you mean that those deported to Siberia believed in Stalin?"

"Many deportees, over a short period of time while being worked to death, became very strange. Some went so far as to say that should they die in the Gulag, their very death would contribute to the glory of the Mother Land. To them, this was far better than making no contribution at all."

"Were you prepared to die for Stalin?"

"It never occurred to me. But, I remember one member of the Communist Party saying to me in an exasperated manner, after I pressed him on why so many went along with the horrors of the Communist regime, that the trouble with the world today is that people who have never been tested go around making judgments about people who have been tested."

The train whistle signaled the end of the stop in Perm. As Mikhail watched Pyotr hurrying back to his railway car, he was saddened with the realization that he might never see his brother again. The very thought of Pyotr going to a camp in Novosibirsk conjured up images of the prisoners so ragged and lice-ridden that they posed a sanitary danger to the others in the camp—prisoners who deteriorated to the point of losing any resemblance to human beings. Mikhail prayed that things would improve for all those being repatriated to the Soviet Union.

As the train pulled out of the Perm railway station, Mikhail was left with this strange feeling that things were about to change. The question was, in what direction? And, would they change in the same direction for him as for Pyotr. The answers to his questions would soon be found. Unfortunately, not everyone would be happy with the outcome.

Chapter 17

A SIBERIAN ROMANCE

Darya, my love for you is as boundless as the Siberian sky

As the cattle train left Perm, Siberia, Mikhail once again examined his repatriation papers. What information did the SMERSH officials have in their possession when he was repatriated from a German prisoner of war camp to Russia? They would have been aware of his service in the Red Army but were they aware of his work with the Trans-Siberian Railway between 1937 and 1941 under the name of Mikhail Baranov? They would also be aware of his capture by the Wehrmacht in 1942 and his time in a prisoner of war camp in Germany from 1942-1945. However, at this point, it is unlikely that SMERSH would have known that his birth name was Konstantin Kozlov and that he had served time in a lumber camp and a kolkhoz from 1930-1937. Had they known this, his repatriation destination might have been very different.

Had NKVD been responsible for determining the destination for Mikhail, their files might have shown that Mikhail had earlier worked in Tyumen. Were that the case, it is unlikely that Mikhail would have been repatriated to a location in which he had previously served as a railway worker. After all, it was unusual to send any person charged with war crimes to the same camp location from which they had come. On the other hand, it is not unreasonable to assume that the authorities had their hands full processing thousands upon thousands of those being repatriated to the Motherland. They simply did not have the luxury of examining each person's background. In all likelihood, it was sufficient for the authorities to know that Mikhail had railroading experience and that his talent could be utilized in the coming days on the Soviet Union's most important railway system. Whatever the process, no one ever really knew how the selections were made.

Arriving at a railway work camp in Tyumen, Mikhail was informed that the incentive scheme put into place before the war for deportees was still in place. However, the conditions in camps deteriorated towards the end of World War II. Quotas had been increased, rations cut, and medical supplies approached zero. During the war, Mikhail had attained the rank of *mladshiy serzhant* (junior sergeant). As a result, he thought that he might receive preferential treatment from the *General-Mayor* (Major General) in charge of the surveillance and repair of the railway system in the Oblast of Tyumen.

Since Mikhail was a prisoner of war in Germany, it was now necessary for him to serve a two-year sentence of re-orientation and re-education. Had he been drummed out of the Red Army, he would have been able to seek work as a civilian. But, that was not to be. In the eyes of the NKVD, Mikhail was still in the military and his re-education would have to take place within the structure and surveillance of the military. The one blessing was that the Tyumen railway crew did not have in its ranks those who were dedicated criminals. All workers were ordinary kulaks, osadniks, and ukazniks who had been sentenced for violating various state laws.

As soon as Mikhail got settled into the railway work camp in Tyumen, his thoughts turned to Darya Dominova. Unlike so many other detention and work camps, this particular camp was not enclosed by barbed wire and was not under constant guard. Tight security was not necessary because the workers were either members of the Red Army or those who were considered by the NKVD to be of low flight risk. This meant that Mikhail did have some time each weekend to pursue activities other than work related. With thoughts of Darya ever on his mind, he decided to seek permission to visit the local hospital. After all, her parting words were, *"Why don't you look me up at the hospital in Tyumen?"*

Permission to leave the work camp was granted by the Brigadir. Approaching security at the entrance of the hospital, his first question was, *"Does this hospital have a nursing station?"*

"Nursing station? What is your business here? Are you a patient?"

"Nyet, I am not a patient. I served with a nurse on the Eastern Front. Her name is Dominova. Darya Dominova. Do you know the name?"

"Nyet. I know no such name. How would I know the name of any individual in this hospital? My job is security, not entertainment."

"Well then, would it be possible for me to make an enquiry in the hospital's nursing station?"

"Where are your credentials? Your passport?"

Once the security agent was satisfied with Mikhail's identification, he waved him into the hospital. As he proceeded to the nursing station, he noted that the hospital was much larger than he had imagined. *"Excuse me, my name is Baranov. I am looking for a nurse by the name of Dominova. Does she work here?"*

"Da," he was told by a matronly woman, *"Nurse Dominova does work here but she has left for the day."*

"Does she work tomorrow?"

"Da, she does. She starts work at seven in the morning."

"Can I get to see her tomorrow?"

"Is she a member of your family?"

"Nyet, she is not. I first met Darya in 1937 in Kazan."

"In Kazan? Why, just yesterday she talked about a person by the name of Mikhail she met in Kazan and later in Germany. Your name wouldn't be Mikhail, would it?"

"Da, that is my name. I am happy that she remembered my name."

"Why don't you come by tomorrow at seven o'clock in the evening. I'll ask Nurse Dominova to wait for you. This is none of my business, but I think that she really likes you."

Hearing those words of encouragement, Mikhail's heart skipped a beat. The next evening, Darya greeted him warmly, not with the customary handshake but with a warm embrace. Taking a deep breath as he looked her over from head to foot, Mikhail felt that he was the luckiest man in Siberia. *What a contrast,* he thought, *to her appearance on the repatriation train.* Obviously, she had sufficient time to recover from her ordeal in Germany.

"You look beautiful, like a spring flower," stammered Mikhail.

"You look different as well, Mikhail. More relaxed."

"I thought of you countless times in the past eight years. I must confess that my nights were much happier with you in my thoughts and dreams. But, I never dared to think that we would ever see each other again."

"This is all so strange to me. How is it that we both ended up in Tyumen?"

"Da, my repatriation to Tyumen is unusual because my family has lived in this region for many years. It is rare that a prisoner of war in Germany would be repatriated by Soviet authorities to their place of birth."

"Well, perhaps the NKVD was not aware that your roots are right here."

"When SMERSH screened me for my repatriation to Russia, they did not ask me for my place of birth. They asked me my last place of work in Russia. It happened to be Perm. That, perhaps, is why they thought that my professional training would be well suited to a hospital in Tyumen."

"I feel very lucky to be in your company, Darya. I want to learn more about you and your family. I want to get to know your city better."

"Da, I know, Mikhail, we have talked about many things but never about ourselves"

Wanting to get caught up about each other's past, they spent the better part of the evening talking about family, the war, and their time in Germany. Things seemed to go quite well until he heard Darya ask, *"Mikhail, just who are you? Are you really Mikhail Baranov?"*

"That is an interesting question. Tell me, Darya, do you have any information that would lead you to believe that I am not Mikhail Baranov?"

"Nyet, I do not have any information either way. However, you already know that I did work for my Motherland before the war. I did some special work for the NKVD."

"You worked for the NKVD? Did you work for them in 1937, in Kazan?"

"Da, I did. But, I don't want to talk about that tonight, especially not here in the hospital. Why don't we meet in the marketplace on Sunday afternoon, the marketplace in Old Town. Can we do that?"

Before departing that evening, Mikhail and Darya walked along the banks of the Tura River and talked about the contributions that Tyumen made to the war effort where over 20,000 townspeople were sent to the front lines between 1941 and 1945. *"Sadly,"* commented Darya, *"only 12,000 returned safely from the conflict. Our hospital continues to be home to many war heroes who are still recovering from their wounds. Some will never recover from the pain and human destruction. Many have lost the use of their limbs."*

They ended their walk in Central Square, the traditional site for events related to various national celebrations and regional events. At that point Darya, after giving Mikhail's hand a gentle squeeze, assured him that she could find her own way home. With her parting words of, *"I shall see you on Sunday,"* Darya hurried off to catch a bus that would take her home. Watching Darya as she boarded a bus, Mikhail imagined bringing Darya home to his own flat. He had to admit that love was in the air. Back at the railway work camp, Mikhail promised himself that things would soon change.

When Mikhail met Darya at the marketplace on Sunday afternoon, she was accompanied by her brother Anton. After introducing Anton, and upon seeing the worried look in Mikhail's eyes, she explained, *"Don't worry about Anton. He is my brother and my best friend. He can be trusted."* With the introductions and small talk out of the way, Mikhail realized that she knew very little about him. At the same time, he knew nothing of her role with the NKVD.

"Why do you suspect, Darya, that my name is not Mikhail Baranov?"

"The NKVD office in Perm had information about counterfeiters providing fake documentation to our citizens and to foreign workers. You were identified by our NKVD Serzhant as having visited one of the unscrupulous artists involved in such work. From that, the NKVD office assumed that your visit to a fake artist was not without some purpose."

"Are you now under the employ of the NKVD?"

"Nyet, I have never been an NKVD operative. However, when I belonged to the Leninist Young Communist League, I heard stories about this kind of illegal activity. At the moment, my situation is much like yours. Since I was an Ostarbeiter in Germany, I must now spend two years in re-orientation. I am no longer a member of Komsomol."

"Are you saying, Darya, that I can trust you and Anton? That I am free to speak the truth fully without fear that you will report to the NKVD?"

"Da, you have that assurance."

"What about Anton. Can I trust him?"

'Da, you and I can trust him with our lives.'

Even with that, Mikhail could not be sure that Anton was not an agent of the NKVD. To make sure, he asked for his internal passport. Upon examination, Mikhail was satisfied that Anton was not a member of the dreaded NKVD. Still, Mikhail knew that he was now on the horns of a dilemma. Unsure and sometimes suspicious of Darya's role when they first met, he now had his answer. However, this did not make life any easier. If he were to admit that his name was not Mikhail, he would have to consider the possibility of correcting the record. As they went their separate ways, Mikhail promised Darya that he would tell her more about his family and about himself at their next meeting. Since his work on the railway frequently took him away from Tyumen for several days at a time, he would not see Darya until the end of the month.

At the end of the month, Mikhail once again went to the local hospital late Saturday to arrange a date with Darya in the city's main market on Sunday. Relaxing in Central Park near the market, Mikhail decided to tell Darya only as much as he thought she should know about his past.

He told her about his family's deportation to Siberia and about his work in the timber logging operation near Omsk. Although against his better judgment, he concluded with, *"Tak, I did approach a counterfeiter in Kazan to prepare my transfer papers to Moscow. I should not have done that."* But, even as he told her about himself and his attempt to escape the Gulag, it seemed as though she already knew about his background. After some encouragement, she admitted that as a Komsomol member, she also served as a novice agent of the NKVD, tracking and recording the methods by which deportees frequently tried to escape the Gulag.

"Were you aware, Darya, that I had obtained a new internal passport and a new identity?"

"Da, I was aware of it when you were working in Kazan. But, that was not unusual since the NKVD was informed in the first instance by the counterfeiter."

"The NKVD was informed by the counterfeiter? You mean Parsimov was a fake?"

"Da, it was not unusual for the counterfeiter to be paid twice, once by the victim for their services, and a second time by reporting it to the NKVD. This was particularly true where a prisoner or deportee was not able to pay the counterfeiter for his services."

"Was that the situation with me? Did the counterfeiter turn me in?"

"Nyet, the counterfeiter did not have to turn you in. The NKVD officer was aware of the situation. The officer tracked your movement from Omsk all the way to Kazan. In the end, it was Stalin's re-armament plan and your work ethic that saved you."

Learning the truth about what took place in 1938 during the period of time that he attempted to escape the Gulag made life easier for Mikhail. The next day, he approached Leytenant Podgorny who was in charge of the railway repair camp telling him about his fake passport. To his relief, Podgorny seemed not to be surprised to learn that he had approached a counterfeiter with a request to obtain fake transfer papers. As for the internal passport with a new identification obtained in Omsk, Podgorny admitted that he was also aware of these types of subterfuges. In response to Mikhail's story, the Leytenant posed an important question, *"Would you like to take your case to the NKVD and have the record corrected?"*

"Is this possible? Do you think that I can do this without incurring additional re-orientation time somewhere deeper in Siberia?"

"Nothing is certain. Do you want to continue to live under an assumed name? Would you not like to search for your family? Return to Ukraine after your sentence is over?"

After several sleepless nights, Mikhail made up his mind. *"Leytenant Podgorny, I have made a decision to make a confession to the Soviet authorities."*

"So, you want to confess that your name is not Mikhail Baranov?"

"Da, I want to tell the NKVD authorities about my attempt to escape from the Gulag. That before the outbreak of the war, I made a foolish decision to change my name to facilitate my escape."

Making the decision to come clean on the issue of change of name was the easy part. However, the process used to correct the record took much more effort than Mikhail anticipated. It took a considerable amount of work to uncover the methods used by the counterfeiter ring to accomplish their illegal deeds. In his search for answers, Mikhail discovered that there was no such person as Parsimov. He, too, had been using a fictitious name. Although most of the Brigadirs in charge of local railroad work crews were honest, several of them were also duped by counterfeiters whose only motivation was the opportunity to make a few rubles as a result of an illegal activity.

At his hearing, Mikhail provided the NKVD Troika with the formula given to him by Parsimov to identify his contacts in Tyumen, Sverdlovsk, Kirov, Kazan, and Moscow. He reasoned that if he did not provide this information, his chances of getting the authorities to change his name back to Kozlov might be doomed.

Three hours after the hearing was over, the NKVD Troika called Mikhail into their chamber. *"Baranov, the NKVD has a decision on your appeal. You did attempt to escape from Siberia in 1938 by changing your name from Kozlov to Baranov. That illegal activity was not unusual. Your file also shows that you served the Motherland in the Battle for Moscow before being captured by the Nazis."*

"The NKVD is aware of this?"

"Da, it is a part of your file. Had you not served for the Red Army, your situation today might be very different. Correcting your name back to Kozlov can be accomplished."

"This can be done without additional re-education time?"

"Da, the NKVD is not looking for additional punishment. Your past misdeeds will be a part of your re-education program."

Mikhail was relieved that his confession was over. *Can you believe it,* he thought, *that no additional time was added to my re-education sentence? Actually, these Communist assholes are not as stupid as I thought. This Troika is really quite smart!*

Not only did Mikhail decide to continue with his re-education program as a railway worker, but he also made another decision. He got permission from Podgorny to enrol in an evening class in railway economics, a program made available to railway workers. Meanwhile, Darya Dominova consumed most of his thoughts.

As a railroader, Mikhail had a lot of information about the movement of POWs and Soviet citizens being repatriated or re-habilitated. Not all returning POWs and Soviet citizens were treated with the same level of regard. Those who had any complicity with the Nazis, nationalistic movements of any satellite Soviet country, criminal record, or contributing in any way to social or political unrest were kept under guard. Most were headed for the Irkutsk region of Siberia.

Thinking about his own time in Siberia, Mikhail could see why the NKVD would consider him to be a reliable prisoner. The knowledge that he tried to escape the Gulag was not unusual. A part of the blame could be placed squarely on the shoulders of an unscrupulous and enterprising counterfeiter. The NKVD was well aware of this, and worked hard to prosecute not only those taking on a new identity but especially the dishonest counterfeiters, many of whom suddenly found themselves a victim of the Soviet prison system rather than profiting from their misdeeds.

Even as he considered various plans to search out his brother, Mikhail was soon made aware that any movement from one oblast to another was forbidden. In turn, this meant that any request to serve any portion of his two-year re-habilitation period in another oblast would not be possible, especially at a time when his very identity and citizenship were in question. Mikhail knew, however, that he had at his disposal another way to set out in search of his brother Pyotr and that was through his contacts within the Trans-Siberian Railway System.

As the summer days of 1946 turned to the colours of fall, Mikhail sent word to the railway work camp in Novosibirsk.

> "Railway Work Camp, Novosibirsk, Brigadir: Would you please undertake a search for my brother, Pyotr Dutkewycz? He may be working for the Trans-Siberian Railway in your region. If you are successful, please contact me at the railway work station in Tyumen. Signed, Baranov, Mikhail."

If Mikhail thought that an answer would be forthcoming in short order, he would have been greatly disappointed. It would not be until the following summer that he would get word as to the location of Pyotr's rehabilitation process. In the midst of all of the difficulties in tracing his brother's location, there was some welcome news. By the fall of 1946, Mikhail was successful in correcting his identify and once again embraced his birthright. Beside himself with joy, he immediately left the NKVD office with a new passport in hand to see Darya at the hospital. Sunday could not come too soon for another meeting with Darya in Central Park.

Walking along the banks of the Tura River while holding Darya's hand, he told her about his meetings with the local offices of the NKVD. At the end of his confession, he announced, *"Darya, from now on, I want you to call me by my christened name. From now on, I shall be known as Konstantin Aleksandrovych Kozlov."*

"Konstantin Kozlov? Konstantin? Why, I simply love that name!"

"Are you being truthful? You're not mad at me?"

"Mad at you? Nyet, I am relieved."

"Darya, there is one other thing I want to tell you. My love for you is greater than the expanse of Siberia. Will you marry me?"

Darya did not respond for the longest time. At first, Konstantin thought that she had not heard his proposal. Then, as big tears of joy welled up in her eyes, she suddenly threw her arms around Konstantin, exclaiming, *"My grand Ukrainian Cossack, do you really mean that? Are you saying that you want to marry this little Russian girl?"*

"Da, that embrace you gave me the first time we met has captured my heart. I am completely without power."

"Do you know that I have had a very special place in my heart since I first met you in Kazan? That I prayed that God would bring us together?"

"You did? Maybe I was not dreaming after all!"

"Dreams sometimes do come true, you know."

"Will you accept my proposal?"

"Konstantin, no matter what I say today, it is a Russian custom to get permission of one's parents before a girl can accept a proposal for marriage. I will first have to ask my mother."

"What about your father? Do I not need your father's permission as well?"

"Nyet, my father is no longer with us. Will you join us next Sunday so that you can meet my mother? She will want to know about your future plans for us in Tyumen."

As they parted that evening, Konstantin had a lot to think about, especially Darya's words, *"My mother will want to know about your future plans for us in Tyumen."* Even though Leytenant Podgorny helped him get his name back, there was no guarantee that Darya's mother would consent to the marriage.

During the next week, Konstantin explained the change of name to railway officials. Even in doing so, he could not quite figure out why Podgorny would want to help him. Was there a change in the policy of the NKVD? Was his work important enough to deserve special treatment? *I wonder,* he thought, *did Darya have anything to do with the NKVD giving me preferred treatment?* Consideration of his circumstance was obviously at variance with that meted out to other POWs and Soviet citizens being repatriated. And, speaking of repatriation, since the authorities now knew that he was an offspring of a kulak deported to the Gulag and not a Russian-born citizen, how could his love affair with Darya ever see the light of day?

His mind turned to the warmth of love as he hugged the bouquet of flowers he was about to present to Darya's mother. As he wound his way up the well-worn steps to the 4th floor of a typical 4-storey Soviet-style apartment, he could feel that the life of a typical Russian was very different than was his own life. Since leaving Ukraine in 1930, he realized that a good portion of his life had transpired. The realization of what he had missed during the best years of his life overwhelmed him.

Arriving in the flat of the Dominova family, he was suddenly witness to a typical Russian scene: a home headed up by a mother whose husband, a career Red Army officer, had long ago disappeared from the scene, now living with her children. Perhaps the modest flat reflected the difficulty in finding separate accommodation for the offspring. They take care of their children and, in many cases, their grandchildren, knowing that homes in a city are very expensive and must be shared with family members.

Recovering from the travails of war, Valentina Dominova struck Konstantin as being no different than was his own mother. Working part-time in a local museum, Valentina, with the help of her two children, was able to provide for the daily needs of the family and the education for Darya and Anton. To augment the family's income, the family had a small garden plot in a dacha outside the city. Whenever possible, they sold excess garden produce at the metro station.

Konstantin immediately took a liking to Darya's mother, telling her, *"Panyi Dominova, you remind me of my mother. As a little boy living in Ukraine, our family had a large garden. Unlike people living in Tyumen, many of whom have a garden in their country dacha, our garden was next to the family home."*

"Da, we do have a modest vegetable garden on the outskirts of the city. This year we took in some cucumbers, parsley, berries, potatoes, and tomatoes. We jarred mushrooms and jams. Sometimes, I go to the Trans-Siberian Railway stop to sell home-baked cakes to travelers."

"Home-baked cakes? What kind of cakes?"

"Home-baked cakes filled with potatoes or cabbage and special sweet waffles. At other times, we sell bags of tomatoes or boiled potatoes."

Having worked on Russia's railway systems for some time, Konstantin was well aware of *babushkas* selling boiled potatoes, smoked or salted Baikal fish—dishes that are especially tasty to hungry and weary travelers. It was also not unusual to find old men, the *dedushkas*, playing their accordions and the *babushkas* singing and dancing their traditional Russian songs in parks near the major stops on the Trans-Siberian Railway System.

The cuisine at the Dominova home was far different and much tastier than Konstantin had experienced in a very long time. Some say that the way to a man's heart is through his stomach. If this was the intent of Darya, Konstantin was quickly became a willing victim.

To his surprise, Valentina seemed not to be shy about raising an important question, *"So, Konstantin, my daughter tells me that you asked for her hand in marriage. Is that true?"*

"Da, that is true. Perhaps Darya told you that I first met her in Kazan. Since that first meeting, I have not been able to put her out of my mind. It's as if there was divine intervention in my meeting her. Your daughter is very special." But, even as he made reference to divine intervention, he wished that he had not made the remark. It occurred to him that the Dominova family might not be of any religious persuasion. Maybe the family, having embraced Bolshevism, did not believe in a Higher Power.

"Can you fall in love and get married during your period of re-education? How do you intend to provide for her? Where do you intend to live?"

"I have thought long and hard about these questions. My period of re-education is nearly over and I get paid for the work I do. I love Darya and I seek your approval for the marriage."

"In that case, you shall have to first discuss the matter with Darya. She is my life, a very sensible young woman. I will have an answer for you once my daughter considers your proposal in light of your answers to my questions."

As Konstantin embraced Darya before departing, he had to admit that he had not thought carefully about his proposal. Darya's words reverberated in his head as he fumbled his way back to the railway camp, *"My mother's heart would be broken if I did not take up residence in Tyumen. So, to win my heart you must make a commitment to stay in Tyumen after your rehabilitation period is over."*

Even as he considered other alternatives, he already knew what his decision would be.

PART 5

REPATRIATION TO UKRAINE

Chapter 18

VICTIM OR TRAITOR?

From POW in Germany to a war criminal in Russia

A s the train wound its way from Perm to Novosibirsk, Pyotr Dutkewycz reflected about the time he spent in Germany, not really as a prisoner of war but as an Ostarbeiter, an eastern worker slaving for the enemy. Although on the same cattle train but in different carriages, Pyotr was certain that his brother, Mikhail Baranov, had a similar aversion to going to Siberia. He could not get out of his mind that his journey to the Gulag was Stalin's plan to re-orient and re-educate anyone who might have come into contact with western ideas or expressed any sympathy, in thought or deed, to any nation other than the Soviet Union. There was no question in Pyotr's mind that this trip was alarmingly similar to that taken by his parents some fifteen years earlier. In the midst of a daydream, he was roused by a question from another repatriate, *"Tovarisch, what is upsetting you?"*

Pyotr thought long and hard before answering. After all, the very fact that the stranger addressed him as *tovarisch* spoke volumes, making him feel uneasy. It is a word that was frequently used by Bolsheviks and Communists as an indication of recognition and acceptance that the person receiving the address was a comrade in arms, a fellow Bolshevik. Pyotr would have preferred that the stranger had addressed him with the more familiar *patsani*, a greeting of familiarity used by boys, or even the word *rebyata*, used not only to refer to one's buddies but also used commonly by those in opposition to the Bolsheviks.

"Upsetting me? It is about my family. My brother."

"Your family? Your brother? Where are they?"

"My brother's destination is the oblast of Tyumen. But, the real problem is with my family, my father and my two sisters."

Having spoken briefly to the stranger, Pyotr retreated into silence once again. Yet, not all of his time was spent thinking about the past and what might have been. Hunger was a constant companion on the journey and conversation with perfect strangers who were all in the same boat seemed always to turn to one's basic needs. Through these discussions, one was able to make a connection with various individuals from Soviet Satellite countries being repatriated to Mother Russia. Each was now on a journey of forced rehabilitation.

Despite their sentences, many continued to be a celebratory mood. To them, winning the war and bringing the Nazis to their knees was the most important event in their lives, especially so since many on the repatriation train had a hand in that victory. It was not a time to belittle in any way the great achievement of the Soviet Union during those terrifying, difficult, and unforgettable years. Above all else, even those who harboured nothing but disdain for Stalin and his wayward policies embraced the memories of all the fallen soldiers and civilians.

As was the case with every transport train, not all of those being earmarked for rehabilitation ended up in the same camp. By the time the train arrived in Novosibirsk, nearly half of the railway cars had been dropped off at earlier camps. Only ten cars were uncoupled at the railway siding at the outskirts of Novosibirsk. The remainder of the carriages continued on their journey to the outer reaches of Siberia.

To no one's surprise, the three camps in Novosibirsk appeared to be packed to the limit and, as a result, after only three days in a Novosibirsk camp, Pyotr got word from the Camp Commandant that he was being immediately transferred to another camp.

Those being transferred to a work camp beyond Novosibirsk were briefly addressed by the Commandant, *"The record shows that in each of your cases the sentences for anti-Soviet activity is five years. Since your re-education sentences are longer than two years, you are being transferred to Karaganda, Kazakhstan. These are the instructions from the regional office of the NKVD."*

That was all there was to it. No time for questions and no answers would have been forthcoming anyway. Each name on the list of transferees was read out by the Commandant, at the end of which the group was marched to another railway siding under heavy guard. At least each now knew that their destination was a work camp in Kazakhstan.

Traversing some of most barren land that Pyotr had ever witnessed, the train finally arrived in the Central Asian steppe and the village of Spassk, just south of the city of Karaganda. It would be here that Pyotr would enter Stalin's notorious system of forced labour concentration camps and internal exile, a multi-national victim of World War II. What he had escaped when his family was taken in 1930 was now his to experience.

During the war, the camp had operated as a POW camp, while between the 1930s to the end of the war, Spassk had been operated as a division of the Gulag forced labour camp known as Karlag. Initially, the camp was developed as a part of a vast agricultural enterprise, but recently changed to a special camp (Steplag). In addition to agriculture, the camp was quickly becoming famous for the extraction of copper from local mineral deposits.

Pyotr was assigned to work in an open quarry where the steppes of Kazakhstan stretched for miles and miles. The very nature of the topography turned out to be a breeding ground for fiercely cold winds and extreme winter temperatures. As he worked to remove the muck from frozen stone with a pick axe and shovel during the winter months, even his thick winter coat and several layers of clothing could not quell the piercing wind. That first winter in Spassk seemed to go on forever and any thought of escape seemed impossible in an area without trees or hills to hide you. Several prisoners who tried to escape were soon re-captured and brought back to the work camp and assigned a longer sentence. Those prisoners of the camp who risked escape and were not re-captured likely became victims of the Gulag.

If nothing else, Pyotr learned very early during his detention in Spassk just how important it was to say as little as possible at the best of times. Upon meeting a young couple and out of earshot of others, curiosity got the best of him, *"Tell me, why are you a prisoner of the Soviets?"*

"Prisoner? Nyet, we are not prisoners. We are here to receive a re-education."

"A re-education? Why?"

"Well, it is no secret that my husband is an ethnic German from Ukraine."

"And you? What about you?"

"I am from Kharkiv, Ukraine. My only crime is that my husband's mother had a sewing machine."

"Well, is there something wrong with that? What about that sewing machine?"

"I made the mistake of telling my neighbour that my mother's sewing machine, made in Russia, was not as good as the sewing machine of my husband's mother."

"Your mother-in-law's sewing machine was made in Germany and your mother's machine was made in the Soviet Union? And, that is why you were sent to Siberia, for making a comparison?"

"Da, for that unpatriotic sentiment I was sentenced to five years of corrective education. I was told that saying that a Soviet sewing machine is inferior to a German sewing machine is treasonable." As Pyotr began his re-education sentence in Kazakhstan, he would never forget that conversation.

Karlag was established at the beginning of the 1930s, during Stalin's so-called *Great Break.* The Gulag emerged as the major institution in the Soviet Union's drive to collectivize agriculture, to industrialize a largely agrarian country, and to transform an entire people's culture in the hopes of catching up with the West. By 1928, Stalin had accepted that the West was more advanced and was profoundly hostile to the construction of socialism in the Soviet Union.

During his first year in Karlag, Pyotr was witness to the staggering loss of life. Death played no favourites. Prisoners died as a result of food shortages, malnutrition, disease, and brutal hard labour. Much like Mikhail before him, Pyotr learned that the Gulag was, in fact, a place of mass death as evidenced by the number of deaths that first winter. Of those who survived the first winter, the NKVD statistics point out that, as a result of Stalin's evolving policies, about 40 percent were released during the fall of 1946. The number of inmates released from imprisonment in the Gulag camps between 1945 and Stalin's death in 1953 ranged from 115,000 to 500,000. The reason for this significant range in statistics has more to do with the absence of definitive reporting procedures than with accuracy. Surprisingly, many prisoners released from work camps elected to stay in Siberia as free workers or returned to Siberia of their own volition after being rejected in their own communities back home. This made the task of determining who was or was not repatriated all the more difficult.

Spassk, consisting of a series of labour camps in the flatlands and hills near Karaganda, housed as many as 60,000 inmates at any given time in its agriculture and mining operations. It is here that the Soviet Union had the facilities and the will to exterminate any number of prisoners who came through its meagre facilities. Yet, the Soviets did not conceive of their concentration camps as instruments of genocide. The most salient feature of the Gulag was an apparent paradox: forced labour, high death rates, and an oppressive atmosphere of violence, cold, and constant hunger, all of which coexisted with camp newspapers and cultural activities. Prisoners were constantly confronted with a barrage of propaganda, re-education in the ideals of communism, and a steady release of a significant portion of the prisoner population.

Pyotr had to accept that his only chance of survival was to re-make himself into a fit Soviet citizen. Through this process, the Bolsheviks were of the opinion that the radical project would lead to a utopian socialist society. Those identified by the NKVD as implacable enemies were executed outright. Others were kept alive in the Gulag by virtue of their capacity to contribute their labour to the cause of socialism. The Bolsheviks could not escape their fundamental belief in the malleability of the human soul and that labour was the key to re-forging criminals as well as those with anti-Soviet leanings. The very harshness of the Gulag was seen as essential to break down a prisoner's resistance in order to rebuild him or her into a proper Soviet citizen. If a prisoner refused correction, the brutality of the Gulag would lead to an inevitable death. After all, the Bolsheviks were no humanitarians. If mistakes were made, they accepted that it was better to kill too many than too few.

The key feature of the Spassk labour camp system was reflected in myriad practices that affected a prisoner's daily life and ultimately determined a prisoner's capacity for surviving the camp. Gulag practices were designed around a categorization matrix based on who a prisoner was upon arrival in the camp and who he had become while in the camp. These categories placed prisoners into a hierarchy according to their perceived level of danger, redemption, and re-education. Complex hierarchies of living and working conditions, differentiation of food rations, and practices of early release tied survival directly to one's place in the hierarchy. Spassk, like all other Gulag camps, served as a crossroads, constantly redefining the line between those who could be reclaimed for Soviet society and those who were destined to die.

The Karaganda region is described by Russians as being an isolated region in a vast area of an uninhabited steppe. Many like to poke a bit of fun about its location by saying that it is *in the middle of nowhere*. During Stalin's reign, the region was certainly ripe for development, especially its natural resources such as coal. The region's natural resources, while known in the Tsarist era, remained underdeveloped until the 1930s. The development of the Karaganda region's natural resources proceeded hand in hand with the growth of Karaganda's Gulag. The history of corrective labour camps in the Karaganda region begins with the arrival of a handful of Chekists and their prisoners in 1930. Karlag, headquartered in the village of Dolinka, was the center of the Gulag system in Kazakhstan, a network of notorious camps which would become one of the largest and longest-lasting camps in Stalin's Gulag system.

Karlag was primarily an agricultural camp established to transform the semi-desert of the steppe into a productive agricultural base for the provision of livestock and crops to the region's growing population engaged in the extraction of natural resources. Russian historians look upon Karaganda as being an offspring of the October Revolution of 1917. They point out that Stalin dispatched Communists, Komsomols, miners, and builders to Karaganda. However, Karaganda can be characterized more accurately as being an offspring of the Gulag.

After having served in the quarry and a coal mine for the first two years of his rehabilitation sentence, Pyotr was assigned to a kolkhoz where the agricultural task was no less daunting. It became the aim of the Communists to develop this semi-desert into an agricultural giant that would exceed many European countries in area. Despite many misgivings on the part of skeptics, opportunists, and pessimists, many were caught up in the atmosphere of revolutionary times of socialist construction. Many embraced the belief that there were no fortresses that the Bolsheviks could not storm.

Karlag's prisoners faced harsh living conditions, particularly because the region was sparsely populated and lacked building materials. Since the construction of living space lagged behind the expansion of the prisoner population throughout its history, many prisoners lived in tents, mud huts, and even under the open sky. There was no such thing as inmates coming to Karlag and finding ready accommodation. In all but a few cases, the inmates built their own camps.

With the extreme living conditions during his first four years in Karaganda, Pyotr felt lucky just to survive. But, he had to admit that Karlag had somehow established the basis of mechanized agriculture in the steppe. The Soviets brought combines, tractors, and automobiles to what they thought of as an empty steppe. Prisoners built massive irrigation works and dammed up regional rivers. NKVD authorities frequently bragged about Karlag's success.

Approaching his fifth year in Karlag, twenty-eight year old Pyotr listened to the Commandant as he addressed the inmates with yet another pep talk, *"Every ravine, every gully, every stream presented itself as a kind of fortress that was stormed in battle by the hero-organizers of Karlag agriculture. Yesterday's wreckers, bandits, thieves, and prostitutes gathered from the various ends of the Soviet country under the able and experienced Communist leadership accomplished great things. Burning with the flame of constructive enthusiasm, valuing highly and proud of that faith placed in them, the former lawbreakers stormed the semi-deserts of Kazakhstan."*

This kind of pep talk to the prisoners of the camp was not unusual. Although it was, in part, a great exaggeration and self-promotion, it actually did contain the tenor of the age. The camp's practices were not simply about its economic role to introduce a huge territory into the stock of socialist agriculture but also to return tens of thousands of former lawbreakers, re-forged in the hearth of collective labour into the ranks of the genuine shock workers of socialist construction.

Pyotr, now no more than a shell of his former self, had to admit that Karlag was quickly becoming an integral part of the approach to the reclamation of the semi-desert. In those criminals who survived the first year of hard labour, Pyotr saw evidence of a re-forging into honest Soviet citizens. Agriculture on local kolkhozes in the vast desert-steppe of Central Kazakhstan was taking hold. Products from the kolhozes were used to support the emerging industrial centers of the region where prisoners were being re-educated. Unfortunately, as the Karlag authorities attempted to complete the often competing penal and economic tasks set before it, a great many of those being rehabilitated would die. Yet, these deaths, too, were seen as an integral part of its work. Those who failed at their own rehabilitation reached the end of the line in an unmarked grave.

By the summer of 1950, Pyotr believed that he had completed his sentence of five years in the Gulag, two years in a labour camp followed by three years on a kolkhoz. However, the NKVD office told him that they needed more time to review his particular case. The NKVD wanted to make sure that he had truly embraced the principles of communism. Only then would Pyotr be ready for re-entry into the communist state. According to the camp Commandant, the NKVD needed time to examine the extent of Pyotr's participation in the Ukrainian Insurgent Army during the war.

"Commandant," was Pyotr's question, *"haven't I completed my sentence of five years?"*

"Have you completed your sentence? What kind of a dummy are you? Don't you know what Article 58 of the Russian Penal Code says? Are you not aware that the Ukrainian Insurgent Army was a group of nationalist partisans, that your participation in the Ukrainian Insurgent Army could carry a death penalty?"

"Da, I know that, but I took up arms against the Nazis not the Red Army."

"Don't lie, you scoundrel. Why don't you confess that you participated in guerrilla warfare against the Soviet Army?"

"That is not possible. How could I take up arms against the Red Army in 1942? Ukraine was occupied by the Nazis. I took up arms against the German Wehrmacht."

"That is another lie. When you were captured by the Nazis, you would have been eliminated had they known that you were taking up arms against them."

"How would they know that, as a teenager, I was taking up arms against anybody? At any rate, the Nazis knew that many in Ukraine wanted a free and independent state."

"We'll see. We execute all traitors, you know that, don't you?" was the curt reply from the Commandant.

The NKVD was well aware that the goal of UPA, the military wing of the OUN, the Organization of Ukrainian Nationalists, was to create an independent and self-governing Ukrainian state. To the NKVD, it was one thing if Pyotr acted against the Nazis; however, it was quite another if the record showed that he acted against the Soviet Army. Even at this stage in the re-orientation process, it was not unusual for a deportee to be executed.

In his request to the NKVD to be repatriated to Ukraine, Pyotr pleaded his case by saying that he was captured by the Nazis in 1943 and given the option of military service with the Nazis after being transferred to Germany to work as an Ostarbeiter. The alternative was a transfer to a POW camp where his fate might well have been sealed.

The NKVD Troika hearing his case seemed quite sympathetic to his claim that as a young worker in a Ukrainian kolkhoz he was forced to join the insurgent army. *"Our anti-German actions,"* explained Pyotr, *"were limited to situations where the Germans attacked the Ukrainian population. The UPA units fought against German administrative agencies, the German police, and the Sondercommandos. It was the aim of UPA to establish an independent Ukraine controlled neither by Moscow nor by Germany."*

As Pyotr went about his duties in the kolkhoz, he anxiously awaited the decision of the NKVD authorities. However, a letter from his brother suddenly brought a ray of hope to his life.

My dear Pyotr, I have known for some time that you were serving your sentence in Karaganda. I am now married and we have a son named Eduard Konstantinovych Kozlov. When you have served your time in rehabilitation, I invite you to visit us. You can get my address from an agent at the main train station in Tyumen. Your brother, Konstantin.

As Pyotr absorbed the contents of the letter, it occurred to him that his brother must have known something he did not know. If so, what was the source of his information?

All too soon, Pyotr would get the good news and the bad news. There would be no shortage of either.

Chapter 19

REPATRIATION TO UKRAINE

You are now a worthy Soviet citizen

A ll kinds of negative thoughts entered Pyotr's head as he considered the official communiqué from the NKVD headquarters in Dolinka, hand delivered to him by a security guard, *"Pyotr Dutkewycz, you are ordered to appear before a Committee of the People's Commissariat for Internal Affairs at 1400 hours on August 12, 1950."*

Having served a sentence of five years pursuant to *Article 58* of the *Penal Code*, Pyotr felt that he was now fully re-educated into the image of a Soviet citizen and was ready for repatriation to Ukraine. But, he was not the only repatriate scheduled to appear before the committee on that fateful day. The NKVD official ordered the driver to pick up eleven other labourers from the kolkhoz for their interviews.

En route, Pyotr thought about what he had heard from others who had been rejected for release and the likely questions that could nullify his release from bondage. Most of all, he feared that the officials would question him about his involvement with the Ukrainian Insurgent Army and once again accuse him of taking a position against the Red Army. He felt that if he were unsuccessful in convincing the NKVD that his involvement was limited to anti-Nazi activity, his banishment to the Gulag could well be extended for another period of time. Anger quickly overcame his fear as he loudly voiced his opinion to no one in particular, *"How many damn times do I have to prove that I am innocent of these charges."* His outburst startled those around him. No one had a response to his question.

Map of Ukraine showing its borders after World War II.

Upon arrival at the NKVD headquarters, Pyotr was surprised to discover that each of the deportees about to be interviewed was searched by a guard before proceeding to the admission room. In the admission room, it seemed that those waiting to be interviewed were on the brink of a nervous breakdown. Two Red Army officers doing the scheduling were standing behind a counter and an additional armed guard was inside the door of the room. One inmate about to be interviewed looked too comfortable to the guards when they noticed that he had crossed his legs and rested his head in the palm of his hand. A guard pointed to his position on the bench saying, *"Straighten up, you piece of shit."* If nothing else, all of the other inmates immediately took most respectful positions.

When it came Pyotr's turn for the interview, he was a nervous wreck. He could tell by the three stars on the shoulder strap of the officer about to lead the interrogation that he held the rank of a Polkovnik (Colonel). Instead of what he believed would be an exit interview, the questions raised by the NKVD officer were, at first, the normal ones of *name, place of birth, marital status, family members, and the work in Karaganda.* However, the tension reached its peak when the Polkovnik made reference to a section of the Penal Code having to do with anti-Soviet agitation and his time with the Ukrainian Insurgent Army. This precipitated a question, *"Did you, Dutkewycz, join a Ukrainian Insurgent group?"*

"Da, I did. But, that was only to take up arms against the Nazis."

"Just answer the question. Did you at any time express a desire for Ukraine to gain its independence?"

"Da, I did. When I joined the partisan group in Zhitomir, I was only 17 years of age. I did not have any political opinions about Ukraine. All I knew was that I wanted to help my friends take up arms against the Germans who were occupying Ukrainian lands."

Instead, what should have been a three-minute exit interview turned out to be a far more intensive interrogation. Finally, the questions turned to his time on the kolkhoz, *"So, Dutkewycz, what have you learned since coming to Karaganda?"*

"What have I learned, Polkovnik? I have learned a lot about the Soviet way of life."

"Do you now understand the advantages of the collective farm? Do you or do you not agree that the kolkhoz is far more efficient than are the small plots of land operated by those money-grubbing kulaks?"

"Da, Polkovnik, I have learned my lessons well. I have learned about the advantages of pooling the labour of many. I have also learned how to operate those big efficient tractors and threshing combines."

As the NKVD official examined his work record over the previous five years in Karaganda, had an uneasy feeling that the decision of the Polkovnik could go either way, particularly in light of rumours that there could be a labour shortage in the Karlag. *"My office will have a decision to you by tomorrow noon. You will either be released if, in the view of our officials, you have fulfilled the terms of your sentence and accepted the principles of communism. If not, your sentence will be extended so that you might continue with your education before being eligible for repatriation."*

Leaving the NKVD office, Pyotr kept his thoughts to himself. *Those stupid communist murderers, they know that I have fulfilled the terms of my re-education. I've worked like a slave for them, starting as a common labourer to that of a tractor operator without ever complaining about their dumb collectivization policies. I even told them what they wanted to hear about their kolkhoz and the soviet system. I'd like to ship a few of those evil bastards to a labour camp in Vorkuta, to give them back some of their own medicine. I don't need any more of their stupid lessons in torture. Their whole system is no more than a slave-labour prison system.*

As events unfolded, it was a good thing that Pyotr kept his thoughts to himself. Soon, it became common knowledge that some of the labourers were interviewed by the Polkovnik while others were being interviewed by an NKVD Troika. In an increasing number of cases, the Troika rejected a labourer who was eligible for repatriation. *Why were they being rejected for repatriation* was the over-riding thought in Pyotr's mind when he received word that the Polkovnik wanted to meet him the following Monday. *"The commanding officer will have a decision for you at that time,"* was the noncommittal comment from the official.

On the one hand, Pyotr was aware that Stalin continued to release a percentage of the prisoners from local labour camps each month because they had fulfilled the terms of their re-education. On the other hand, rumours persisted that there were looming labour shortages. Suddenly, more and more prisoners were being refused repatriation to their homeland. Even with the refusals, rumour had it that the number of labourers being held back was not sufficient to meet the Gulag's labour needs. With the labour shortages, Stalin instructed the NKVD to declare that an increasing number of prisoners as not being fully re-habilitated. They would be held back to meet the Gulag's ever-increasing labour needs. All of this worried Pyotr.

It was common knowledge in Karaganda that those prisoners charged with carrying out espionage, diversionary activities, or terrorist plots against the Soviet Union were condemned to death and the sentences promptly carried out. At the same time, the authorities were not above announcing these executions to other prisoners to put the fear of God in them. By this time, some of the facts about the brutality were beginning to come to light. Many prisoners ended up in Karaganda as a result of transfers from *Operation Keelhaul* camps in Germany. Other prisoners came under the purview of *Operation Eastward* and were entrained to other work camps in Western Siberia. Even the knowledge that many of them were being sent to their deaths elicited little, if any, sympathy from NKVD officials.

As Pyotr awaited the decision of the NKVD, he reflected once again upon the rumour that the Gulag was running short of workers. This thought made him very nervous. *Could it be that those criminals will detain me for additional re-education? Will I become an Ostarbeiter right here in Kazakhstan?* His unsettling thoughts were suddenly interrupted when the guard announced, *"Polkovnik Voznik is ready to see you."* Upon entering the NKVD office, Polkovnik Voznik motioned Pyotr to a chair.

"The NKVD Troika has its decision. I have here important documentation for you."

"What is the decision of the Troika? Will I be free to leave the Karlag Kolkhoz?"

"Da, you have served your sentence and the NKVD believes that you have been rehabilitated. However, the Karlag Kolkhoz has a need for your expertise. You are being invited to stay. I am told by the Brigadir that you are a good tractor operator. He wants you to stay as a member of the kolkhoz with full pay. Will you stay?"

"This invitation is a surprise for me. I will need a few days to think about it."

"Let me know within one week. I strongly urge you to become a free worker right here. If you decide to return to Ukraine, I will have an envelope waiting for you with your train billet and sufficient funds for your return."

With time on his hands to think about the NKVD's proposal, Pyotr set out to find out if the rumours about labour shortages were true. From various sources he was able to confirm that a large number of prisoners were being released and repatriated to their home towns, creating a labour shortage throughout Kazakhstan. To make matters worse, the NKVD realized that the number of POWs being repatriated to Siberia from Germany and Poland after the war had fallen far short of expectations. Many of those being repatriated as civilians were convicted of complicity in the Soviet war effort and immediately sent to labour camps. This further depleted the number of workers available to agricultural kolkhozes.

It was now obvious that his release from bondage was not taken at the local level but as a result of a review by the Main Administration for Affairs of Prisoners of War and Internees, a department of the NKVD in charge of the handling of foreign civilian internees and POWs in the Soviet Union during and in the aftermath of World War II. Many of those sent to the Gulag for purposes of rehabilitation were invited to remain in the Gulag. In addition, the kolkhozes and work camps became a major source of recruitment of future communist activists for communist states such as the German Democratic Republic (East Germany), the People's Republic of Poland, and Soviet Ukraine. In fact, this recruitment activity was not limited to seeking out candidates for committees dealing with the ideological re-forging of labourers, but also to the indoctrination of teenagers in young people's clubs.

Having made his decision to leave the Gulag behind, Pyotr approached the NKVD officials in Karaganda. Looking at Polkovnik Voznik, it could not escape Pyotr that the famous blue cap worn by the officials reflected the ultimate in control. It was a cap that would ever remain in his mind as a symbol of the evil within the Bolshevik Empire. Putting his thoughts aside, he addressed the Polkovnik, *"I want to thank the NKVD authorities for inviting me to stay, but I am duty bound to return to my family."*

"Return to your family? Where is your family?"

"That is the question. I do believe that I have one brother in Tyumen who works on the Trans-Siberian Railway. As to the other members of my family, I do not know."

"What is the name of your home village?"

"It is Horodok. But, I do not know if it still exists."

"Well, Dutkewycz, you are free to travel anywhere in the Soviet Union but you cannot take up residence in any city. Here are your passport and your transfer papers. You are free to return to Ukraine."

With the release papers consisting of a certificate of release signed by two administrators of the MVD office in Karaganda and a second-class train ticket to Kyiv, Ukraine, in hand, Pyotr packed his few personal possessions into a burlap sack and caught the next train bound for Tyumen, now home to his brother Konstantin. As he counted his meagre possessions, he felt fortunate to have been paid a small pittance for his work on the kolkhoz.

To his surprise, the passenger train which would take him to Tyumen was quite a contrast to the cattle train that brought him to the Gulag five years earlier. Looking around, he could see that each railway car was packed with what appeared to be rehabilitated citizens and prisoners, most of who seemed to be containing their elation at being released from the Gulag while at the same time perhaps being somewhat apprehensive about what the future held for them.

Pyotr was not surprised to note that a train traveling in the opposite direction was also filled to capacity with a new batch of prisoners and citizens bound for the Gulag and an uncertain future of incarceration, labour, and rehabilitation. But, that did not matter because for the first time since the outbreak of World War II, Pyotr tasted freedom and was able to relax.

Arriving in Tyumen within a week, Pyotr took out the letter he had received from his brother. Following Konstantin's instructions, he approached the station master, *"Excuse me, my name is Pyotr Dutkewycz. I am looking for my brother Konstantin Kozlov."*

"Konstantin Kozlov? Da, of course. He said that you might be arriving. Your brother is a train engineer. He should be arriving in Tyumen from Novosibirsk in about an hour. Why don't you wait for him in this train station."

Within the hour, another train pulled into the railway siding. At that point, the station master waved to him exclaiming, *"He is here. Your brother Pyotr is here."*

Konstantin, wearing a train engineer's uniform, waved from the locomotive shouting, *"Pyotr, it is me, Konstantin. Wait over there and I will join you in a few minutes."*

Shortly, Konstantin emerged from the train locomotive and rushed to embrace his brother, in the tradition of Russian siblings who had not seen one another for a long time. Stepping back and looking Konstantin over from head to foot, Pyotr showed his delight, *"You look great, brother. Life must be good to you!"*

"My dear brother, considering what you just went through, you look gaunt but at least you survived your re-education."

They had much to talk about to get caught up on the news of the family. However, even the talk of family was undertaken in quiet tones. One could never be too certain as to who might be listening.

"You know, Pyotr," confided Konstantin, *"I have seen and heard so many things. Stalin has acted, not through persuasion, explanation, and patient cooperation with people, but by imposing his concepts and demanding absolute submission to his opinion. I very nearly lost my life during Stalin's Reign of Terror during those two awful years of 1937 and 1938."*

"How did that happen?"

"That was the period of time when I decided to escape from the Gulag. My timing was bad, very bad. Without a little bit of luck, I would have been a goner."

"You have seen Stalin liquidate his enemies?"

"Tak, and much more. Whoever opposed Stalin or tried to prove his point of view or the correctness of his position was doomed to be removed from the collective and subsequently subjected to moral and physical annihilation."

"Is it true that Stalin used and continues to use the political charge of 'enemy of the people' to impose cruel repression on citizens?"

"I hear almost every day from deportees that those suspected only of hostile intent were suddenly eliminated."

Eventually, the conversation turned to that of family when Konstantin asked, *"Pyotr, you said that you saw our father when he returned to Horodok. How did he look? Was he healthy?"*

"I had not seen our father for eight years. When he arrived in Horodok, I hardly recognized him. He looked so old to me. Emaciated and gaunt. It took me several weeks to get over what he said about Siberia and the Gulag."

"Are you still upset with what father said to you about Stalin's repressive measures?"

"At the time, had I been able to get my hands on that son-of-a-bitch Stalin, I would have torn him limb from limb!"

"What did father say about Katusha and Nikolashya?"

"The loss of our mother and the disappearance of Katusha and Nikolashya completely destroyed father. He was never the same person. Life seemed to have little meaning for him."

"So, father confirmed that our two sisters did not return to Ukraine with him?"

"Tak, that is what he said. He tried to contact them when he received his release from the Rodina Kolkhoz. Nothing official came of father's enquiries, except that our sisters were suddenly secreted out of Iskra Kolkhoz by several Red Army officers."

"Was he able to get any information about their destination?"

"Nyet, father was never able to get any information as to their destination once they left Iskra. There was a rumour that Katusha married a Red Army officer and that Nikolashya joined them when they left the Iskra Kolkhoz."

"Sad, so very sad. Perhaps I will undertake a search for them in Siberia," was Konstantin's thoughtful response.

In considering the political situation in the Soviet Union, Konstantin had earlier discovered that finding work was just as hard as was finding a place to live. *"Soviet officials,"* observed Konstantin, *"are generally mistrustful of former prisoners, and many employers continue to regard them with suspicion as potential trouble-makers and enemies of the people."*

Unfortunately, political prisoners were being released from work camps and repatriated to their home villages and cities at the same time as were thieves, scoundrels, and common criminals. As a result, the mass of the Soviet population did not distinguish between political deportees and criminals. They associated the rise in crime and hooliganism with the releases from the Gulag. Even after their rehabilitation, many former prisoners were refused work. The very fact of their rehabilitation was frequently a cause of prejudice and suspicion among employers who did not want to run the risk of taking on a person who had been labeled as a political criminal only a few years earlier.

Pyotr spent the evening in Tyumen in the company of Konstantin, Darya, Valentina, and their two-year old son Eduard. The contrast between his life in Karaganda and that of his brother and his family in Tyumen was stark, to say the least. The smell of home cooking immediately reminded him of his aunt's cooking in Lisovody. Although the 4th floor apartment was small by any measure, it was ample for Konstantin and his family.

Although the two brothers had met briefly while en route to Siberia for their rehabilitation sentences in 1945, they did not get an opportunity to discuss their own lives or the lives of their families for fear of discovery by the NKVD. Even during their time together in Tyumen, there still existed that innate fear that something untoward could happen that would lead to arrest and more hard labour. Neither brother wanted to be transferred to a work camp in Siberia ever again.

While visiting a local market and out of earshot of any eavesdropper, Konstantin wanted to know how Pyotr spent his time with his aunt and uncle between 1930 and the outbreak of the war. *"Well,"* responded Pyotr, *"as you know, the very first thing that my aunt and uncle did was to change my name from Pyotr Kozlov to Pyotr Dutkewycz."*

"What about your school? What name did you use?"

"I attended school under the name of Dutkewycz, but always with the fear that the police would knock on our door and take me away."

"What made you join the Ukrainian partisans?"

"When the Nazis attacked Ukraine, there was much talk about an independent Ukraine. At first, many people in the village of Horodok supported the Nazis. However, we soon learned just how cruel were those Nazi subaky (wild dogs). This is why I joined the Ukrainian partisans. I wanted to help exterminate those crazy vbevtsi (killers)."

After a long silence, Konstantin asked, *"Braty (brother), why don't you look for work in Tyumen? You're not obligated to return to Ukraine."*

"Work in Tyumen? That may not be possible because the NKVD officials told me that I could not take up residence in any major city. Tyumen is a major city. Anyway, what would I do in Tyumen?"

"New industries are coming to our city. The railway has been a good employer for me. Do you want me to try to find you permanent work and a flat, perhaps near the city?"

Staying in Tyumen until the following weekend, Pyotr was torn between Konstantin's invitation to stay in Tyumen and his return to Ukraine. He even discussed his dilemma with Konstantin's wife and her mother. In the final analysis, the pull of Ukraine was far greater than was the invitation from Konstantin to stay in Tyumen. Besides, he very much wanted to return to his roots and his family.

With a heavy heart, Pyotr bade his brother and his family farewell, knowing full well that he might never see them again. Still, he knew that the great geographic distance between them would not stop them from communicating with one another. It was now time for Pyotr to try to put his own life together, not in the Gulag, but in his ancestral homeland of Ukraine. As Pyotr took his leave from his brother's home in Tyumen, he was suddenly attacked with a feeling of emptiness. Not only would he leave behind a brother but, in a strange way, the fellowship created while working in the quarry and more recently in a kolkhoz in Kazakhstan.

Arriving in Moscow on a Trans-Siberian train, Pyotr decided to spend a few days taking in the sights and sounds of Russia's capital city, even though it was contrary to the policies of the NKVD. By this time the war had been over for nearly six years and it was quite evident that the Soviet Union was well on the road to recovery. However, that was not to say that Pyotr wanted to take up residence in this major city even if he was permitted to do so. Red Square was a beehive of activity and he found comfort in meeting many others, much like himself, who were wending their way back home. They, too, had completed their re-education sentences in Siberia. Most had that vacant look in their eyes, searching for meaning after having experienced man's inhumanity to man.

After three days of wandering the streets of Moscow, Pyotr boarded a train bound for the oblast of Khmelnytsky and the village of Horodok.

Located in the southwestern plains of Ukraine, the Khmelnytsky Oblast had no shortage of streams and rivers, among them the large Dniester River and the historic South Buh River. One of the 20 districts in the oblast was Horodskiy, which was home to the small village of Horodok. Pyotr tried hard to recall the moment in his life in 1941 when all hell broke loose as the Nazis marched across Ukraine.

As a 17 year old, he had listened with great interest to an agitator speaking about the liberation of Ukraine. Being a youngster of impressionable age, it did not take much to convince him that he should join a Ukrainian partisan group located just north of Rivne. In making a decision to join the partisans, he recalled listening to stories from his *gido* (grandfather) about how a narrow strip of the Chernivtsi oblast at the south separated it from nearby Moldova and Romania, while the Polish border shifted much farther to the east. Ukrainians, according to his grandfather, wanted to once again incorporate these regions with a free and independent Ukraine.

Arriving in what was once Horodok, he discovered that the Nazis had done a good job of decimating the village. However, only positive thoughts entered his consciousness as he absorbed the unique landscapes, reserved territories, rocks, caves, and lakes of his beloved Ukraine. Even though the war had been over for five years, the devastation from the three major battles in and near the small city of Khmelnytsky left an indelible mark. Very few of the original houses in the village of Horodok remained standing. Not surprising, the Kozlov family home was totally destroyed. But then, that seemed not to matter because after the purges of the 1930s, most villagers took employment in one of several kolkhozes in the region while others sought employment in state industries. Not only did the devastation of war leave its marks on most buildings, but on the human element as well.

Now 26 years of age, Pyotr's first challenge was to set out in search of his aunt and uncle, the Dutkewyczes, who had brought him up since he was eight years of age. Although he had tried to contact them when he was an Ostarbeiter in Germany and during his rehabilitation in the Gulag, he received no response to his letters. Upon questioning the local residents of the village of Lisovody, it was confirmed that his aunt and uncle were victims of the war.

His grandparents, who lived in the Kozlov family home in 1930, perished in 1933 during Holodomor, the man-made famine perpetrated by Stalin's collectivization program. Even more devastating was the news from a survivor of Horodok that Aleksandr Kozlov, repatriated from the Gulag in 1938, perished in Zhitomir in 1944. Although Alexei survived the initial Nazi attack on Ukraine in 1941, he was a victim of the Red Army as it marched through the region in hot pursuit of the Wehrmacht.

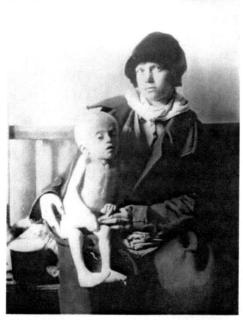

Victims of Holodomor (hunger famine) in Ukraine.

Monument to victims of Holodomor in Kyiv, Ukraine.

Pyotr's first challenge was to find gainful employment in one of the local kolkhozes, the fledgling food industry, or a manufacturing plant. The war had created a great demand for machine-building and metalworking. In turn, these factories would produce machine tools, forging and pressing machines, transformers, farm machinery for plant growing, and equipment for food processing. In particular, the state was interested in extending the oblast's capacity to produce sugar from sugar beets, bakery products, confectionery, macaroni, canned vegetables, meat and dairy products, alcoholic beverages, and flour-grinding mills.

Residents of Horodok talked about the oblast of Zhitomir starting to process such local raw materials as leather for the footwear market. As well, the garment industry showed signs of growth when materials from other regions of Ukraine found their way to Zhitomir. However, having worked for two years doing hard labour in a quarry in Karaganda, Pyotr did not have the stomach for more physical punishment. He preferred to examine employment alternatives that did not require strenuous labour.

Realizing that no members of his immediate family survived the war, Pyotr tried hard to develop new friends. At the same time, he wanted to get a better handle on the structure of the local kolkhozes as contrasted to those in Kazakhstan. Similar to those in Kazakhstan, the internal organization of the local kolkhozes was divided into a number or working groups generally known as brigades. The larger kolkhozes employed from 200 to 400 households, most of who lived in nearby villages or on the kolkhoz itself. In other cases, a kolkhoz had temporary or permanent work units within its operation which provided work for another 15 to 30 households. In carrying out its agricultural operations, each kolkhoz took charge of its personnel, land, equipment, and draught horses. Looking to the future, the oblast of Zhitomir was in the process of re-organizing the kolkhozes into larger and more streamlined operations.

One of the reasons Pyotr was not able to immediately find work on a kolkhoz was that each kolkhoznik was paid a share of the farm's product and profit according to the number of workdays. The pay could be in cash, grain, or vegetables. Each kolkhoz was required to sell its crop to the state at a fixed price, often set at a very low value to generate more income for the state. Adding Pyotr to a kolkhoz's workforce would result in having to share limited resources with yet another worker. Those in management were reluctant to approve such an addition.

Members of the kolkhoz were required to do a minimum number of days of work per year on both the kolkhoz and on other government work such as road building. The remuneration among its membership was in the form of a cooperative-style distribution of the kolkhoz's earnings in cash or in kind. If a kolkhoznik failed to perform the required work, the penalties could involve confiscation of the farmer's private plot, a trial in front of the People's Court, or up to a year in a corrective labour camp. A system of internal passports prevented movement from rural areas to urban areas. In contrast, if he were to find work on a *sovkhoz,* headed by a state-appointed director on land confiscated from former large estates, his wages would be regulated.

As for the concept of remuneration, in 1950 the government charged wholesalers 335 rubles for 100 kilograms of rye, but paid the kolkhoz roughly 8 rubles for the same amount of rye. For this reason, profits generated by a kolkhoz were relatively small. As a result, kolkhoz members were allowed to hold a small area of private land and one or two animals. The size of the private plot varied but was usually set at about one acre.

Until 1969, all children born on a collective farm were forced by law to work there as adults unless they were specifically given permission to leave. In effect, farmers became tied to their kolkhoz in what can be described as a system of neo-serfdom. With the emergence of the Soviet Union, the former landowners were replaced by communist bureaucracy.

In time, Pyotr realized that those who survived the harsh conditions in the labour camps tended to be more supportive of each other because special bonds of trust and mutual reliance had developed between them. This was quite a contrast to the attitudes of relatives and friends back home where former prisoners were frequently the victims of prejudice and malice. While the prisoners did not talk to their families about the camps, they did talk with other labourers from the Gulag who shared similar experiences. Many would correspond, meet on holidays, visit one another, and arrange reunions. Some prisoners returned home with new husbands or new wives whom they had met on the other side. For women, in particular, these marriages had sometimes been motivated by the struggle for survival, while others were based on the understanding and trust that frequently did develop between prisoners.

With memories of the horrors of World War II still ringing in his ears, Pyotr settled down in Zhitomir determined to find a new meaning to his life. The war ended in a clear-cut victory for the Soviet Union. Some went so far as to say that the victory would bring positive and enduring results by opening doors to a new and better way of life. In setting a course for himself, Pyotr wanted to open one or two of those doors for himself. Oh, yes, there was one other thing on his mind, Pyotr wanted to know if his childhood sweetheart, Ulyana, survived the war.

With memories of deportations and rehabilitations receding in his mind, Pyotr was about to get another dose of reality. Unfortunately, there were precious few rays of sunshine.

Chapter 20

THE END OF A TYRANT

Stalin saved a nation from the Nazis while murdering millions

A s Pyotr settled into the role of a kolkhoz labourer in Zhitomir in 1950, Stalin's fourth Five-Year Plan had just come to an end. Under this plan, the Soviet Union had planned to refurbish its factories and attain the level of production seen before the outbreak of the war. However, in order to ensure the survival of manufacturing plants during the war, much of the manufacturing capacity had been moved beyond the Ural Mountains. Stalin now wanted to move these plants back west closer to Moscow. But, these efforts were frustrated by labour shortages. Even Stalin's agricultural collectivization plan had mixed results as a result of a European drought in 1946. Exasperated, Stalin hoped that his fifth Five-Year Plan, scheduled for 1950-1955, would bring better results.

In watching the movement of people on trains through Zhitomir, Pyotr noted that repatriation was not flowing in a westerly direction only. Even five years after the end of the war, those prisoners of war and citizens who found themselves in Western Europe continued to be rounded up by the NKVD and repatriated to their Motherland. Many of them continued to be sent to the Gulag labour camps on a variety of trumped-up charges. Whatever their background, Stalin wanted all of them back home, even if they didn't want to go back home. When the workers of the world won their fight against Nazi totalitarianism, the world was once again confronted by evils they had fought to eradicate. This came in the form of Josef Stalin and his plan to deal with those opposed to communism or even those suspected of being opposed to his dictatorial rule.

Realizing the impact of a labour shortage in Siberia, Stalin began putting into place a new plan to control all those being released from bondage. As a result, the NKVD was strengthened and re-organized into two factions: the MVD which continued control of the Gulag and the exile villages, and the MGB (renamed the KGB in 1954), the *sword and shield of the Communist Party*. Recognizing Stalin's political motives, the Brigadir of the Zhitomir kolkhoz had a word of caution for Pyotr, *"I know that you served your sentence in Siberia, but, I warn you, there is a new NKVD policy."*

"A new policy? A policy that would impact me?"

"Tak, it could impact you. There is a labour shortage in Siberia. All those who served time as prisoners of war or Ostarbeiters in Germany, repatriated to Russia, and then returned to their villages may be at risk."

"How is that, Brigadir?"

"Well, the rumour is that the NKVD is extending the sentence of all those who were repatriated to the Soviet Union after the war. In fact, those arrested during the Great Terror are being re-arrested and forced to remain in Siberia."

It did not take long for these rumours to come to fruition. The NKVD suddenly took the position that all those arrested and exiled during the Great Terror of 1937-1938 would now be re-arrested. Even as many of them were in the process of being returned from Siberia to Ukraine, many others were rounded up and deported right back to the Gulag. In essence, Stalin decreed that they and their families would be exiled in perpetuity. Stalin's plan seemed clear—no one who had received a sentence for spying, sabotage, or any form of political opposition during those two years of terror would ever be allowed to return home.

Pyotr felt most fortunate to have escaped re-arrest when the NKVD authorities in Moscow had examined his repatriation papers and noted that he was not a prisoner who had been deported to Siberia during Stalin's Reign of Terror, but rather a Nazi prisoner of war. Perhaps Pyotr had second thoughts about having spent three days in Moscow while on his journey back to Horodok.

Other pieces of important information about the conduct of World War II came to Pyotr. A long-time resident of the Zhitomir region explained it this way, *"When Hitler attacked Ukraine, Josef Stalin ordered the local residents to move all of their livestock and burn all buildings in advance of the Wehrmacht."*

"You survived the war living right here?" asked Pyotr in astonishment.

"Tak, I barely survived the war even though I was twice wounded."

"Your family burned their farm buildings to the ground?"

Of course, not everyone living in the region followed Stalin's order. However, in the end this mattered little because those buildings left standing were destroyed by the Nazis for fear that rearguard or partisan action by nationalistic Ukrainians would delay the Wehrmacht's march on the capital city of Moscow.

In early spring of 1951 and just before the planting season on the Zhitomir kolkhoz, Pyotr was given a week off by the Brigadir to visit his boyhood village of Lisovody. He had a mission in mind, and that was to re-connect, if possible, with childhood friends. As well, he wanted to see his childhood sweetheart, Ulyana Shymkiv. *Is it possible,* he thought, *that she survived the war?* After much searching, he met an elderly man who was raised in the village of Lisovody and who knew its history. When Pyotr asked the villager if he was a resident of the village in 1930, the villager had a question of his own, *"A resident of Lisovody? Why do you ask? We have had enough of these questions from the NKVD."*

"I ask the question because I was born in the nearby village of Horodok."

"In that case, I can tell you that I am a resident of this village. What about you? Where did you come from?"

"I have recently returned from a prisoner of war camp in Germany. I am searching for a girl I once knew."

"You had a sweetheart? What was her name?"

"Her name was Ulyana Shymkiv. Do you know of the family?"

"Tak, I do know them. Ulyana is now married and has two children of her own."

Pyotr could do nothing to hide his disappointment. After a long silence, Pyotr had another question for the villager, *"What about the Kozlov family, do you recall that name?"*

"Tak, tak, I do. That was the kulak family that was deported to Siberia a long time ago."

"You remember them? When did you last see them?"

"The last time I saw Kozlov was in 1938, just before the outbreak of the war. Alexei Kozlov told me that he had just returned from a labour camp in Siberia. He said that he would go to Zhitomir to look for work on a kolkhoz."

A survivor of the gulag, Horodok, 2012.

Interviews conducted in Horodok and
Lisovody, 2012.

Entry to the village of Lisovody,
Ukraine, 2012.

Entry to the village of Horodok, Ukraine, 2012.

"Why didn't Kozlov stay in the village of Horodok on his farm?"

"He had no farm. Any property that he had before 1930 was seized by the Soviets and absorbed into an agricultural cooperative. All private land in this region was collectivized by force."

"Did you know my aunt and uncle, the Dutkewycz family?"

"Yes, I do recall the name. But, they were not from Horodok. They lived right here in the village of Lisovody. They all perished in the war."

When Pyotr told the villager that Alexei Kozlov was his father and that he, too, had served time in the Gulag, the villager's demeanour suddenly changed. This confirmed what he had heard from others: once you had served time in the Gulag, you were forever tainted. Some felt that you had actually committed a crime and that your deportation to the Gulag was well deserved. Others wanted to avoid any contact for fear of guilt by association. This attitude was very common and was taken into consideration in advance of any response to questions being asked. It appeared as though locals did not want to be seen as associating with any person who was sentenced to the Gulag.

Thereafter, Pyotr decided not to tell anyone that he had been banished to the Gulag for the purpose of re-education after the war. He found it more useful to tell strangers that he was captured by the Nazi Army, taken prisoner, and served time in a prisoner of war camp in Germany. He concluded that this explanation precipitated far more sympathy than did any mention of the Gulag. Only in cases where he met a person who had also served time in the Gulag did he mention that he, too, had been rehabilitated by Stalin's henchmen.

Even as Pyotr raised questions about what happened to the villages of Lisovody and Horodok during the war, he already knew that the answers would be heartbreaking. He recalled the shock of seeing his father in 1938 and what the Gulag had done to him. It had been a sorrowful time for Pyotr as he listened to the stories of the Kozlov family's time in the Gulag, especially the story about the loss of his mother, now laid to rest somewhere in Siberia. Their time together had been short when his father decided to leave Lisovody and join an agricultural kolkhoz in Zhitomir. Pyotr continued to live with the Dutkewycz family in Lisovody, working on a local kolkhoz as a herdsman. It was also a time when the dark clouds of an impending war were gathering momentum.

Alexei Kozlov had decided to seek employment in a kolkhoz in Zhitomir in order to minimize the pain associated with the loss of the modest farming operation he worked so hard to develop. Meanwhile, Pyotr had promised his father that he would make every attempt to join him in the future. However, with the outbreak of the war in 1939 and Operation Barbarossa in 1941, world events unfolded in such a way as to make a reunion impossible. The war changed everything and it would not be until 1950, long after the hostilities of the war had ended and his own banishment to Siberia was over, that he would learn about the fate of his father.

Upon his return to Zhitomir, Pyotr said a prayer at the grave that was now the final resting place of his father, a father that he knew only as a child and briefly again in 1938. It took Pyotr a long time to come to grips with what had happened to his family. With the loss of his aunt and uncle as well as his parents and grandparents, he now had something in common with so many others who lost their families. Simply put, there was no one left in his family to come home to. Even Ulyana, his childhood sweetheart, was now married.

As Pyotr learned more about the atrocities committed by the Nazis, he realized that there was another tyrant in his midst—Josef Stalin. After the war, people in the countryside lost all confidence in his form of law and justice and used every opportunity to escape to the city. It was their way to protest against the arbitrary rule of local authorities and their own miserable lives. To stop this migration, the Supreme Soviet issued a decree in 1948 saying that, *"Those persons who deliberately evade work and seek a parasitic lifestyle in a city will be punished."* As a result of this decree, thousands of peasants were thrown behind bars. Many more were exiled to Siberia.

After organizing the kolkhozes, the government determined the sizes of personal plots for the collective farmers and factory workers, as well as the number of cattle and poultry each family could have. These norms were repeatedly reduced. Starting in the 1930s, the Soviet authorities closely watched every collective farmer's family lest it have an extra hen, calf, or piglet. This allegedly would have been counter to the principles of socialism. The Soviet regime did its utmost to make the peasants completely dependent on the kolkhoz and the state. Its aim was to prevent corruption and any attempt by the peasants to become prosperous by selling products on the side. This is why the Supreme Soviet passed a decree that a family was permitted to own one cow, one calf under one year of age, and one pig or three sheep.

Stalin did not mellow with age. He executed a Reign of Terror, carried out purges, executions and exiles to the Gulag, and persecuted prisoners of war after World War II. He suppressed all dissent and anything that smacked of foreign influence, especially if the influence came from Western Europe.

To the great relief of many, Stalin died of a massive heart attack on March 5, 1953. Even as he was dying, he must have reflected on his own words, *"I trust no one, not even myself."* Many remembered him as the man who helped save his nation from Nazi domination, while others remembered him as a mass murderer of the century.

Even with access to NKVD records, it is difficult to say with any certainty the number of citizens Stalin murdered during his reign. Some researchers place the figure to be in excess of 80 million, while others conclude that his policies led directly to the death of no fewer than 8 million of his own people. It seems to matter little which figure one embraces. Ultimately it is a portrait of a monster in blood responsible for the death of millions through assassination, purges, imprisonment, and deportation to labour camps which stretched through eleven time zones. If a dictator has people imprisoned or sent to camps, then he is ultimately responsible for their fate.

As a result, there is little distinction between killing people deliberately and letting them die of neglect. We can only speculate that Stalin, as he lay there dying, must have been forced to eat his own words, *"Death is the solution to all problems. No man, no problem."*

It was during Pyotr's third year working on the Zhitomir kolkhoz that Josef Stalin died. Pyotr wanted some assurance that the tyrant was really dead. Out of curiosity, Pyotr asked a fellow worker, *"What happened to Stalin? How did he die?"* A response was slow in coming as if the tyrant were still listening with great anticipation to every word.

"Comrade," was the guarded response from Anatoli as he spat in the general direction of Moscow, *"I hope he died a thousand deaths before going to hell."*

"Was he assassinated by one of his Ministers?"

"Could be, the rumour is that he retired to his dacha near Moscow on the very first day of March with four of his trusted murderers. He died four days later. Some say it was his heart. His murderous heart gave out."

With tears of happiness in his eyes, Pyotr couldn't think of anything important to say. He said nothing.

By mid-March of 1953, the fertile soil in Zhitomir began to spring to life and so did the rumours. Would the next dictator be another tyrant or a benevolent despot? Would Stalin be replaced by his trusted heir apparent Lavrentiy Beria or the quiet but scheming Nikita Khrushchev? Unlike his predecessor, Vladimir Lenin, Josef Stalin had not designated a sole successor. Consequently, immediately after his death strategic power struggles between the five members of the Presidium commenced. However, it did not take Khrushchev long to solve the succession question.

Immediately after Stalin's death, Khrushchev, assisted by Marshal Zhukov's military forces, arrested Beria and charged him with treason. Beria was taken to Moscow's Lubyanka Prison where, along with his closest associates, he was shot.

Looking back, when Soviet troops, pursuant to the Molotov-Ribbentrop Pact, invaded the eastern portion of Poland on September 17, 1939, Khrushchev, at Stalin's direction, accompanied the troops. Khrushchev's role was to ensure that the occupied areas voted for a union with the Soviet Union. On November 1, 1939, Western Ukraine became a part of the Ukrainian Soviet Socialist Republic. Despite Khrushchev's efforts to achieve unity, staffing Western Ukrainian organizations with Eastern Ukrainians, many of whom were ethnic Russians, and giving confiscated lands to collective farms rather than to peasants soon alienated Western Ukrainians.

During World War II, Khrushchev served in various fronts and was attached to the Soviet troops at the Battle of Kursk in 1943. This was a decisive battle which turned back the last major German offensive on Soviet soil.

After the war, Khrushchev became increasingly involved in reconstruction work in Ukraine. He was appointed Premier of the Ukrainian Soviet Socialist Republic, a country where one of every six Ukrainians had been killed during the war. In an effort to increase agricultural production in Ukrainian kolkhozes after the war, Khrushchev instituted a program of expelling to Siberia those who were not pulling their weight. Even though his first initiative was to consolidate the kolkhozes in order to gain better control, he was instrumental in getting the NKVD to go after the members of the Ukrainian Insurgent Army who wanted independence for Ukraine. In 1953 after several effective political moves, Khrushchev became the First Secretary of the Communist Party.

In time, Pyotr was becoming more and more disillusioned with his repatriation to Ukraine. He was especially disturbed to learn that the NKVD did not hesitate to torture members of the Insurgent Army by cutting off their skin, nailing suspects to the cross, cutting off their sex organs and the breasts of women, cutting out their eyes, and breaking a bone or two in their bodies. These atrocities were discovered and reported by the German Army as early as 1942 when several mass graves were discovered near Rivne, each of which held over five thousand bodies.

As Pyotr thought about the horrors of the war, he wished that he had family with whom he might share his pain. However, that was not to be. The realization suddenly came to him—the only family he had was his brother Konstantin, now living in Tyumen.

What to do, that was the question. With the death of Josef Stalin, the character of the Soviet Union began to change. A person could now spend more time thinking about his role in the community and how he might fulfill the dreams he had for himself. Not only that, but some of the restrictions upon travel within the Soviet Union were being eroded, thereby making travel much easier. With this in mind, Pyotr made a momentous decision. Unfortunately, his decision would lead to unintended consequences. Nikita Khrushchev's *Cold War* foreign policy was about to have quite an impact upon his life.

After a sleepless night in the kolkhoz, Pyotr penned a letter to his brother Konstantin. His brother was about to receive the shock of his life.

Chapter 21

A TOP SECRET MISSION

Tsar Bomba, the largest most powerful weapon ever detonated

The letter Pyotr wrote to his brother Konstantin was already in the mail as he hurried to put all of his affairs in order. Coincidentally, the contemporary form of *Murphy's law* which said, *'Anything that can possibly go wrong, does,'* was being coined. Unfortunately for Pyotr, he was now on his way to prove this hypothesis to be true.

At this particular stage in his life, Pyotr could not have guessed that Novaya Zemlya was about to figure prominently in his future. For some very obvious reasons, Soviet citizens knew very little about this island. Those living outside Russia knew virtually nothing about this isolated place. Very soon, Pyotr would learn a lot about the island.

Novaya Zemlya is an archipelago in the Arctic Ocean in the north of Russia which contains two main islands, Severny and Yuzhny, which are separated by the Matochkin Strait. It was not until July of 1954 that most of the territory of the Novaya Zemlya Islands was declared as the Novaya Zemlya Test Site of the Ministry of Defense of the Soviet Union. In the view of the Soviet Military, the islands provided an ideal site for nuclear testing. The indigenous population of only 536 people could be easily resettled out of harm's way on the mainland of Russia.

The initial code name of the nuclear testing project was *Object-700* and the corresponding Moscow address was *Moscow-300*. In due course, the official name of the test site would become the Sixth State Test Site of the Ministry of Defense. From the beginning, the Novaya Zemlya Test Site was under the authority of the Soviet Navy. As early as 1953, the Soviet Union began recruiting construction workers to put the necessary infrastructure for the nuclear tests into place. The secrecy of Novaya Zemlya was also used for other purposes. When the Soviet authorities did not want to grant leave for some person abroad, they could send him to Novaya Zemlya for work or service. That secret work implied that the person could not leave the USSR for some foreign country even within the next five years after his period of service or work on the island expired.

By some strange coincidence in September of 1954 Pyotr Dutkewycz boarded a train in Zhitomir and set his sights on a reunion with his brother, Konstantin Kozlov, in Tyumen, Siberia. It was just two weeks earlier that he had penned the letter to his brother telling him of his intention to journey to Tyumen.

Arriving in Moscow two days later, Pyotr made his way to Yaroslavsky Vokzal, the railway station that would launch his journey to Tyumen on a Trans-Siberian passenger train. Over the previous four years he had saved sufficient funds to purchase a railway ticket and start a new life in Siberia. The trip from Zhitomir to Moscow was without incident and he was looking forward to a leisurely train ride to see his brother. At the train ticket wicket in Moscow, things began to take a turn for the worse when three armed KGB guards singled him out for special attention, *"Police! Stop! Don't move! Your identification, please."*

Looking at the KGB officers in a state of shock, Pyotr nervously handed over his passport saying, *"I am on my way to visit my brother in Tyumen."*

After a brief examination of Pyotr's passport, the KGB operative declared, *"What the hell are you doing? Your passport does not allow you to travel to Siberia. The passport in your possession was issued to you in 1950 to allow you to return to Ukraine. It does not allow you to travel anywhere you want to in the Soviet Union. For you to travel to Siberia requires a special passport and permission from authorities."*

"This is chush' sobah'ya (bull shit). I was told by the NKVD authorities in Karaganda that my passport is good in Russia and Ukraine. If my internal passport does not allow me to return to Siberia, how will I go about getting the proper credentials?"

"Not so fast. Whoever gave you this information in Karaganda was wrong. You'll have to come with us and explain yourself to the KGB authorities. You are under arrest for breaking our federal laws."

Pyotr spent the next three days in detention in Moscow being interrogated by the KGB. Most of their questions centered around his desire to travel to Siberia, *"Why do you want to travel to Tyumen? Don't you know that your passport does not permit you to travel to Siberia?"*

"I want to join my brother, Konstantin Kozlov, in Tyumen," was Pyotr's response.

"You have a brother in Tyumen? What work does he do in Tyumen?"

"Konstantin Kozlov works for the Trans-Siberia Railway. He lives with his wife and son in Tyumen."

"You say your brother's name is Kozlov and your name is Dutkewycz? Why are you giving me this bullshit? Do you take me for a crazy person?"

"I took the family name of my aunt and uncle's family during the war."

It took the KGB a full day to review Pyotr's file at which time he was called into the interrogation room. *"Well, Dutkewycz, we have reviewed your file and the KGB has some good news for you and maybe some bad news. You can spend a couple years in jail in Moscow, or two years in a slave labour camp in Irkutsk, or you can elect to work in Novaya Zemlya."*

"A slave labour camp? You mean in Irkutsk? Near Lake Baikal?"

"You know about Irkutsk? The Soviet government began the construction of a hydroelectric power station in Irkutsk in 1950 and wants to complete that important project. They need more workers."

"Nyet, thank you. I have had enough of work in Siberia. What about Novaya Zemlya? Where the hell is that place? I have never heard of it."

"Novaya Zemlya is up north, near the Arctic Circle. Our Motherland has a special construction project, a military project up there. That is all this office knows. Give it some thought, Dutkewycz. You are a lucky man to have choices!"

After spending a night under tight security, the next morning Pyotr appeared once again before the KGB officials. *"It doesn't look as though I have much choice,"* was Pyotr's response. *"Jail time and hard labour are most distasteful to me. Maybe this Novaya Zemlya is the best choice."*

"You are a very wise man, Dutkewycz. Tomorrow you will board a military aircraft that will fly you and several other workers to a military base in Arkhangelsk. From Arkhangelsk you will take a navy ship to Novaya Zemlya. That is all I can tell you. Once you arrive in Arkhangelsk, you will be provided with additional information."

"But," continued Pyotr, *"I do have one request."*

"You have a request? Well, go ahead. What is your request?"

"I want to write a letter to my brother Konstantin to tell him of my change in plans."

364

"Have you gone crazy? You will be going to a top secret location, a location from which mail is not delivered. How can the KGB allow you to tell anyone where you are going?"

At the time of the assignment, Pyotr would not have known that the construction of the nuclear test site, including the relocation of the more than 500 members of the indigenous population, would soon begin. Nor would he have been aware that the Soviet Union had earlier considered the construction of a nuclear test site in Kazakhstan, only to change their minds because that location would be too close to human habitation. Soviet authorities wanted a remote and secret site for the development of their nuclear program.

On the flight from Moscow to Arkhangelsk, Pyotr could not get out of his mind how bad luck seemed to follow him no matter where he went. However, to his surprise and relief, the navy vessel which would take him and hundreds of other workers from Arkhangelsk to Novaya Zemlya was quite comfortable. Not only that, but the construction workers were actually treated as human beings and not slaves, a significant change from being in a labour camp in the Gulag. This, perhaps, came about as a result of the construction skills that many of them possessed—professional skills that would be required for the project. *But,* thought Pyotr, *what the hell do I have to offer these bastards? What do I know about construction?* If Pyotr had doubts about his own talents, he was about to learn that many of those joining him had even less to offer.

The first stage of test site construction began in October of 1954, at which time Pyotr was joined by several battalions of military construction workers who arrived from Arkhangelsk with their equipment. In all, as many as 7,000 civilians and military personnel endured that first winter season of 1954-1955 in tents. Their main goal was to build the support facilities necessary to carry out the first Soviet underwater nuclear tests. Since the island of Novaya Zemlya extended from 470 to 1,150 kilometers north of the Arctic Circle, the ice cover reached five feet at the end of the winter in the southwest coast of the southern island. This made it necessary for the Soviet Union to deploy the icebreaker *Baikal* to establish an all-season connection between the various parts of the test site and the mainland. The main port for supplying the testing operations was Arkhangelsk, near the Kola Peninsula, 900 kilometers away.

Virtually forced into the Soviet Navy, Pyotr, along with many others, was now assigned to a work crew responsible for the construction of the administrative and command center in Belushya, the airport in Rogachevo, the command center on board the ship *Emba*, and all the facilities needed for conducting and monitoring an underwater nuclear explosion in Chernaya Bay. It is little wonder that so large a construction crew was required!

Test site operations involved a large organization of thousands of employees. By the end of Pyotr's first year on the island, a modern airport was constructed near Rogachevo with a 2,400-meter runway. Here, almost any type of military or civilian aircraft could land. A large ocean steamship, serving as a floating hotel for business travelers and as a restaurant for generals and other military officers, arrived during the fall season of that same year.

Nuclear testing in the Soviet Union, where the majority of warheads used were dropped by parachute from bombers, started in 1957 and the last nuclear test was conducted in August of 1962. The Russian-made Tu-95 heavy bombers were loaded at the Olenye airbase on the Kola Peninsula about 1,000 kilometers from the test site.

On October 30, 1961, the most powerful atmospheric bomb code named *Big Ivan* (generally known as *Tsar Bomba* within military circles in the Soviet Union) was exploded. Dropped from a height of 10.5 kilometers over Mityushikha Bay (Sukhoy Nos Zone C), the bomb was detonated at a height of four kilometers above sea level. The resultant mushroom cloud reached a height of 65 kilometers. Throughout this period of nuclear testing, Pyotr served on a squadron charged with the responsibility of preparing the bombers for their missions.

Time passed quickly as Pyotr was shuttled from one construction project to another on the island. Construction fatalities were minimal at best and Pyotr had his hands full just staying alive and healthy. Approaching his fourth year of service, he had a feeling that things were about to change. Seemingly out of the blue, he was called aside by the Chief Marshal of Aviation, General Golovanov who, in a most direct way, raised this question of him, *"Serzhant Dutkewycz, would you be interested in heading up a special mission?"*

"Special mission? What kind of a special mission?"

"Da, da, a top secret special mission. I want you to take charge of a squadron to modify the appearance of our Tu-95 Bomber for a flight to an unknown destination."

"Did you say, General, that you want to dress up the plane to look like a passenger aircraft?"

"Da, that is it. Top secret. If you accept, you will meet with Commander Korab. He will coordinate the loading of the nuclear warhead."

"I accept the challenge, General."

Since the operation was top secret, the camouflaging of the aircraft took place in a large enclosed hangar away from prying eyes. During the process of making the military aircraft look like a commercial passenger plane, curiosity got the better of Pyotr Dutkewycz. As a result, during a brief progress meeting with Commander Korab, he felt compelled to ask, *"Commander, tell me, where the hell are you flying this beast? What is your destination?"*

"I'll be damned if I know," responded Commander Korab. *"The destination is top secret. And, even if I knew the destination, I would not be able to tell you. It is my understanding that General Golovanov will provide our flight crew with our destination once we are over the Barents Sea."*

"It's an important mission, isn't it?"

"Important and dangerous," ventured Commander Korab with a great deal of pride as he stuck out his chest. *"And, these Soviet military leaders are smart. Smart because they chose me for the mission."*

It would not be until the following week that Commander Korab's flight crew got word that they would be leaving on the special mission the following day. Meanwhile, Pyotr got to know Commander Korab much better during that week, especially since both came from the same region of Soviet Ukraine. They talked about their families and the circumstances that led them to Novaya Zemlya. Most of all, they talked about the Soviet Union and the Cold War with the United States of America. *"Dutkewycz,"* confided Commander Korab during one of their conversations, *"if something happens to me on this mission, I want you to contact my family in Buczacz, Ukraine. Tell my parents that I love them."*

"That may be difficult. You know that all mail going to the mainland is being read by the KGB. In fact, I am told that very little, if any, mail gets to the Russian mainland."

"Da, I know that, Dutkewycz. But, I recently heard a rumour that the Soviet authorities are loosening their grip on the military personnel in Novaya Zemlya."

"Da, da, Commander Korab. I promise to write a letter to your parents if something happens to you. However, there is one condition."

"One condition? What is that condition?"

"That you should do the same for me if I should come to an unfortunate end here on the island. Would you do that for me?"

"Where does your family live, Pyotr?"

"I have no immediate family in Ukraine. All perished during the war. I have only one brother in Tyumen."

"In Tyumen? How is that?"

"Our family was deported from Ukraine to Siberia in 1930. I remained behind as an eight-year old where I lived with my aunt and uncle. My family name is Kozlov, but my aunt thought it best that I assume the name of Dutkewycz. My brother's name is Konstantin Kozlov. He works for the Trans-Siberian Railway in Tyumen."

After exchanging comradely hugs, they promised each other that should either perish during these trying times, their respective families would be informed.

As the Tu-95 bomber lifted off the ground, the special mission under the code name of *ANADYR* set its sights for the Barents Sea and the eastern coastline of Greenland. One hour into the flight, Commander Korab got the rest of the details for the mission. The flight would take him and his crew from the airport in Novaya Zemlya, over the Barents Sea to the southern tip of Greenland, before setting a course over the

North Atlantic to Havana, Cuba. Unknown to Commander Korab, he was about to become a participant in the Cuban Missile Crisis.

On October 22, 1962, American President John F. Kennedy informed the world that the Soviet Union was building secret missile bases in Cuba, a mere 90 kilometers off the shores of Florida. Kennedy immediately demanded that the General Secretary of the Soviet Union, Nikita Khrushchev, remove all the missile bases and their deadly contents.

For seven days, the two most powerful leaders in the world stared each other down until Khrushchev blinked. On October 28, Khrushchev acceded to Kennedy's demands by ordering all Soviet supply ships away from Cuban waters and agreeing to remove the missiles from Cuba's mainland. After several days of teetering on the brink of nuclear holocaust, the world breathed a sigh of relief.

Although Commander Korab might have guessed that he was a participant in international incident, it would not be until years later that he would learn the full extent of his involvement in the Cuban Crisis. When Commander Korab returned to the cold and desolate island of Novaya Zemlya at the end of October, his thoughts turned to his friend Pyotr Dutkewycz. He wanted to tell Pyotr just how happy he was to return to the Soviet Union in one piece. Most of all, he wanted to tell him that he would not have to write that letter to his parents in Buczacz, Ukraine.

However, the news was not all good. Earlier nuclear tests on the island of Novaya Zemlya began to take their toll when several hundred military personnel were evacuated to a hospital in Moscow. Unfortunately, Commander Korab soon learned that among that group of evacuees was Pyotr Dutkewycz. He had suddenly taken ill and had been airlifted to a military hospital in Moscow. Although the officials did not talk about the fatalities as a result of the nuclear tests, Korab knew that the news was not good. A KGB security guard confirmed that there were three accidental releases of significant radioactivity in Novaya Zemlya during the underground nuclear testing program. Two of these resulted in what the Russian officials described as emergency situations.

The Soviet Union exploded the most powerful nuclear weapon (Big Ivan) ever detonated on the Island of Novaya Zemlya on October 30, 1961.

Fidel Castro and Nikita Khrushchev, Cuban Missile Crisis, 1962.

When Commander Korab returned to the Russian mainland from Novaya Zemlya early in 1963, he wanted to check with the KGB authorities in Moscow about the health of Pyotr Dutkewycz. Of course, the KGB head office, because of national security, would not release any information about the survival of those evacuated from the island. Even his approach to the Soviet Military Intelligence Unit Directorate, a unit that worked with the KGB to gather intelligence abroad, drew a blank. Commander Ostap Korab knew better than to pursue the matter further with the KGB or the health authorities in Moscow. Relying upon his acquaintances within the Soviet Party, it took considerable time for Ostap to ferret out sufficient reliable information to determine what happened to his friend Pyotr. And, the news was not good.

Once Commander Korab confirmed what had happened to Pyotr, he was obliged to carry out a promise he had made. It was now time to write a very important letter to Konstantin Kozlov in Tyumen.

Chapter 22

THE THREE LETTERS

Putting together the final pieces of the puzzle

It is now over eighty years since the Kozlov family was deported from Soviet Ukraine to Siberia. Knowing that the vast reaches of Siberia had swallowed millions of deportees never to be heard from again, what were the chances of finding any survivor of the Kozlov family? The NKVD of the Soviet Union did not always maintain accurate records of who was deported to Siberia, who perished, and who was repatriated to their homeland. In the absence of any reliable records in Russian archives, I wasn't overly optimistic about my chances of finding a surviving member of the family. In the end, and not without a considerable amount of luck, it is unlikely that any descendant of Alexei Kozlov would have been discovered.

The final pieces of the puzzle of what happened to various members of the Kozlov family, deported to Siberia in 1930, began to fall into place in the spring of 2010 when my search for family took me to Tyumen, Russia. It was here that I met Eduard Kozlov, the grandson of Alexei Kozlov. To my surprise, Eduard had in his possession three very important letters that made little sense to him at the time. Yet, these were the essential pieces of the puzzle that established a connection between our two families. In reality, the letters were a genealogical DNA test to establish a link between two branches of one family.

When we were in Tyumen, Eduard Kozlov had reflected upon the discovery of those letters. *"You know, Steven,"* he said at the time, *"those letters have been a mystery to me for a very long time. In fact, my father once told me that he wished he had never seen those letters. All they gave him was a headache."*

"Well," I had assured Eduard, *"I am glad that you kept those letters. Perhaps the pain that your father experienced with the content of those letters will find a silver lining with us."*

The first letter in Eduard's possession was written by Pyotr Dutkewycz from a kolkhoz in Zhitomir, Ukraine to his brother Konstantin Kozlov in Tyumen. The letter was very short and simply informed Konstantin Kozlov that he planned to take a Trans-Siberian train to Tyumen:

August 15, 1954

Dear brother, I accept your invitation to come to Tyumen. We no longer have any immediate family living in Ukraine. I plan to visit you and your family and hopefully find work in Tyumen. I will be taking the Trans-Siberian train and expect to see you in about three weeks. Your brother, Pyotr.

We now also know that Eduard's father, Konstantin Kozlov, did respond to the letter from Pyotr Dutkewycz on at least two occasions. *"My father,"* explained Eduard, *"told me that he never did receive a response from my uncle, Pyotr Dutkewycz."*

"Do you have any evidence that Pyotr actually received any of the letters?"

"Nyet, I don't. My father never did find out if the letters were actually delivered to Pyotr in Zhitomir or in the village of Horodok. Even though Stalin was dead and gone by this time, my father continued to fear the NKVD. He never did make any official enquiries about the letters or the whereabouts of Pyotr."

We now had the evidence that the short letter penned by Pyotr Dutkewycz did arrive in Tyumen; however, Pyotr never did. Meanwhile, and according to Eduard, his father wrote at least two letters addressed to Pyotr Dutkewycz with the hopes of reaching him in Horodok or Zhitomir. A response to these letters was never received by Konstantin. This raised several important questions. *Did Pyotr receive either of these two letters? Did he respond to them?*

Although we do not have any definitive answers to these questions, it is reasonable to assume that the letters were not received by Pyotr because he was no longer living in Ukraine. By this time he was well on his way to Tyumen before being deployed to Novaya Zemlya. As a result, the postal authorities probably elected to destroy the letters rather than to return them to Konstantin. On the other hand, it is not out of the realm of possibility that the two letters were initially intercepted by the KGB and never did arrive in the villages of Horodok, Lisovody, or Zhitomir.

The next piece of important evidence in Eduard's possession was an official looking envelope with a Soviet Union Air Force logo prominently displayed on it and with a postmark of *Moscow Military District, Air Defence Forces, Moscow, Russia.* Addressed to Konstantin Kozlov in Tyumen, Russia, the letter was written on Russian Air Defence Forces letterhead paper. It contained the following message:

October 26, 1963

Gospodin Kozlov, It is my sad duty to inform you that your brother, Pyotr Dutkewycz, recently perished in Novaya Zemlya while on special duty with the Soviet Union Air Force, I send my regrets. Commander Ostap Korab.

It is not so much what the letter said but rather what was left out. The letter contained no information about the circumstances surrounding Pyotr's death. Perhaps, the reason for this is now quite apparent. Had the letter contained any sensitive information, such as the fact that Pyotr may have died as a result of the nuclear tests on the island of Novaya Zemlya during the Cold War, it is unlikely that the KGB would have allowed the letter to proceed to its intended destination.

Taking into consideration these two important letters, the first one from Pyotr and the second one from Commander Korab, I had a question for Eduard, *"Do you believe in the strangest of coincidences?"*

"Do I believe in strange coincidences? In what way do you refer to coincidences?"

"For example, if you and I observe a chance occurrence of events which are remarkable either for being simultaneous or for being connected, that, in my view, would be a strange coincidence, would it not?"

"Are you," Steven, *"referring to the letters?"*

"Tak, I am referring to the letters. There are several things that occurred which cannot be explained by natural or scientific law. First of all, is it not Commander Korab who wrote the letter to your father about the loss of Pyotr? Do you not agree?"

"Of course, I agree. The letter was signed by Commander Korab."

"Well, I have met Commander Korab."

At first, Eduard had that startled look of incredulity on his face. It seemed as though he wanted to say something but was at a loss for words. Looking at me intently as if not believing what he had heard, he finally stammered, *"Are you fooling me? Do you really mean that you have met Commander Korab?"*

"Tak, I have. I met him by sheer accident in Lviv, Ukraine, in 2004. He mentioned that he wrote a letter to a Konstantin Kozlov in 1963."

"And you immediately thought of your father's family?"

"Well, since my assignment in Ukraine had to do with genealogy and family searches, tak, I did think of the possibility of a connection to our family."

"How did Korab get to write that letter?"

"Commander Korab told me about working with Serzhant Pyotr Dutkewycz in Novaya Zemlya. Korab learned that Pyotr had a brother in Tyumen. He was duty bound to write that letter to Konstantin Kozlov."

"What did you say to Commander Korab that led him to tell you about the letter to my father?"

"In my discussions with Korab, we talked about our respective families and family names. We also talked about family searches and genealogy."

"You talked about family names? For what purpose? To prove what?"

"Well, I wanted to mention to Commander Korab the family names of various relatives I had in Ukraine."

"And, what were your conclusions?"

"I pointed out to Ostap that the name of Dutkewycz was on my father's family tree. This was the comment that led Ostap to tell me that he worked with a Serzhant Dutkewycz in the Soviet Air Force."

"Commander Korab worked with a Serzhant by the name of Dutkewycz?"

"It was at this point that Ostap told me about his special assignment in Novaya Zemlya where he met Pyotr Dutkewycz."

"How did they meet?"

"Korab told me that they met while he was on special assignment having to do with the Cuban nuclear missile crisis of 1962."

"What happened during this special assignment?"

"Commander Korab and Serzhant Dutkewycz made a pact. Whoever survived their special assignments was to notify the deceased person's next of kin."

"Korab was made aware of the loss of Pyotr?"

"Tak, that is what happened. He was then obliged to write that letter to your father."

"Steven, do you believe that this is what happened?"

"I believe this to be true. When we left Lviv in 2004, I assured Ostap that I would investigate the destination of that letter. I felt that it was my duty to find out if Pyotr Dutkewycz was related to me. At that point I would not have known that Pyotr Dutkewycz was related to Konstantin Kozlov."

For a long time, I gently held the letter penned by Commander Ostap Korab, as if wanting to make sure that all of this was not a dream. However, there was no mistaking the postmark, *Military District, Moscow, Russia.* And, there was no doubt in my mind that the translation provided by Eduard was accurate.

The third letter that we examined was written by Konstantin Kozlov and addressed to Commander Ostap Korab. Like the first two letters, this letter was also very brief, acknowledging receipt of Commander Korab's letter saying,

November 15, 1963
Commander Korab
Soviet Armed Forces
Moscow

I am saddened with the information you are providing me about my brother Pyotr. Is it possible for you to make more information available to me about Pyotr's death? Konstantin Kozlov.

The letter, addressed to Commander Korab, never did reach its destination. It was returned to the sender by Russian Postal Services. During those years of the Cold War, mail from Siberia to any satellite Soviet country was monitored by the KGB. One can only speculate that any letter of a sensitive nature would have been destroyed by the KGB. However, in this case, it appears as though the KGB did not destroy the letter but elected to return it to its sender. Maybe they simply wanted to get a message to Kozlov. On the other hand, the KGB might have concluded that the letter contained no information of a sensitive nature. As a consequence, it was not destroyed but returned to its sender.

I felt that I should now carry out one more important mission. In July of 2011, my wife and I boarded an Air Canada flight to Lviv, Ukraine, where we would once again meet with Commander Ostap Korab. When we arrived in Lviv, we telephoned Commander Korab. The Commander picked us up at the Lviv airport and after the normal small talk, my first question to him was, *"Commander, do you recall that in 2004 you told me that you wrote a letter to Konstantin Kozlov in 1963? A very important letter?"*

"Why, I'll be damned, you have a great memory. Tak, of course, I remember that conversation."

"Well, after a journey to Tyumen last year, I am able to confirm that Pyotr Dutkewycz did have a brother in Tyumen. His brother's name was Konstantin Kozlov."

"Tak, tak. I do remember writing that letter in 1963."

"What did you say in that letter? Do you remember?"

"Not much, just the truth. The truth about what happened to Serzhant Pyotr Dutkewycz."

"Pyotr had a military rank?"

"Tak, he did. He attained the rank of a non-commissioned officer in the Soviet Air Force as a result of his work. He had a non-commissioned rank of Mladshiy Serzhant."

"How were you able to confirm the death of Pyotr Dutkewycz?"

"The information about Dutkewycz's death came to the Soviet Air Force from official sources. Of course, this information was not available in the public record. To tell you the truth, many brave soldiers died as a result of the nuclear tests in 1961-1962."

"You're the lucky one. You survived those nuclear tests?"

"Tak, I was very, very lucky. I was not on the island at that time. You know, Steven," explained Commander Korab, *"two nuclear charges were detonated in 1961 where the charges were sufficiently large to cause the level of gamma radiation to jump to several hundred roentgens per hour."*

"Roentgens? What are those?"

"Well, a roentgen is a unit of measurement for exposure to ionizing radiation such as x-rays and gamma rays. An exposure of 500 roentgens in five hours is usually lethal for human beings."

"Are you saying that Pyotr Dutkewycz died as a result of these nuclear tests?"

"The typical exposure to normal background radiation for human beings is about 200 milliroentgens per year or about 23 microroentgens per hour. Many members of the test personnel were exposed to the resulting radiation hazard when they were exposed from 40 to 80 roentgens of radiation. I am convinced that Pyotr was a victim of that radiation."

"What happened to other military personnel? Did they survive?"

"Well, only those who survived the initial blast were evacuated to a safety area about an hour later. Over 400 test crew members were transported for treatment to Moscow. Unfortunately, hundreds of the workers died before they could be evacuated."

"Did you receive any word about Pyotr Dutkewycz? Was he one of the fatalities?"

"As a result of Soviet policy," explained Commander Korab, *"no official explanation for this radioactive release has been published. However, further enquiries convinced me that Pyotr was one of the fatalities of those tests."*

"You know this, Commander?"

"Tak, that is my understanding. I served in the Soviet Air Force from 1955 until just before the breakup of the Soviet Union in 1991."

"Commander, you had great respect for the Soviet Air Force?"

"I have learned a lot while serving our country. I served the Soviet Union when Nikita Khrushchev was the General Secretary of the Communist Party."

"After the death of Stalin, did Khrushchev change the political environment?"

"Almost immediately after Stalin's death in 1953, many of his policies were dismantled and political controls relaxed under the leadership of Nikita Khrushchev. Under Khrushchev, the Soviet Union suffered reverses in foreign relations with the United States, nearly causing a nuclear war in the Cuban Missile Crisis."

"How do you remember your mission to Cuba?"

"The mission to Cuba was very secret and involved very few personnel. This is why I kept in touch with many of my colleagues. Dutkewycz was a colleague of mine. Although information about his demise was never publicly released, members of the ANADYR flight mission were made aware of the tragedy."

"The ANADYR flight mission? What was that?"

"Operation ANADYR was the code name used by the Soviet Union for their 1962 secret operation of deploying ballistic missiles in Cuba."

"Since you were quite certain that Dutkewycz was a victim of the nuclear tests, did you write that letter to his brother Konstantin Kozlov in Tyumen?"

"Tak, I kept my promise to write him in the event that Dutkewycz lost his life. But, I never did receive a response from Kozlov. One thing is

for certain, if Dutkewycz survived the nuclear tests, I would have known about it."

"Was it possible for anyone to find their way to the mainland without detection?"

For the longest time Commander Korab did not answer. Perhaps he was thinking about those who tried to escape the loneliness of the island and found a certain death. On the other hand, maybe he had knowledge of someone who did make it off the island. Whatever the answer, Commander Korab was not about to reveal his inner thoughts. Like so many who served in the Soviet military, it was for certain that the Commander knew how to keep his inner thoughts to himself. The closest I came to getting an answer from him was a shrug of his shoulders and a noncommittal, *"Anything is possible."*

"Ostap, did you mail that letter to Konstantin in Novaya Zemlya or from mainland Russia?"

"Well," replied Commander Korab, *"there is no way I would have mailed that letter from Novaya Zemlya. Because of military security, I knew that all mail would be opened and read by authorities before it left the island."*

Ostap went on to explain how every letter leaving Novaya Zemlya would likely have been opened by the KGB, and it is virtually certain that any letter of a sensitive nature would never reach its intended destination. The reason for this close surveillance was national security. On the eve of the Great Patriotic War the Soviet military industrial complex created a number of new towns and cities for weapons development and manufacturing. The Soviet military industrial infrastructure was relocated beyond the reach of Hitler's advancing armies. Stalin called these military outposts as *Naukograds,* the Science Towns charged with the responsibility of providing the technical foundations for Soviet military technology such as long-range missiles, thermonuclear warheads, the enriching of plutonium, and military intelligence work.

"And, you say, Commander, that Konstantin never responded to your letter?'

"Regrettably," replied Commander Korab, *"that is what I am saying."*

Before boarding a plane in Lviv for my return to Edmonton, I had one more surprise, a surprise that I wanted to personally deliver to Commander Ostap Korab. To do this I invited Ostap to *Veronika's*, perhaps the finest pastry restaurant in Lviv. It was here, over a cup of tea and poppy-seed delicacies that I declared, *"Ostap, I have a surprise for you."*

"A surprise for me? And here I thought that I had all of the surprises for you!"

"Well, Ostap, perhaps I should have told you this before, but I wanted to be sure that I had all of the facts correct."

"Can I take a guess? You have some information for me about Pyotr? Am I right?"

"Tak, Ostap. I do have some wonderful news for you. You do remember writing that letter in 1963 to Konstantin Kozlov in Tyumen, don't you?"

"Why, of course I remember it. It feels as though it happened just yesterday."

"Well, Ostap, I don't have the original letter but I do have a copy of it and I want to present it to you."

"Are you kidding me? How did you come by that letter?"

"After the pleasant surprises you had for me, I wanted to share one with you. Most important, if it were not for you, it is doubtful that I would have been able to put the last pieces of this puzzle together. I now know what happened to Pyotr and the Kozlov family."

On the return flight from Lviv to Edmonton, I had to pinch myself to make certain that my search for the Kozlov family was no more than just a dream. I now knew the truth. The Kozlov family was exiled from Ukraine to Siberia in 1930. Eighty years later, there is one descendant family of the Alexei Kozlov family—Eduard Kozlov, now the head of a proud Russian family living in Tyumen. Even more shocking is the realization that without the discovery of these three letters, it is unlikely that I would have been able to solve the mystery of what happened to the Kozlov family. For certain, I would not have discovered what happened to Pyotr Dutkewycz. My only regret was that the Gulag swallowed any trace of Katusha and Nikolashya Kozlov. They left no footprints.

Looking back and starting with Stalin's first Five-Year Plan in 1928, I do know that the NKVD Troikas did not get stuck in the need of public trials or in arguments between political sides to arrest and deport the Kozlov family. In that initial interrogation and operation, the NKVD did not seek evidence and proof that the kulak family acted in word or deed against the Bolshevik power. Their first questions might have been, *What is your class? Are you a kulak?*

Of course, Brigadir Getnikov's unit already knew the answers. The NKVD was also aware of the family's origin, education, and upbringing.

The answers to these questions were placed in the hands of the military unit whose primary and principal distinguishing feature was that of taking decisions behind closed doors. In essence, they were closed courts for the convenience of quickly putting into place Stalin's first Five-Year Plan to collectivize agriculture.

In the eyes of Stalin's henchmen, it was a case of, *If it is necessary to shoot you, you'll be shot, even if you're completely innocent.* There was never any thought given to the possibility of exercising punishment only on those who committed certain crimes. In reflecting upon the work of the NKVD military units, it was permissible for them to merely carry out orders. Their conscience, if they had one, was obviously committed to someone else's keeping. In other words, the NKVD operatives carried out their orders without any ideas of their own about good and evil, right or wrong. Their orders were derived from the printed instructions and verbal orders of their superiors. That was good enough for them.

Millions upon millions of people were tried behind closed doors and deported to Siberia during the 1930s and 1940s. The whole reason for Stalin's exiles and deportations was the creation of social structures for the ruthless utilization of millions of free-of-cost slaves. According to Stalin, hard labour was one of the highest forms necessary for the passionate and conscious creation of the individual. To him, the processing of the human raw material, although considerably more complicated, was no different than was the processing of lumber. The Gulag turned out to be the social structure for the ruthless enforcement of political dissidents, real or imagined.

Given the deplorable and inhumane working conditions in the Gulag, the result was a narrowing of the deportee's mental and intellectual horizon to the level of an animal. Recognizing the extremely low survival rates in the Gulag, Eduard Kozlov characterized them as slave labour camps where the workers were dying alive. Isolated from humanity in work camps, the inmates became so used to their plight and the innate desire for survival that they developed a fear that their enemies would find out about any transgression causing them to clamp their heads between their own knees and work themselves to death.

The tragedy of the Gulag was further compounded when during the first days of World War II, prisoners frequently wrote petitions to their superiors expressing a desire to be sent to the front. This desire to be sent to the front line to defend and die for the camp system, and the Soviet Union, is hard to understand and explain. Could it be that prisoners hated the stinking camp swill served up as food more than was their fear of service in the military where the survival rate was low? This decision was not ideological—it came from the heart and expressed the Russian character—better to die in the wide field than to decay in a narrow shanty.

For those who were captured and ended up in Nazi prisoner of war camps, it mattered little as to the individual circumstances, all were promptly repatriated to Mother Russia and the Gulag at the end of the war for the purpose of re-education in the ideals of communism. Perhaps, this policy, more than any other, demonstrates the Soviet Union's worst crime—to betray their own people and proclaim them as traitors.

As Eduard Kozlov expressed it, *"It mattered little whether a person was in prison and in solitary confinement or outside solitary confinement, a human being had to confront his grief face to face."*

"It seems to me," was my response, *"that your father's grief was a mountain."*

"Da. It was a mountain with which he had to familiarize himself, to digest it, and it him. This is the highest form of moral effort, which has always enabled every human being to carve out a path in order to move forward."

As I consider what Russians have said to me during my journey to Siberia, there is little doubt that within the Russian soul can be found several opposing points of view. Some say that the deportations and exiles to Siberia have had both, intended and unintended consequences. Many are of the view that the development of the vast expanses of Siberia would not have been possible without the deportation of millions of its own citizens. In fact, some go so far as to say that the very defeat of Nazi Germany would not have been possible without the help of Gulag prisoners and the creation of munitions factories beyond the Ural Mountains.

As I bring to a close this story about my search for any surviving members of the Kozlov family, I may have solved one mystery but many questions remain. Unfortunately, with the loss of upwards to twenty million innocent people in the Gulag, there are many more stories that will never be written.

That, in my view, is too bad. May they rest in peace.

EPILOGUE

As I pause to consider the deportation of the Kozlov family to Siberia so many years ago, it is clear that exiles were not limited to criminals and political dissidents. It was a Russian law of 1736 which declared that if a village decided someone in its midst was a bad influence on others, the village elders could divide up the culprit's property and order him to move elsewhere. If that person failed to find another domicile, the state could send him into exile, all too often to the frozen wasteland of Siberia. This practice continued throughout the 19th century. Such administrative exiles required no trial and served to punish troublemakers, political opponents, religious objectors, members of secret societies, and any other identifiable group as selected by the state. Perhaps a good example of how slave labour was utilized in the early 18th century, one need only look at how Peter the Great used convicts and serfs to build roads, canals, fortresses, factories, ships, and the city of Saint Petersburg itself.

In its time, Peter the Great's use of forced labour was considered to be a great economic and political success. Even though many died during those times, the forced labour program had an enormous impact on future generations, especially upon Josef Stalin's Five-Year Plans. The deported labourers were forced to live in exile, and it was they, and not the convicts labouring in chains, which gradually populated Russia's empty mineral-rich wastelands. The wealthier exiles and ex-prisoners sometimes built up large estates, while the more educated became doctors, lawyers, and ran schools. It is in this way that the Gulag became an integral part of both Soviet and Russian history and is inseparable from European history. In the final analysis, deportations to Siberia resulted in millions of tragedies and, in the eyes of some, a handful of triumphs over evil.

Historians point out that the primary purpose of the Gulag was economic. This, however, did not mean that the treatment of labourers was humane. Like millions of others who were deported or exiled to Siberia, the Kozlovs were treated as cattle, shuttled from labour camp to labour camp, weighed and measured, fed if it seemed that they might be useful, starved if they were not. Unless productive, their lives were worthless to their masters. But, unlike those who were expelled from a village by their peers, it was Josef Stalin who identified the Kozlovs as belonging to an identifiable group, the kulaks, thereby making them eligible for immediate removal to the Gulag to make way for collectivization.

During my time in Siberia, I interviewed dozens of Russians, most of who continue to view Stalin in a positive light. They are of the view that without his iron fist, the Soviet Union could not have carried out its *overtaking* development to catch up to the West. Even of greater interest to me was that too many of my interviewees continue to believe that Russia requires an authoritarian ruler, someone like Vladimir Putin to regain its rightful place among the powerful nations of the world. They look at the grandeur of Saint Petersburg and Moscow and conclude, *how could we have built these United Nations heritage sites without the slave labour? Without the Gulag system?* Perhaps they choose to see only the few positive features of Stalin's policies as opposed to their cruelty and inhumanity.

When Stalin died in 1953, more than a quarter of the adult Soviet population had been a victim of Stalin's repression. Less than one-quarter of the millions of those exiled could be considered as criminals in other societies. From this, one can only conclude that Stalin's repressive measures can in no way be compensated for by the so-called economic achievements of the Bolsheviks and their successor, the Communist regime.

Even of greater interest to a Westerner is that Russians seldom want to debate, discuss, or even acknowledge the Gulag. There are few monuments to the victims of Stalin's execution squads and concentration camps. True, there may be a few scattered memorials, but no national monument or place of mourning. Here it is, nearly a quarter century since the collapse of the Soviet Union, and there are no trials, no truth and reconciliation commissions, no government inquiries into what happened in the past, and no public debate. This is truly amazing!

The reasons for this are not hard to fathom. Russians, particularly in Siberia, have pointed out to me that life is genuinely difficult in Russia today, and most spend all of their time trying to cope and eke out a living. In their minds, the Stalinist era was a long time ago and a great deal has happened since it ended. The memory of the labour camps is diffused by other atrocities such as war, famine, and collectivization. Further to this, the Russian psyche was further damaged with the collapse of the Soviet Union. Perhaps the old system was bad but at least the Soviet Union was once powerful.

The old system was run by the Communists and what continues to surprise is that on this day, 13 out of the 15 former Soviet Republics are run by former Communists. These former Communists have no interest in discussing the past. It tarnishes them, undermines them, and hurts their image. It is for certain that my distant cousin Eduard Kozlov portrayed this attitude. For me, the ever heavy presence of the secret police was sufficient testimony that the past lives on in the Russian hierarchy. It is for certain that the Soviet legacy does not haunt Russia's criminal police, secret police, judges, jailers, or businessmen. Few people in contemporary Russia feel the past to be a burden or an obligation at all.

For many Canadians whose roots lie in Poland or Ukraine and who lost loved ones to the Gulag, their memory of the Soviet past is far different. For them, it is not only a memory of the Gulag but also of the Ukrainian *famine genocide* (Holodomor) of 1932-1933 which was triggered by Stalin's deportation of kulaks to Siberia. These tragedies can be laid squarely at the doorstep of Josef Stalin, the focus of concentrated evil. No television cameras ever filmed the Soviet camps or their victims.

With but a few exceptions, the deportees left no footsteps. No footsteps and no images, in turn, meant that the subject, in our image driven culture, didn't really exist either.

Since the Soviet Union was our ally during World War II, does make it more difficult to characterize it as an evil empire. All of this contributed to our firm conviction that this war was a wholly just war. We remember our war veterans, but we do not remember that the camps of Stalin, our ally, expanded just as the camps of Hitler, our enemy, were liberated. No one wants to think that we defeated one mass murderer with the help of another mass murderer.

If we forget the Gulag, sooner or later many of us will forget the history of our own extended family. After all, any family coming to Canada from Eastern Europe most likely had a member of their extended family shipped off to Siberia, never to be heard from again. Perhaps the reason that we do not know of this kind of a deportation is that we have not searched sufficiently hard. Maybe it is because the Soviet Union put up walls around its member states from 1939 to the disintegration of the Soviet Union in 1991 that makes it impossible to keep in touch with members of an extended family.

If we do not study the history of the Gulag, some of what we know about mankind itself will be distorted. Every one of the 20th century's mass tragedies was unique, be it the Gulag, the Holocaust, the Ukrainian Holodomor, or the Armenian massacre. Every one of these events had different historical and philosophical origins and arose in circumstances that will hopefully never be repeated.

Above all else, I wrote *Destination Gulag* to help families better understand the tragedy of deportations and exiles to Siberia. Millions have been laid to rest in the frozen tundra of Siberia. Few have left any footprints behind and no one to speak for them. I hope that this one voice will recognize their sacrifice.

SELECTED REFERENCES

Applebaum, Anne, Gulag, A History, Anchor Books, A Division of Random House Inc., New York, 2003.

Cawthorne, Nigel, The Crimes of Stalin, The Murderous Career of the Red Tsar, Arcturus Publishing Limited, London, 2011.

Erickson, Professor John & Liubica, Hitler v Stalin, A Conflict of Evil, Seven Oaks, Carlton Publishing Group, London, 2001.

Figes, Orlando, The Whisperers, Private Life in Stalin's Russia, Metropolitan Books, Henry Hole and Company, New York, 2007.

McDowell, Bart, Journey Across Russia, The Soviet Union Today, Prepared by the Special Publications Division, National Geographic Society, Washington, D.C., 1977.

Misilo, Eugeniusz, Action Vistula, Lviv, Ukraine, 1997.

Polian, Pavel, Against Their Will: The History and Geography of Forced Migrations in the USSR, Central European University Press, Budapest, New York, 2004.

The National Geographic Society, The Soviet Union Today, Washington, D.C., 1989.

Thomas, D. M., Alexander Solzhenitsyn, A Century in His Life, St. Martin's Press, New York, 1998.

Vilensky, Semyon, Volume Editor, Resistance in the Gulag, 1923-56, Memoirs, Documents and Letters, collected and edited by Vozvrashchenie, Moscow Historical-Literary Society, 1992.